KATIE WORKMAN

Photographs by Todd Coleman

DINNER SOLVED!

100
Ingenious recipes that make the whole family happy, including
YOU

WORKMAN PUBLISHING
NEW YORK

To
my mom
and
my dad

Photographs copyright © 2015 by
Workman Publishing Co., Inc.

Library of Congress Cataloging-in-Publication
Data is available.

ISBN 978-0-7611-8187-3 (pb)
ISBN 978-0-7611-8497-3 (hc)

Cover and interior design by Lisa Hollander
Cover and interior photographs by Todd Coleman

Workman books are available at special discounts
when purchased in bulk for premiums and sales
promotions as well as for fund-raising or educational
use. Special editions or book excerpts can also be
created to specification. For details, contact the
Special Sales Director at the address below, or send
an email to specialmarkets@workman.com.

Workman Publishing Co, Inc.
225 Varick Street
New York, NY 10014-4381
workman.com

WORKMAN is a registered trademark of
Workman Publishing Co., Inc.

Printed in the United States of America
First printing August 2015

10 9 8 7 6 5 4 3 2 1

Thanks

Far and away, this is my favorite part of the book to write, mostly because it makes me feel inordinately warm and fuzzy as I think of all the people in my life who help make it all work.

First, my husband and kids. Guys, I love you so much. Gary, you are the most supportive husband around. I am so sorry I generate so many dishes, but I hope you think it's worth it in the end. I will try to remember to line the pan with aluminum foil more often.

Jack, you are an amazing person, so smart, interesting, and insightful. When you like something I make, it's one of my best seals of approval ever. Thanks for keeping me true to the goal of making family-friendly food with optimized kid appeal.

Charlie, being your mom is like going on a different amusement park ride every day—I'm never quite sure what's going to happen, but I know it's going to make me laugh, and inspire me, and keep me on my toes. Thanks for being such an entertaining person.

Cooper, I know we lived a perfectly happy life before we got you, but I'm not sure how. Reaching out with my toes to find you at the end of the bed is the best way I know to start any day. When I am giving you a little piece of chicken or even a slice of carrot, the unbridled admiration and affection in your eyes makes me melt. (I surely hope that it's clear by now that Cooper is a dog.)

My father died a couple of years back and I miss him every day. He was the smartest person I've ever known, and while that wasn't always easy to live with, it certainly raised the bar in terms of what I believed could be achieved. What I know about the importance of hard work and honest quality started with him. I'm forever happy that he was here for the first book.

My mom is one of the most unboring people around. And when she arranges some herbs on a platter, sets up a craft table for the kids on Thanksgiving, or wraps a present, you can bet that whatever extra touch she adds makes all the difference between something that's just fine, and something that's very special.

Much love to my sister, Lizzie, and all of my brothers- and sisters-in-law, parents-in-law, aunts and uncles, cousins, nieces, and nephews.

I count my blessings every single day to have so many amazing friends, who encourage and buttress me in so many ways. Some that need singling out, who really were a support to me as I wrote this book: Jennifer Baum, Jean Witter, David Erlanger, Pam Krauss, Dana Cowin, Catherine and Andy Skobe, Claire and Tim Radomisli, Kate and Chris Carr, Laura Agra, Charlie Masson, Abby Schneiderman, Chris Styler, Christopher Idone, and my entire extended family of friends. I am so grateful.

And without my other family at Workman Publishing, none of this exists. My editor Suzanne Rafer makes it all so much smoother and clearer, and is the kind of detail-oriented partner that authors yearn for. Art director Lisa Hollander for her smart and beautiful design, and the kind, super-conscientious photo director Anne Kerman, who both contributed so much to the look of the book. The sales team led by Walter Weintz is sine qua non (I had to look that up, but I knew there was a good Latin phrase for "kicks ass"): Michele Ackerman, Valerie Alfred, Marilyn Barnett, Angela Campbell, Liz DeBell, Adelia Kalyvas, Emily Krasner, Randy Lotowycz, Jenny Mandel, Steven Pace, Kristina Peterson, Michael Rockliff, Rebecca Schmidt, Jodi Weiss, and James Wehrle. The gracious John Jenkinson and Selena Meere in Publicity. Other brilliance at Workman comes in the form of Vaughn Andrews, Suzie Bolotin, Sarah Brady, Page Edmunds, Andrea Fleck-Nesbit, Moira Kerrigan, Beth Levy, Deborah McGovern, Claire McKean, Barbara Peragine, Julie Primavera, Dan Reynolds, David Schiller, Lauren Southard, Kate Travers, Janet Vicario, Jessica Wiener, and Doug Wolff.

Todd Coleman, you take a mean photo and you are a great friend. The team who worked on the interior photo shoot, led by Mira Evnine, was spectacular, as was Nora Singley, who styled the food on the front cover.

If this was an awards ceremony, the music would have swelled and I would have been forcibly removed from the microphone. I don't care, I would have finished yelling these names over the soaring score as I was being dragged from the stage.

Contents

Happy in the Kitchen

Cooking without eaters is of little to no interest to me. There has to be someone at the other end of the fork or the table. Cooking for family and friends; making something comforting for a colleague having a hard time; surprising someone with a batch of birthday brownies, dropping off a container of fried chicken for a new mom—in short, having people happily eating something I made is my very definition of joy. It doesn't get any better than that.

This book is filled with 100-plus recipes designed to be doable, crowd-pleasing, comforting, flavorful, and family friendly. It's just a honking big batch of very flexible recipes (with some pretty

dazzling photos) that I hope you will want to make over and over again, and that your family and friends will want to eat over and over again.

Fork in the Road

Adaptable recipes appeared throughout my first book, *The Mom 100 Cookbook*, but in *Dinner Solved!* they take a star turn. Almost all of the recipes in this book are open for adaptation. And all are modifiable so that everyone at the table can enjoy the version that works best for them. Picky eaters, vegetarians, the spice-averse—there are ways to make everyone at the table happy without feeling the need to turn into a short-order cook.

Buffalo wings can be made with traditional spicy buffalo sauce or in a sticky honey garlic version (or both!). A batch of Asian spareribs can be made sweet and tangy or with a nice dose of heat (or with both!). Fried chicken can be simple or spicy (or both!). The various components of couscous salad can be served separately, so everyone can put together the salad of their liking. A simple, perfectly cooked steak is great on its own—maybe even greater with a flavorful chimichurri sauce. Pass it at the table and let everyone decide for themselves. You get the idea.

A lot of the recipes included have a

Lo Mein with Chicken

Vegetarian version with tofu

vegetarian option, making it a helpful choice for those who have a vegetarian at the table on a regular, or an occasional, basis. A well-seasoned spicy sloppy joe sauce can be stirred into ground beef or crumbled tempeh . . . (or—wait for it—both!). An orangey stir-fry can be made half with tofu, half with chicken. Lo mein can be made vegetarian or with cubes of chicken or pork.

The Fork in the Road concept is something you can embrace and incorporate into your everyday cooking. The idea is that at some point in its preparation, a dish can be divided with part of it going one way, part of it going another way, so that everyone ends up happy and eating basically the same thing. Appealing, right?

Some Basic Cooking Thoughts

1. **MEASURING.** In almost all cases amounts are suggestions, exactness doesn't matter. Add more broccoli to the Stupid Easy Chicken and Broccoli Pasta (page 202), or use sugar snap peas instead. Add more beans to the Chicken and White Bean Chili (page 247), or more zucchini, or more chicken, or more cumin, or more paprika. Or less.

This is mostly true with the exception (as all recipe writers hasten to add), of baking. But, I will tell you that once my son Charlie was making the Berry Streusel Coffee Cake with Sweet Vanilla Drizzle (page 15), and added a cup less flour than the recipe called for. And guess what? It was fabulous. It was more like a clafoutis than a cake, and it is now an alternate version of the recipe in our house.

2. **SALT.** Use it. Use it in savory food, use it in sweet food. Salt elevates flavor. Use kosher or coarse salt. Unless you have a real issue with sodium, don't be too shy with it, really. Salt is one of the vital elements that makes the difference between food that tastes pretty good and food that tastes wow. Ask any professional cook.

3. **FAT.** Again, use it. Fat is also a flavor booster, a flavor conductor, and just

plain delicious. It adds all kinds of great texture, too. In baked goods it's essential, but that extra tablespoon of oil or butter in savory dishes can elevate a dish to where it should be. And when you're making a pan sauce or a pasta or a grain dish, swirling in a tablespoon of butter or good quality olive oil at the end can really make a dish extraordinary.

4. **CHANGE IT UP**. Make the Asian Rice Bowl on page 189 with a fun variety of add-ins. Make the Chicken Vegetable Potpie Casserole (page 183) with whatever vegetables you have around or are in season. Ditto for the Thai Chicken Stir-Fry (page 176). The scrambled-egg wraps on page 11 are a blank canvas, as is the pasta on page 198, which you can make in about 100 different ways.

5. **HEAT**. Don't be afraid of high heat. Getting a gorgeous sear on a piece of fish or meat provides wonderful texture and flavor. You want to hear a serious sizzle when that chicken, or that steak, hits the pan. Same for roasted vegetables; turn that oven up. There are plenty of exceptions to this rule, and cranking up the heat when you're baking is not advisable, but I have often found that cooking food at a higher-than-you-might-think temperature provides a whole lot of bang for the buck.

6. **ACID**. Adding something tart is another way to coax more flavor out of a dish. Lemon, lime, or orange juice, vinegars of all kinds—a little bit wakes up the other

Good Items That Jack Up the Flavor or the Interest in a Dish

By now you've gotten the gist of the Fork in the Road, or the malleable/flexible/convertible recipe. When you are starting with a plainer recipe—say a grilled or sautéed chicken breast—and want to think about what you can add to provide more interest for the more adventurous eaters at the table, here are some items you'll be happy to have on hand:

Sun-dried tomatoes

Olives

Mushrooms

Roasted peppers

Various cheeses: Parmesan, cheddar, mozzarella, feta, goat, sheep's milk cheeses

Various spices: cumin, paprika (smoked and regular), ground coriander, cayenne pepper

Fresh herbs: basil, rosemary, cilantro, tarragon, oregano

Vinegars: white wine, red wine, sherry, balsamic (red and white), rice vinegar

Citrus: lemons, limes, oranges

Horseradish

Harissa paste

Tapenade

Onion family members: garlic, onions, shallots, leeks, scallions

Pestos store-bought or see page 350

Pickled and fresh ginger

Anchovies

Capers

Sesame oil

Hoisin sauce

Soy sauce

Tahini

Canned chipotles in adobo

ingredients in the dish. And even though you should not skimp on the salt, adding some acid pumps up flavor without adding sodium, so the two together really work some magic.

Urge, Compliment, Criticize . . . or Try to Keep Your Mouth Shut

Push your kids to try new things? Complain that they hardly eat anything? Make comments about how they won't get big and strong if they don't eat some vegetables or broaden their dinner horizons? Lavish them with praise every time a morsel of broccoli passes between their lips. Bribe? Beg? Threaten? Do any of these sound familiar?

If any (or all) of them do, then congratulations, you are a real parent, and I would be pleased for you to sit next to me so we can exchange stories.

What to do?

Well, I have some advice, but it's not foolproof, and I'm not in your house. And furthermore, I need to say loudly and repeatedly that there *are* no foolproof answers, and also reiterate that those few parents who want to share the news that their kids eat everything, from the stinkiest blue cheese to smoked oysters, are not who I plan to hang out with at the next school cocktail party. For the rest of us, this is neither compelling news, nor helpful information. And frankly, I think they might be lying a little bit.

A quick recap of advice from *The Mom 100 Cookbook*:

1. DON'T ASSUME YOUR KIDS WON'T LIKE SOMETHING (AND FOR THE LOVE OF GOD, DON'T SAY IT OUT LOUD).

There are a number of recipes in this book that I know parents might look at and say, "No way this flies with my kids." Maybe they won't. But maybe they will. I am not into challenging what kids will eat for the pure sport of it, BUT I do know that quite often we err on the side of imagining that our kids will never be up for a little push in the new food direction. Let's stop assuming that. Let's serve some foods that we aren't sure they will like, and see what happens. Let's be pleasantly surprised, and let's let them be pleasantly surprised, and a little pleased with themselves for discovering a new food.

We help our kids with their homework, we help our kids practice sports, we help our kids navigate the often tricky world of friends and school and mean kids and peer pressure. So, it makes a bit of sense that we have to help them realize that lentils aren't so bad. I will now get off my soapbox before the mother of an intractably picky eater throws a bag of lentils at my head and lights my car on fire.

2. **TRY SOMETHING NEW.** Try it again. Repeat. There is nutritionist wisdom that says kids on average need to try a new food about 8 to 10 times before they'll embrace it as a "liked food."

3. **DON'T SERVE OVERAMBITIOUS PORTIONS.** Especially when you're trying out a new food, or a food that has been previously on the "meh" or "gross" list.

4. **FINALLY, THINK ABOUT KEEPING COMPONENTS SEPARATE.** Sometimes, keeping the ingredients of a salad or another dish separated in the presentation (see the Cobb Salad on page 83 or the Simple Couscous Salad on page 273), allows kids to pick and choose the things they like, and not get freaked out by a jumble of things they actually like when served individually.

What the Kids Can Do

In each recipe there will be a little section suggesting what tasks might be kid-appropriate. These are just suggestions—only you know your kid, and what they can handle in the kitchen. Some 10-year-olds are proficient with a sharp knife, some 13-year-olds aren't yet comfortable peeling carrots. It's all okay. The rewarding thing all around is just to get them involved, in whatever way feels right.

A couple of details: Supervise, supervise, supervise. Knives, heat . . . let them learn how to handle sharp and hot, but do it with an eagle eye, even after you think they are on top of it.

Handwashing. Before and after food prep. Very warm water, lots of suds, and a good scrub, not a quick rinse after anything that has to do with raw meat or seafood. There is no reason kids can't shape meatballs or flour chicken breasts or peel shrimp. And there are lots of reasons why they should. Just train them from the get-go to be aware of the bacteria factor and wash well.

Why I Do What I Do

If you've got some time to kill, read on.

I was pregnant with my second son when I first started

Charlie, Jack, and our friend Eve, having a penne moment.

thinking seriously about pursuing a long-deferred dream of doing something in the food world. I was looking at various options, and seriously considering getting into the restaurant business, even though I fully (really, fully) understood how grueling and unromantic it was most of the time (I've been a busgirl, a waitress, a hostess, and almost a bartender once, but I couldn't reach the bottles on the top speedrack).

After Charlie was born, my husband presented me with a gift in front of both of our families. The gift was this: For three days I would work, for free, at one of the best restaurants in New York City, and experience the reality of a high-end restaurant kitchen. The rest of the family looked at Gary as though he had given me a backhoe for giving birth to his child, but I was very touched.

Excited but nervous, I put my breast pump in a backpack and headed to work. I did my three eight-hour evening shifts, punctuated with milk pumping sessions in the office of the somewhat discomfited but surprisingly accommodating executive chef. And it was exhausting. But it was wonderful. I did not end up pursuing a restaurant career, but it certainly wasn't the experience that dissuaded me.

Anyway, why am I bringing this up? Because at one point I was dicing potatoes with the chef de cuisine, and I thought I was holding my own. "Watch this," he said, and he stacked up all of the cubes of his diced potato into a perfectly straight column of squares, each cube a perfectly symmetrical marvel of 90-degree angles. Like a stack of actual dice. "You try," he said, and I dutifully stacked up my little mound of cubes. I could say my column was crooked, but that would imply that I was able to pile up enough to justify calling the structure a column.

So, when you go to a four-star restaurant, you are paying for that kind of perfection: flawless balance of flavor, innovation, pristine ingredients, dazzling presentation, and the fact that if you measured the sides of the cubed potatoes on your plate, they would all be equal. And this taught me something about home cooking. The food should taste great, the company should be excellent, and the length of sides of the potato cubes should be beside the point.

"What I love is to cook for someone. To put a freshly made meal on the table, even if it is something very plain and simple . . . is a sincere expression of affection, it is an act of binding intimacy directed at whoever has a welcome place in your heart."

—Marcella Hazan

DINNER
SOLVED!

ORANGE SCONES, *page 13*

Planning a little bit ahead can make the difference between a bowl of cereal and an apple (not that there's anything wrong with that) on a school morning, and something that feels like a more imaginative and enthusiastic start to the day, a break from the usual. Breakfast wraps are but a step beyond scrambled eggs (and you can customize to your heart's content), crostini (savory or sweet) take a couple minutes more than toast, and a healthy smoothie whirls together speedily (and can get spiked with fresh ginger).

Morning Food

But let me be clear and frank. Whenever I see a commercial featuring a cheery family around the weekday breakfast table, I want to call baloney on that (only I don't use the word *baloney* in my mind). A weekend morning is another breakfast story altogether, when the minute hand mercilessly sweeping around the clock doesn't matter so much. Then it's a moment for something freshly baked, maybe scones or a streusel-heaped coffee cake that says, "Yes, you have time for that second cup of coffee and, no, you don't have to get going just yet."

Berry Banana Smoothie

FORK IN THE ROAD: Blueberries, strawberries, other fruits . . . and a bracing burst of fresh ginger if you like.

A basic smoothie recipe is hardly rocket science, but it is just excellent to have as a template to use to create your own smoothies forevermore. You can use whatever berries you like, which makes this the recipe to grab after a berry picking expedition in the summer. But you can also use any kind of soft fruit you want—peeled peaches or nectarines, melons, even grapes (unpeeled)—and puree. You can always add a bit more fruit or ice to thicken it, or a bit more milk to thin it out.

1½ cups strawberries, blueberries, or raspberries, fresh or frozen (see Note)

1 banana, fresh or frozen (see Note), sliced into chunks

1 cup (8 ounces) plain Greek yogurt

½ cup milk

3 to 4 teaspoons honey, to taste

1 cup crushed ice

Place the berries, banana, yogurt, milk, honey, and ice in a blender. Pulse a few times, then puree until it is the desired texture. Pour into glasses and serve.

FORK IN THE ROAD

Ginger Berry Banana Smoothie

The only change you need to make is to add 1 tablespoon minced, peeled fresh ginger to the blender. If you want to serve one plain smoothie, pour out half the mixture after pureeing the fruit, then add 1½ teaspoons minced ginger to the rest of the smoothie in the blender and puree that.

Yield

Makes 2 smoothies

What the Kids Can Do

Choose the berries or other fruit, slice the banana, drop things into the blender, puree with supervision.

Make Ahead

This is best made right before drinking, but you can keep it chilled in a thermos for several hours. Shake before opening the thermos.

Note: **The decision to use fresh or frozen fruit depends on how thick you want the smoothie to be. Frozen will make for a more milkshake-thick smoothie, whereas fresh will be thickened up slightly by the ice but have a thinner texture. I like to freeze the banana, and use the berries fresh.**

VEGAN VARIATION:
Skip the milk and yogurt and use 1 cup orange juice instead.

Strawberry
banana

Blueberry
banana

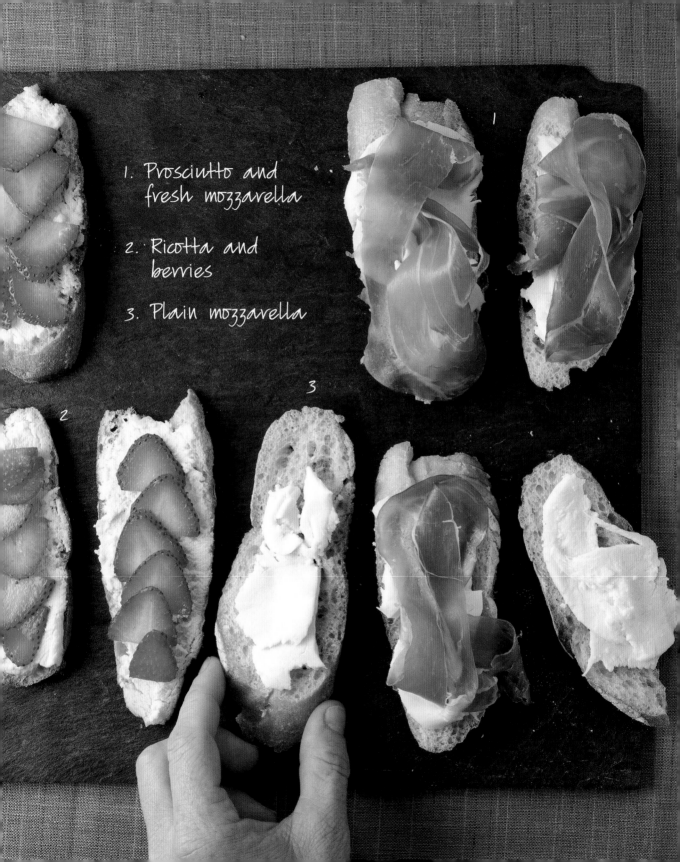

1. Prosciutto and fresh mozzarella

2. Ricotta and berries

3. Plain mozzarella

Ricotta Berry Breakfast Crostini

FORK IN THE ROAD: A little piece of toast can become a base for a sweet or savory handheld breakfast, depending on your mood.

Crostini usually make their appearance as an appetizer. They are merely little pieces of toast topped with anything from a nice brush of olive oil and salt to almost anything on the planet. Although toast for breakfast isn't exactly a new idea, it seemed like a good idea to bring the concept of breakfast crostini into our always-wanting catalog of morning options. They make nice snacks, too.

12 baguette slices, cut on the diagonal for more surface area

½ cup ricotta cheese (if you can get fresh, it's a beautiful thing)

2 teaspoons honey

1 cup sliced strawberries or whole raspberries

1. Toast the baguette slices in a toaster or preheated 350°F oven until very lightly browned, about 3 minutes.

2. ◗━━◖ You can continue with Step 3 or see the Fork in the Road (page 8) for fancy ham-and-cheese crostini.

3. Combine the ricotta and honey in a small bowl.

4. Spread the ricotta mixture evenly over the toasted bread slices and evenly distribute the berries over the tops.

Yield

Serves 4

What the Kids Can Do

Mix the ricotta and honey, top the crostini with the mixture and the berries. In the Fork in the Road version they can brush the crostini with olive oil and arrange the toppings on the crostini.

Make Ahead

The toast can be made 2 days ahead of time and kept tightly sealed at room temperature. You can mix the honey and ricotta 2 days before as well. Refrigerate, covered, until ready to serve.

FORK IN THE ROAD

Mozzarella & Prosciutto Crostini

This sounds highbrow (and certainly prosciutto is more expensive than your everyday ham, which you could also use), but it's one of my kids' favorite sandwich combos, so I knew it would take a crostini topping to make mornings a little brighter. These would also be great as appetizers.

If you want to serve half sweet and half savory, just toast the 12 baguette slices and halve all of the topping ingredients. Spread 6 toasts with the sweet topping and the other 6 with the savory topping.

12 baguette slices, toasted (see Step 1 on page 7)

1 tablespoon extra-virgin olive oil

Kosher or coarse salt, to taste

4 ounces fresh mozzarella cheese, thinly sliced

2 ounces prosciutto (see Bacon, Prosciutto & Other Pork Cousins, facing page), very thinly sliced

Freshly ground black pepper, to taste (optional)

1. As soon as the crostini are toasted, brush them lightly with the olive oil and give them a light sprinkle of salt.

2. Cover the toasts evenly with the mozzarella, cutting the cheese to fit neatly on the crostini, then drape pieces of prosciutto over the mozzarella, dividing it evenly. Top with a grind of pepper at the end, if desired.

Other breakfast crostini notions

- a spoonful of scrambled eggs and grated cheese
- sliced avocado and crumbled bacon
- Nutella and bananas
- cream cheese and sliced peaches with a sprinkle of cinnamon

Bacon, Prosciutto & Other Pork Cousins

Boy, has bacon found its way into almost every dish under the sun at this point. Besides the usual suspects, there is bacon ice cream, bacon peanut brittle, bacon jam, and bacon cupcakes. I saw a recipe for a bacon milk shake recently. No comment. Wait, yes, I do have a comment: No, thank you. And, of course, there are now food people who claim that bacon is "over." Bacon will never be over. And if it's over for you, then I'm sorry to hear it.

I love bacon and don't mind it turning up in interesting places. However, there are a host of other kinds of salted and cured pork products out there that are also amazing on their own and in recipes, sometimes cooked, sometimes not. Here are a few of the most common porky meats:

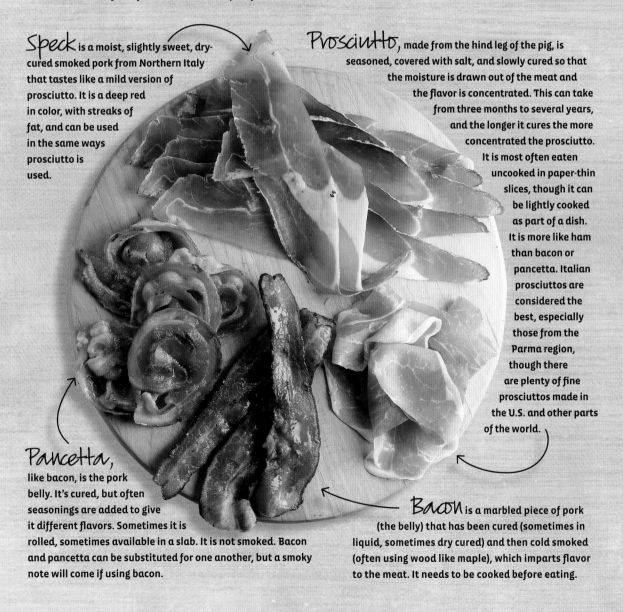

Speck is a moist, slightly sweet, dry-cured smoked pork from Northern Italy that tastes like a mild version of prosciutto. It is a deep red in color, with streaks of fat, and can be used in the same ways prosciutto is used.

Prosciutto, made from the hind leg of the pig, is seasoned, covered with salt, and slowly cured so that the moisture is drawn out of the meat and the flavor is concentrated. This can take from three months to several years, and the longer it cures the more concentrated the prosciutto. It is most often eaten uncooked in paper-thin slices, though it can be lightly cooked as part of a dish. It is more like ham than bacon or pancetta. Italian prosciuttos are considered the best, especially those from the Parma region, though there are plenty of fine prosciuttos made in the U.S. and other parts of the world.

Pancetta, like bacon, is the pork belly. It's cured, but often seasonings are added to give it different flavors. Sometimes it is rolled, sometimes available in a slab. It is not smoked. Bacon and pancetta can be substituted for one another, but a smoky note will come if using bacon.

Bacon is a marbled piece of pork (the belly) that has been cured (sometimes in liquid, sometimes dry cured) and then cold smoked (often using wood like maple), which imparts flavor to the meat. It needs to be cooked before eating.

Spinach and Monterey jack

Black beans, avocado, cheddar, tomato, and red onion

Bacon and cheddar

Spinach, bacon, and goat cheese

Avocado, yellow pepper, tomato, and red onion

Breakfast Wraps

FORK IN THE ROAD: This is a choose-your-own adventure breakfast.

This is one of the many recipes that is a jumping-off point for whatever moves you. If you are making it for, say, a brunch gathering or sleepover, think about putting out a pile of warmed tortillas, a big bowl of fluffy scrambled eggs, and a bunch of toppings and letting everyone do their own thing. You know when you go to a hotel that has a full-on brunch buffet, and there's a person in a white coat standing behind two pans making individual omelets to order? Yeah, that's not you. But this, this could be you.

8 large eggs

Kosher or coarse salt and freshly ground black pepper, to taste

1 tablespoon unsalted butter

4 tortillas (8 inches in diameter), any flavor

¼ cup shredded cheese, such as cheddar, Monterey jack, pepper jack, provolone, a Mexican blend, or crumbled feta

1. Beat the eggs with salt and pepper in a medium-size bowl. Melt the butter in a medium-size skillet over medium-high heat. Pour in the eggs and scramble them, stirring occasionally, until cooked to your liking.

2. Meanwhile, place the tortillas on a plate with a slightly damp paper towel covering them and microwave for 20 seconds.

3. Place about ½ cup scrambled eggs on a tortilla and sprinkle over a tablespoon of shredded cheese. Then, either call it a day and wrap it up, or sprinkle over any of the suggested toppings and roll up. Repeat to make 4 wraps and serve.

Yield

Makes 4 wraps

What the Kids Can Do

Beat the eggs, maybe scramble the eggs with help, choose their wrap fillings, and wrap up the tortillas.

Make Ahead

Not really, but you can wrap these while still warm in aluminum foil and eat on the run.

Optional Additions

Diced avocados

Diced tomatoes

Salsa

Chopped olives

Crumbled cooked bacon or sausage (turkey or pork)

Black or kidney beans, drained and rinsed

Minced raw onion or sautéed sliced onion

Raw or sautéed spinach

Minced raw bell pepper or sautéed sliced bell pepper

Studded with
dried cranberries
and apricots

Orange Scones

FORK IN THE ROAD: Plain for breakfast, all dolled up with cranberries, apricots, and sage for fancier moments.

I love the very word *scone*. So elegant, so dignified, so *Downton Abbey*-ish. And so easy to make. No yeast, no kneading (in fact, like biscuits, the less you handle scone dough the lighter and more tender your scones will be). There are lots of things you can add to scones. All the suggestions in the Fork in the Road can be added, or just one or two. What a great kid project this is: lots of use of hands, lots of room for creativity, and pretty quick from start to finish.

2 cups all-purpose flour (see Note), plus extra for flouring the work surface

8 tablespoons (1 stick) unsalted butter, chilled, cut into small pieces, plus butter for greasing the baking sheet

2 tablespoons sugar

1 teaspoon finely grated orange zest

1 tablespoon baking powder

½ teaspoon kosher or coarse salt

½ cup milk, preferably whole

¼ cup heavy (whipping) cream, plus 2 tablespoons for brushing tops of scones

1. Preheat the oven to 400°F. Lightly flour a work surface. Lightly butter a baking sheet.

2. Stir together the flour, sugar, orange zest, baking powder, and salt in a medium-size bowl. Using your fingers, two knives, or a pastry cutter, cut in the butter (see Cutting in the Butter, page 14) until the mixture resembles coarse crumbs.

Yield

Makes 10 scones

What the Kids Can Do

This has kids written all over it. You have a nice opportunity to talk about kitchen chemistry (not scary chemistry, just kitchen chemistry) with the cutting in of the butter. And, of course, they can measure, dump, mix, cut out circles, brush with cream, and transfer biscuits to the wire rack with a spatula.

Make Ahead

These are best eaten the day they are baked but can be held at room temperature for up to 2 days. At that point they will benefit from a quick warm-up in the oven or toaster.

Note: **If you like, you can use 1 cup all-purpose flour plus 1 cup whole wheat flour, preferably whole wheat pastry flour, which has a lighter texture than regular whole wheat flour.**

3. Add the milk and the ¼ cup cream and using a fork or your fingers toss the mixture just until combined.

4. ◄═══ You can continue with Step 5 or see the Fork in the Road for a souped-up version with dried fruit.

5. Transfer the mixture to the floured surface and pat it into a 1½-inch-thick round (it doesn't have to be a neat shape). Use a 2-inch biscuit cutter or a glass with a thin rim to cut out circles and place them at least 2 inches apart on the prepared baking sheet. Collect the scraps, pat them together, and repeat the cutting process. If there is still a bit of dough left over, gently shape it into a couple of 2-inch circles. Brush all of the scones with the remaining 2 tablespoons cream.

6. Bake the scones until puffed and golden, 13 to 15 minutes. Cool on a wire rack, and serve warm or at room temperature.

FORK IN THE ROAD

Orange, Cranberry, Apricot & Sage Scones

These gorgeous and slightly autumnal scones are hardly everyday morning fare. Breakfast or brunch, sure. Afternoon snack or tea, yup—if you're a tea kind of person; I aspire to be a tea kind of person. Next life. They are also a show-off quick bread to whip up during the holiday season, working as an accompaniment to a meal. Leave out the sage if the herby/fruity thing doesn't work for you.

After incorporating the milk and cream into the flour mixture in Step 3, add ½ cup dried cranberries, ½ cup chopped dried apricots, and, if you like, 1 teaspoon minced fresh sage (or ½ teaspoon dried). Toss just until they are evenly distributed through the scone dough. Continue as directed with Step 5.

If you would like to make some with and some without, separate out half of the plain orange scone mixture, and add half of the above ingredients to it. Continue as directed with the two versions.

Cutting in the Butter

Various baking recipes will instruct you to "cut in" butter or shortening—usually when you are making a baked good that needs to be flaky. Unlike creaming the butter, cutting in the butter means incorporating the butter into the dry ingredients in such a way that little lumps of the chilled butter are distributed throughout. During the baking process, these little lumps create little air pockets as they melt, which is what makes the pastry flaky.

You can use a pastry cutter (cheap and useful if you make a lot of biscuits, pie crusts, scones, and the like) to cut the butter into the flour mixture. You can also use two knives, scissoring them (hold a knife in each hand and cut through the butter by pulling the knives in opposite directions); a fork (mashing the ingredients together just until pebbly); or your fingers (rubbing the flour against the chilled butter).

Cold butter is critical, as warm butter will just blend into the flour, making a paste. The bigger the lumps of butter, within reason, the flakier the pastry, so use a light hand and refrain from kneading the dough.

Berry Streusel Coffee Cake with Sweet Vanilla Drizzle

FORK IN THE ROAD: One showstopper of a cake, or a batch of berry muffins (guests can choose blueberry or raspberry) for snacks or a brunch buffet.

Seriously, cake for breakfast? Yes, when it is coffee cake. The word *coffee* preceding the word *cake* makes it all okay. It's a fact; you can look it up.

I grew up making coffee cakes from Bisquick mix, and was extremely pleased with myself each time I turned out one of those moist, crumb-topped treats. On the weekend, I'd bring it up to my parents for breakfast in bed, who seemed pleased but not as pleased as they would have been if I had let them sleep later.

Fast-forward to now, when I am drawn to baking from scratch, though no less drawn to eating cake for breakfast. Combine that with the fact that my husband spent his childhood and most of his adulthood ripping open a package of store-bought crumb cakes for breakfast on the way to school/work. And top all of *that* with the notion that raspberries are my kids' most lusted-after member of the berry family, and this recipe practically willed itself into creation.

Some of the berries are fully blended into the cake batter, and some are sprinkled on top as a bright, juicy layer right underneath the streusel, providing little pops of color peeking through the crumbs.

Yield

Serves 10 to 12

What the Kids Can Do

The usual baking tasks—measure, mix, crack the egg—plus cut in the butter, sprinkle the berries and streusel on the cake or muffins, and drizzle on the drizzle if desired.

Make Ahead

The cake or muffins can stay covered at room temperature for up to 3 days.

Unsalted butter, for buttering the baking pan

FOR THE CRUMB TOPPING

½ cup packed light or dark brown sugar

½ cup all-purpose flour

½ teaspoon ground cinnamon

Pinch of kosher or coarse salt

6 tablespoons (¾ stick) unsalted butter, chilled, cut into small pieces

FOR THE COFFEE CAKE

2 cups all-purpose flour

2½ teaspoons baking powder

½ teaspoon ground cinnamon

½ teaspoon kosher or coarse salt

4 tablespoons (½ stick) unsalted butter, at room temperature

¾ cup granulated sugar

1 large egg

½ teaspoon pure vanilla extract

¾ cup milk, preferably whole

3 cups fresh raspberries or blueberries

FOR THE VANILLA DRIZZLE (OPTIONAL)

⅓ cup confectioners' sugar

1½ teaspoons hot water

½ teaspoon pure vanilla extract

Note: If you don't have a springform pan you can use a regular pan. Cool the cake in the pan completely, but don't attempt to turn it out of the pan, because it will fall apart. Just cut it in the pan.

1. Preheat the oven to 350°F. Butter a 9-inch springform baking pan (see Note).

2. Make the topping: Combine the brown sugar, flour, cinnamon, and salt in a small bowl. Add the butter and using your fingers, a pastry cutter, or 2 knives, combine everything until the butter is cut into the dry mixture, and the whole thing is quite crumbly (see Cutting in the Butter, page 14). It should not be a paste; there should be little pieces of butter throughout.

The mere word "streusel" can make the day better.

3. Make the cake: Combine the flour, baking powder, cinnamon, and salt in a medium-size bowl. Beat the butter and granulated sugar together in a large bowl with an electric mixer until light and fluffy. Add the egg to the butter mixture and beat until incorporated, then beat in the vanilla. Add half the flour mixture and beat just until almost incorporated. Beat in the milk just until blended. Add the remaining flour mixture, beating just until everything is combined but not any more than that.

4. ◼━◀ You can continue with Step 5 to make the coffee cake, or see the Fork in the Road to make streusel muffins.

5. Gently fold in 2 cups of the berries, then spread the batter in the prepared pan (it will be very thick). Sprinkle the remaining cup of berries on top, then sprinkle the crumb topping evenly over the berries.

6. Bake the cake until golden brown, 45 to 50 minutes. A wooden skewer inserted into the middle might have some berry stuck to it when you pull it out, but there should not be any uncooked batter.

7. Let cool on a wire rack for 15 minutes, then release the side of the pan and continue to cool the cake on the pan bottom on the wire rack.

8. While the cake is cooling, make the drizzle, if desired: Combine the confectioners' sugar, hot water, and vanilla in a small bowl. When the cake has cooled completely, use a teaspoon to lightly drizzle on the drizzle.

Dual Berry Streusel Muffins

Makes 18 muffins

Line 18 muffin cups with paper liners. Instead of 3 cups of one berry, use 1½ cups blueberries and 1½ cups raspberries. Follow the recipe through Step 3, then divide the batter between two bowls. Fold 1 cup raspberries into one half of the batter and 1 cup blueberries into the other. Scoop the batter into the muffin cups, filling each a little more than halfway, making about 9 muffins of each type. Sprinkle the rest of each type of berry over their rightful muffin type and divide the streusel evenly over the tops of the muffins. Bake for about 25 minutes, until a toothpick or a wooden skewer inserted into the middle of a muffin comes out clean, except for maybe a bit of berry. Cool the muffins in the cups on a wire rack. Drizzle with the drizzle, if desired.

Fresh mozzarella is a gorgeous, creamy, delicate base for an infinite number of sandwich possibilities.

THE MOZZARELLA SANDWICH, *page 27*

Ah, the perennial lunchtime dilemma. A few slices of cold cuts layered between a couple of slices of bread usually works, but it doesn't take too long before tedium sets in. Start with the condiments—it's fun poking around the shelves at a specialty store; harissa, tapenade, aioli, curry pastes . . . inspiration awaits. And when you are making rémoulade (page 143), pesto (page 350), or chipotle mayo (page 355), you will be so happy to have extra to transform turkey and roast beef sandwiches later in the week.

CHAPTER 2

Serious Sandwiches

These recipes bridge the span between perfectly respectable and simple sandwiches and sandwiches with oomph. Plain egg salad or a variety of options, chicken salad with or without some great tangy add-ins, a mozzarella sandwich that is unadorned or ornate. Also an old-school sloppy joe (with a vegetarian option!) and a shrimp roll, straight up or smacked with some Creole seasoning. See you later, lunchtime blues.

Egg Salad Sandwiches

FORK IN THE ROAD: A total comfort food sandwich, with some optional twists.

There are few things better than a perfect egg salad sandwich. It has the same appeal as a deviled egg (see page 48), only in sandwich form. Even as a scoop on a plate, there is something almost moving in how trustworthy it is. It's a Boy Scout-type quality I don't look for in foods on a regular basis, but when it comes along every once in a while, it's like pulling an old holey, favorite sweater over your head and it should be embraced.

However, on the days when you do want a little zing in your world, egg salad is also perfectly capable of talking smack. See the Fork in the Road versions with some imaginative add-ins for an edgier egg salad. And if none of the bread options below strikes a chord, you could spread the egg salad on a tortilla and make it into a wrap or pile it onto several crisp lettuce leaves, or serve it with crackers for scooping.

6 hard-boiled eggs (see Making Perfect Hard-Boiled Eggs, page 50), peeled and roughly chopped

⅓ cup chopped celery (optional)

2 tablespoons minced shallots or ¼ cup minced onion

¼ cup mayonnaise, or more to taste

Kosher or coarse salt and freshly ground black pepper, to taste

4 to 6 slices bread (white, sourdough, whole wheat, pumpernickel, or rye), toasted if you like

Lettuce, sliced tomato, and/or Other Add-ins (optional; see facing page)

Yield

Makes 2 fat sandwiches, or 3 more restrained sandwiches

What the Kids Can Do

Peel and chop the cooled eggs, measure the ingredients, and mix the salad, picking any of the add-ins. They can also assemble the sandwiches.

Make Ahead

This salad is best made the day it is eaten, but if you skip the celery it can last for at least 3 days in the refrigerator (or fold in the celery just before serving so it doesn't make the salad watery). To prevent the bread from getting soggy, if you are packing a lunch box, you can either place a piece of lettuce between the egg salad and each piece of bread, or pack the egg salad in a container, the bread in a plastic bag, and any lettuce or tomatoes in a separate bag. Then your kid can assemble it just before eating, which is kind of fun.

1. Gently combine the eggs, celery, shallots or onion, mayonnaise, and salt and pepper in a medium-size bowl until well blended. If you like a smoother egg salad, you can pulse the mixture in a food processor.

2. ◄━━€ You can continue with Step 3 or see the Fork in the Road for some optional add-ins.

3. Pile the egg salad onto 2 or 3 slices of bread or toast, add lettuce, tomato, and any other add-ins if desired, and top each with another slice of bread. Cut in half and serve.

FORK IN THE ROAD Add any one of the following to the egg salad mixture at the end of Step 1. (Or divide the egg salad into two equal portions, keep half plain and add half of any one of the following ingredients to the remaining egg salad!)

2 teaspoons curry powder

2 teaspoons minced fresh dill, basil, or tarragon, with or without 1 teaspoon rinsed and chopped capers

2 tablespoons sweet relish or minced cornichon pickles

1 teaspoon minced seeded jalapeño pepper

Creamy vs. Chunky

Few things are more personal than food texture. Bumpy vs. smooth—whether it's peanut butter, pasta sauces, or egg salad, people often have strong opinions, especially kids. I like a chunky but not too chunky egg salad, which of course I usually get because I am the maker of the egg salad, and I know where that perfect line is. So, keep it chunky, chop it like crazy, or even pulse it into a coarse puree in the food processor, if that makes you happier.

Other Add-ins

Beyond doctoring up the egg salad, the construction of the sandwich itself offers a nice blank canvas for pile-ons, such as watercress, arugula, halved olives, thinly sliced radishes, onions (red, yellow, or sweet), cucumbers, or pickles.

A Portable Egg Salad Sandwich Kit

With jalapeño

With dill and capers

With curry powder

With chopped pickles

Mozzarella and . . .

Basil Pesto (page 350)

proscuitto

and , 'onions 'peppers 'tomatoes roasted

carmelized onions (page 42), tapenade,

and arugula

Sun-dried Tomato Pesto (page 351) and basil

tomatoes and tapenade

The Mozzarella Sandwich

FORK IN THE ROAD: The simple combination of fresh mozzarella and ripe tomatoes on a baguette is hard to beat . . . but there's no harm in trying.

I know, I know, you don't need a recipe for a mozzarella sandwich. But if you'll just humor me, maybe you'll find some new thoughts for add-ins, or even just be reminded that fresh mozzarella is one of the most delicious sandwich stars around. And now it's everywhere, available at almost every supermarket, or deli, or specialty or cheese shop.

One more thing to mention—a little trick that elevates sandwiches from "why-doesn't-this-taste-as-good-as-the-sandwich-I-buy-from-a-deli?" to "now-this-sandwich-tastes-as-good-as-the-kind-I-buy-from-a-deli": The trick is simply olive oil and salt and pepper. I didn't say it was a fancy trick. Brushing nice crusty bread lightly with olive oil, and giving it a good sprinkle of kosher salt and freshly ground pepper turns most sandwiches into something much more special (skip the pepper if your kids aren't pepper kids).

Oh, and if you have a panini machine? Go for it. Melty and crusty equals another layer of supreme mozzarella sandwich love.

4 pieces (each 6 inches long) of baguette, white or whole wheat

Extra-virgin olive oil, for brushing

Kosher or coarse salt and freshly ground black pepper, to taste

4 thick slices fresh mozzarella cheese (about ⅔ pound; see Note)

4 thick slices ripe tomato (1 very large tomato)

12 fresh basil leaves (optional)

Balsamic vinegar for drizzling (optional)

Yield

Makes 4 sandwiches

Note: If you have a big fat ball of mozzarella and a big fat tomato, then a thick slice of each is all you need. Smaller tomato and mozz? Layer on a couple of slices of each.

Slice the baguette pieces in half horizontally. Brush the insides of both the top and bottom halves with olive oil and sprinkle them with salt and pepper. Layer the cheese and tomato slices on the bottom halves. Top the tomatoes with 3 basil leaves per sandwich, if using. Drizzle a bit of balsamic vinegar over all, if desired. Close up the sandwich with the top baguette half and that's it. Or not: ●━━◗ See the Fork in the Road.

The Mozzarella Sandwich & Then Some

Like chicken, like eggs, fresh mozzarella takes kindly to all kinds of seasonings and flavors. My kids are bonkers for it. Do you know how your dog or cat can hear you open a can of food with the can opener and come flying into the kitchen? If I start slicing fresh mozzarella, Jack can hear it from anywhere in the house, and appears in the kitchen to pinch pieces off the cutting board.

Optional add-ins to the mozzarella sandwich, alone or in combination:

Prosciutto

Sun-dried tomato paste

Basil Pesto (page 350) or Sun-Dried Tomato Pesto (page 351)

Sliced or crushed avocado

Roasted tomatoes, in place of or in addition to the fresh

Roasted peppers

Baby kale leaves

Tapenade (olive paste)

Sautéed onions

About Mozzarella

Fresh mozzarella is soft and silky and has a delicate milky flavor with a tiny tang. It is much creamier and softer than the blocks of commercial mozzarella available in most grocery stores. Fresh mozzarella is usually found in the deli section or fancier cheese section of the market.

Most mozzarella available in the U.S. is made from cow's milk, but traditionally it is a buffalo-milk cheese. If you find it, buy it.

Real fresh mozzarella is made daily. It can come salted or unsalted, so pay attention to that when seasoning your dishes.

You can store fresh mozzarella in the fridge in the brine solution it came in, or, if it is wrapped in plastic, transfer it to a container of water with a teaspoon of salt mixed in. It will last for 3 to 4 days. Best to bring it to room temperature—as with all cheeses—before eating it.

Commercial mozzarella is much lower in water content, sturdier, and it melts very well.

Smoked mozzarella is fresh mozzarella that has been smoked over wood. Refrigerate wrapped.

Lastly, there is burrata. It's essentially a big ball of mozzarella with a creamy center. Imagine a molten chocolate cake, only it's mozzarella. Now, you're going to try that, aren't you?

Sloppy Joes

FORK IN THE ROAD: One basic sauce can be divided to make both beefy and vegetarian sloppy joes.

Every once in a while one or the other of my kids would mention having eaten a sloppy joe for lunch in school, and I was somewhat skeptical about the whole concept: "Really? Did you like it?" The reply? A resounding "YES!" I've always thought that meat loaf didn't get the respect it deserves, but I harbored a secret disdain for sloppy joes. So, I set about unraveling the mystery appeal of this cafeteria classic, and now I fully understand. The slightly sweet and tangy sauce, the soft buns, the glorious messiness of it— what's not to love? And what took me so long to get on board?

I asked my husband what he topped a sloppy joe with when he was a kid, and he said, fairly mulishly, *"Nothing."* My kids agree. I did spend a good amount of time thinking about this and discussing it with others, and you'll see a list of suggestions. One bacchanalian individual suggested kielbasa, which I cannot in good conscience recommend.

Our friend Sarah is a vegetarian, and when she tasted the veggie joe, she was fairly ecstatic. I think it's partly because it was really good, but also partly because she might have assumed that she would never know the pleasures of a sloppy joe again, having eschewed meat. Nothing like a little childhood food flashback to whet the appetite.

Yield

Serves 8

What the Kids Can Do

Measure the ingredients, dump them into the pan (with supervision), put the buns on the plates, spoon the sloppy joe mixture onto the buns.

Nonstick cooking spray

2 pounds lean ground beef,  or see the Fork in the Road for the vegetarian version

1 tablespoon olive oil

1 cup chopped onions

1 teaspoon minced garlic

1½ cups ketchup

1 can (6 ounces) tomato paste

1 tablespoon Dijon mustard or mustard powder

1 tablespoon light or dark brown sugar

1 teaspoon chili powder

½ teaspoon kosher or coarse salt

Freshly ground black pepper, to taste

1 cup water

2 tablespoons Worcestershire sauce (see Note)

1 tablespoon cider vinegar

8 hamburger buns, white or whole wheat (toasted, if desired)

FOR THE TOPPINGS (OPTIONAL)

Pickles

Onions, raw, sautéed, pickled, or fried

Grated cheese

Creamy Coleslaw (page 281)

Potato chips

Fried egg

Pickles and coleslaw are rarely a bad idea on a sandwich.

1. Spray a large skillet with nonstick cooking spray and heat over medium-high heat. Add the beef, and cook, using a spoon to stir and break up the meat into crumbles, until it is browned, 6 to 8 minutes. Drain the beef in a colander.

2. Wipe out the skillet and return it to the burner. Add the olive oil and heat over medium heat. Add the onions and garlic and cook until the onions are tender, 4 minutes. Add the ketchup, tomato paste, mustard, brown sugar, chili powder, salt, and pepper and stir until well combined. Add the water, Worcestershire sauce, and cider vinegar, then return the beef to the pan. Bring to a simmer, adjust the heat if necessary, and simmer uncovered until the liquid has reduced and thickened into a sauce, about 5 minutes.

3. Place an open bun on each plate, and using a large spoon, scoop some of the beef filling onto the bottom half of each bun. Add toppings, if desired, top with the other half of the bun, and dig in.

Make Ahead

The filling is, in fact, even better when you make it a day or two ahead and reheat it; heat the buns right before you serve. This is a good recipe to remember if you are going to have an onslaught of teenagers coming over. Both fillings also freeze well for up to 3 months, well sealed.

Note: Most Worcestershire sauces contain anchovies, and therefore are not vegetarian, but you can find anchovy-free versions. Annie's and The Wizard's are two brands, and any Worcestershire labeled kosher will also be vegetarian. You could also substitute 1 tablespoon balsamic vinegar and 1 tablespoon soy sauce for the 2 tablespoons of Worcestershire.

FORK IN THE ROAD

Vegetarian Joes

If you want to make a vegetarian—actually even vegan—version, use tempeh instead of beef. With your fingers, crumble 1½ pounds of packaged tempeh (usually three 8-ounce packages) into really small pieces. Proceed with the recipe at Step 2, using the tempeh in place of the browned beef (no need to brown the tempeh).

If you want to make both beef and vegetarian sloppy joes, brown, drain, and set aside 1 pound beef. Wash out the pan. Crumble ¾ pound tempeh (1½ 8-ounce packages), and set aside. Continue with Step 2 and after blending the vegan Worcestershire sauce (see Note) and vinegar into the sauce, transfer half the sauce to a second pan. Add the crumbled tempeh to one, and the beef to the other, and simmer for 5 minutes each. Fill the buns according to who wants what.

Tangy Chicken Salad

FORK IN THE ROAD: A chicken salad dressed up with radishes, pickles, and olives, or a classic plain chicken salad—or some of each.

A few piquant and crunchy add-ins turn everyday chicken salad into something you would pay hard-earned cash for at a gourmet deli or specialty food counter. And it's awfully pretty, too. That said, there never has been, and never will be, anything wrong with a straightforward chicken salad. And that's the way many people like it. You can toss a scoop on a green salad, use it to make a sandwich or a wrap, or serve it on crackers.

Yield

Serves 4

What the Kids Can Do

If they can handle a knife that's up to the task, kids can do some cutting and chopping. They can blend together the basic dressing (Step 1), and help mix everything together.

This sandwich is an excellent reason to roast a couple of extra chicken breasts.

½ cup mayonnaise

½ cup chopped celery

¼ cup minced onion

2 teaspoons Dijon mustard

2 teaspoons minced fresh tarragon or 1 teaspoon dried

Kosher or coarse salt and freshly ground black pepper, to taste

3 cups shredded or diced cooked chicken

4 medium-size radishes, cut into matchsticks (see Sidebar)

¼ cup chopped cornichons or sweet pickles

¼ cup chopped pitted black olives, such as Greek or Niçoise

1. Mix together the mayonnaise, celery, onion, mustard, tarragon, and salt and pepper in a large bowl. Add the chicken and stir to combine well. ➤⊷ See the Fork in the Road for a plain-Jane (or fruity) chicken salad.

2. Mix in the radishes, cornichons, and olives. Taste and adjust seasonings.

Plain Chicken Salad

Stop before adding the radishes, pickles, and olives and serve just as is. Or remove as much plain chicken salad as you like, and adjust the amount of the remaining ingredients as needed, depending on how much chicken salad you are working with. Exact amounts are really irrelevant here.

VARIATION:
Red or green grapes are a sweet, fresh, and wonderful addition to chicken salad. Skip the radishes, cornichons, and olives and fold in 1½ cups halved seedless grapes.

How to Cut Radishes into Matchsticks

Trim the tops and roots off the radishes and cut each into ⅛-inch-thick slices. Stack up the slices and cut them into ⅛-inch-wide matchsticks. That's it. If this still seems like too much, just chop them.

Creole Shrimp Rolls

FORK IN THE ROAD: These feature punchy Southern seasoning, but you can separate out some of the shrimp filling and keep it classic.

New Englanders and New England vacationers don't consider it a summer unless there is at least one lobster roll involved. However, wrestling the lobster meat out of its shell and getting it into lobster roll form is usually left to the experts at seafood shacks—and we appreciate it mightily.

But a shrimp roll is much more accessible on every level, and slakes the craving pretty nicely. If you can eat these outdoors, they will taste twice as good for unquantifiable reasons. The Creole part is a twist that purists will sneer at, but it is my go-to version. Skip it if you are just looking for the platonic ideal of a shrimp roll, or if you have family members who aren't interested in a little heat with their seafood.

This is wonderful made with fresh corn during the summer months, but frozen corn is also great if you have a hankering for the rolls during non-corn months. Corn kernels are one of the vegetables I always have in my freezer; the quality, in general, is excellent.

Kosher or coarse salt, to taste

1 pound large shrimp (21 to 25 per pound), peeled and deveined

2 tablespoons unsalted butter, at room temperature

1 cup corn kernels, fresh or frozen

2 ribs celery, thinly sliced

¼ cup minced red onion

⅓ cup chopped cornichon pickles

⅓ cup mayonnaise

1 tablespoon fresh squeezed lemon juice

Freshly ground black pepper, to taste

3 tablespoons Creole Spice Paste (recipe follows), or to taste

4 hot dog rolls (buy good ones!)

Yield

Serves 4

What the Kids Can Do

Mix the ingredients together, make the spice paste, and fill the rolls.

Make Ahead

The Creole paste can be made 3 days ahead of time and the shrimp mixture can be made 1 day ahead of time. The rolls should be toasted and filled just before serving.

1. Place a bowl of ice water near the sink and have a strainer or colander ready. Bring a large pot of water to a boil over high heat. Generously salt the water, return it to a boil, and add the shrimp. Cook just until pink throughout, 3 to 4 minutes. Drain the shrimp and add to the ice bath.

2. Melt 1 tablespoon of the butter in a skillet over medium heat. Add the corn, celery, and onion and sauté just until the corn is barely cooked (the celery should still be pretty crunchy), 2 to 3 minutes. Transfer the mixture to a large bowl. (Wipe out the pan, but keep it handy.) Add the cornichons, mayonnaise, and lemon juice to the corn mixture. Season it with salt and pepper to taste and combine well.

3. Drain the shrimp, shake off any excess water, and give them a quick pat with paper towels. Roughly chop the shrimp. Add them to the bowl with the corn mixture, using a spoon to mix well.

4. ━━◀ You can continue with Step 5 or see the Fork in the Road for a traditional shrimp roll.

5. Blend the seasoning paste into the shrimp mixture and set aside.

6. Melt half of the remaining tablespoon of butter in the skillet over medium heat. Open 2 hot dog rolls and press them into the pan so that the insides come in contact with the buttery bottom of the pan. Cook until nicely golden on the inside, about 2 minutes. Repeat with the remaining butter and rolls.

7. Divide the shrimp mixture evenly among the toasted hot dog rolls, heaping it in (these are messy to eat; that's just the cost of doing business). If you've made some traditional rolls, make sure the spice-lovers get the right rolls.

What Makes These Creole?

New Orleans chef Frank Brigtsen explains Creole food (versus Cajun) as "the difference between city and country tables." Creole is the city version, developed over 300 years of New Orleans evolution. It's a blend of French and Spanish with heavy influences from the other European, African, and Caribbean settlers in the town. Peppers, onions, and celery are key ingredients in Creole cuisine, and all are included in this sandwich.

Cajun cooking, he says, "has its origins in the countryside of Acadiana, Louisiana, and is also rooted in French cuisine, but more rustic in nature." So how do we know if this recipe is truly Creole? Or maybe Cajun? Eh. I've said it before, and I'm repeating it now— authenticity isn't necessarily my strong suit, but flavorful, satisfying food is, and these shrimp rolls deliver on that promise.

Creole Spice Paste

Makes ¼ cup

Leftover spice paste is nice to add to chilis or soups, or to rub on chicken breasts or steaks before broiling or grilling them.

- ¼ cup coarsely chopped onion
- 1 clove garlic, peeled
- 1 tablespoon roughly chopped fresh flat-leaf parsley leaves
- ½ jalapeño pepper, seeded
- ¼ teaspoon ground cayenne pepper
- ¼ teaspoon dried thyme
- ¼ teaspoon paprika
- Kosher or coarse salt and freshly ground black pepper, to taste

Place the onion, garlic, parsley, jalapeño, cayenne, thyme, paprika, and salt and pepper in a food processor and process until the spice paste is well blended, scraping down the sides of the bowl at least once. Transfer the paste to a small plastic container. Cover and refrigerate until ready to use.

FORK IN THE ROAD

A Classic Shrimp Roll

If you'd like to make a portion of the shrimp mixture less spicy, scoop out the amount to a separate bowl and head directly to Step 6. Add the spice paste to the remaining shrimp mixture, making sure to adjust the amount appropriately.

Tiny grilled cheese and pretzel bites

CHEESY PRETZEL SNAPS, *page 43*

What makes a good snack? Frankly you're asking the wrong person (not that you actually asked me, but let's gloss over that): I would eat anything for a snack. I would eat two big forkfuls of leftover Carnitas (page 220), a crispy chicken wing (page 61), a cold meatball (pages 169 to 173). And that's not even getting into the sweeter stuff, like or a sliver of coffee cake (page 15).

Snacks

But when kids ask for a snack they're usually not thinking about a little wedge of noodle kugel from the fridge (page 301—oh, would that be perfect right now). Jack once hissed at me, "Mom, when Lucien asks for a snack, he is NOT expecting a bowl of lo mein." Well, excuse me. He seemed quite content with that lo mein.

Anyway, this chapter contains five answers to the eternal, "What do we have for a snack?" question. Beyond these choices, you'll want to consider the recipes in the Appetizers chapter. And beyond that, I humbly submit that a snack is in the eye of the beholder, and when I'm hungry at 10 in the morning or 3:30 in the afternoon, I have no problem picking at that pasta with Bolognese sauce (page 195) from last night.

With sultry caramelized onions (page 42)

Olive oil and a sprinkle of paprika

Hummus

FORK IN THE ROAD: A simple hummus is a crowd pleaser . . . a hummus with caramelized onions is something to show off.

For a long time, it seemed as if everyone else's kids liked hummus but mine didn't, and I felt like they were missing out. Hummus is such a great food—a dip and a sandwich spread; nutritious, ubiquitous, and truly easy to make. And finally it happened: Hummus slid over onto the list of liked foods. I don't know why, but I didn't stop to question it. Probably something else slid off, because that's the way things seem to work. But hey, mission accomplished.

My friend Chris Styler, who is fairly brilliant in the kitchen, was cooking with me one day when I realized I was out of tahini. He said, "Just use sesame oil instead." Can you believe it? It's so crazy and so simple at the same time. Genius. Seriously. I now sometimes use both, which gives the whole thing a deeply rich sesame flavor.

2 cans (15.5 ounces each) chickpeas, drained and rinsed

2 cloves garlic, minced

⅓ cup tahini

2 teaspoons sesame oil (optional)

3 tablespoons fresh lemon juice

¼ cup extra-virgin olive oil, plus extra for drizzling if desired

1 teaspoon ground cumin

Kosher or coarse salt and freshly ground black pepper, to taste

About ½ cup water

Paprika or cayenne, for garnish

1. Place the chickpeas and garlic in the food processor and pulse a few times. Add the tahini, sesame oil (if using), lemon juice, olive oil, cumin, and salt and pepper.

Yield

Makes 3 cups

What the Kids Can Do

Rinse and drain the chickpeas, measure the ingredients and dump them into the food processor, and run the machine with supervision.

2. ✦ You can continue with Step 3 or see the Fork in the Road to make the onion and other versions.

3. Puree all the ingredients. Then, with the motor running add about ⅓ cup of the water. Allow the mixture to process for about 2 minutes (see Cooking Tip), adding more water if you'd like a thinner consistency.

4. Transfer the hummus to a serving bowl, drizzle with a bit of olive oil if you like, and sprinkle with the paprika or cayenne.

Caramelized Onion Hummus

Heat 1 tablespoon olive oil in a large skillet over medium heat. Add 2 sliced or chopped onions and slowly sauté until they are very nicely browned but not too dark, at least 10 minutes, but preferably 15 to 20 minutes. Add most of them to the food processor with the other ingredients in Step 1 and continue with the recipe. Save a small amount to top the hummus.

Or, to make half plain/half onion hummus, sauté just 1 onion in a couple of teaspoons of olive oil. Blend up the hummus as directed above and remove half to a small bowl. Add the caramelized onion to the rest in the food processor and blend for 1 minute; serve in a separate small bowl.

Hummus Plus

You can dress up a plain hummus with other favorite ingredients instead of the caramelized onions. Instead try: roasted peppers, smoked paprika, roasted garlic, artichoke hearts, harissa paste, sun-dried tomatoes, or pitted olives. Add one or more favorites to the food processor with the other ingredients in Step 1 and continue with the recipe.

Make Ahead

This will keep in the refrigerator for up to 1 week. Bring to room temperature before serving if possible, and also know that it will thicken in the fridge, so if you'd like a looser consistency, put it back in the food processor with a couple of teaspoons of water and give it a whirl.

Cooking Tip

I have made hummus for years, but only recently did I figure something out that made me love it even more. Don't just process the mixture until it is blended— let that machine go for 2 or 3 minutes at full throttle for the creamiest texture. And even better, the heat from the motor starts to warm the hummus a bit, so while you can certainly make it ahead, there is something about fresh, slightly warm hummus that is just fantastic.

Cheesy Pretzel Snaps

FORK IN THE ROAD: Filled with cheese, or with a little ham also tucked in, these pretzel sandwiches have some protein and substance.

So many of us stock our snack drawers and pantries with pretzels, feeling like they must be a better nibbling solution than fried chips and the like. But watching our kids (and certainly speaking for myself, us adults) reaching for a handful of plain pretzels over and over again doesn't feel like the best or most nourishing daily solution to the munchies.

A small piece of cheese tucked in between two pretzels makes them into something with a bit more flavor and heft, and you still get that satisfying snacky crunch. Including a piece of ham is another option. And these are quite fun and easy for the kids to put together.

2 thick slices cheddar cheese

40 mini pretzels (if you can get the little square pretzel "snaps," even better)

1. Preheat the oven to 400°F. Line a baking sheet with aluminum foil.

2. Place 20 pretzels on the prepared baking sheet leaving space between each.

3. Cut or tear the cheese slices into small pieces, each the size of a pretzel, 20 pieces in all. Place a piece of cheese on each of the 20 pretzels on the baking sheet.

4. ━━◄ You can continue with Step 5 or see the Fork in the Road for the ham version.

Yield

Makes 20 mini pretzel sandwiches

What the Kids Can Do

Make the pretzel sandwiches!

Make Ahead

These may be made up to a few hours ahead and kept at room temperature.

5. Top the cheese (or ham) with another pretzel. Bake until the cheese is melted, about 6 minutes. Allow the pretzels to cool for a minute or two before serving. Eat warm or at room temperature.

These would be great with a bowl of soup to round out an easy meal.

FORK IN THE ROAD

Ham & Cheese Pretzel Snaps

Top the cheddar with a same-size piece of ham before closing the sandwiches with the second pretzels. Proceed as directed. Another option is to use another firm but melty cheese, like Gruyère or Swiss or provolone.

Salty, savory snackiness.

Tortilla Scoops with Minty Pineapple-Jalapeño Salsa

FORK IN THE ROAD: And don't stop at salsa—check out the list of fillings that would be so happy piled into a tortilla scoop.

This bracing yellow and green salsa is so, so pretty. Even with the slight kick from the jalapeños (and of course the amount of jalapeño can be adjusted as desired), it is really refreshing. Piled into those easy-to-find little bowl-shaped tortilla chips, the salsa makes a lovely salty-sweet snack or appetizer.

Also try the salsa atop quesadillas, a simply grilled chicken breast, or a piece of fish, and absolutely on the Carnitas (page 220) and the Fish Tacos (page 214). Or just serve with pita chips for a bright appetizer. If you don't feel like neatly dicing the ingredients, just give them a rough chop—it might not look as elegant, but it will taste exactly the same.

2 cups diced fresh pineapple (¼-inch dice)

¼ cup diced yellow bell pepper (¼-inch dice)

¼ cup diced green bell pepper (¼-inch dice)

1 to 2 tablespoons chopped fresh mint leaves

1 teaspoon minced fresh jalapeño pepper, or to taste

1 tablespoon fresh lime juice

Kosher or coarse salt, to taste

About 25 scoop-shaped tortilla chips

1. Place the pineapple, yellow and green bell peppers, mint, jalapeño, lime juice, and salt in a medium-size bowl and toss gently until well combined.

Yield

Makes 2 cups salsa, about 25 tortilla scoops

Make Ahead

The salsa can be made up to a day ahead of time. Fill the tortilla shells just before serving or they will get soggy.

The colors of this salsa are so cheery.

2. Scoop a heaping tablespoon of the salsa into each tortilla scoop and serve on a large plate or platter.

FORK IN THE ROAD

Tortilla Scoops Many, Many Ways

You can use these great little tortilla bowls to use up all sorts of leftovers. Any of these fillings would make a great snack, or maybe an appetizer or even just a slightly weird, fun dinner.

Sloppy Joes filling (beef or vegetarian), page 29

Shredded Jerk Chicken, page 127

Shrimp Roll filling (Creole or regular), page 35

Egg Salad filling, page 22

Tangy (or plain) Chicken Salad, page 32

Shrimp or Chicken Taco filling, page 217

Carnitas, page 220

What the Kids Can Do

Chop the ingredients with an age-appropriate knife (if they touch the jalapeño, make sure they don't touch their eyes, nose, or lips, and that they wash their hands very well with soapy water after). Mix everything together. Fill the scoops.

Deviled Eggs Five Ways

FORK IN THE ROAD: Deviled eggs are the best blank slate for all kinds of improvisation.

W ho doesn't love deviled eggs? Deviled eggs know no time or demographic, they are just blissfully democratic appetizers. They are in the same category as pigs in a blanket: Everyone is happy to see them and sophisticated people shed their cool when they appear. You can't be annoyed when there are deviled eggs around; it would be like being irritated in the presence of a puppy or a rainbow.

But while a straightforward deviled egg is always a pretty sight, sometimes a little pop of exciting flavor is called for. Below is a simple, perfect deviled egg. The Fork in the Road offers versions that are something to talk about.

12 hard-boiled large eggs, peeled
    (see Making Perfect Hard-Boiled Eggs, page 50)

⅓ cup mayonnaise

1 tablespoon finely minced shallot

2 teaspoons Dijon mustard

Few dashes of hot sauce, such as Tabasco or sriracha

Kosher or coarse salt and freshly ground black pepper, to taste

Paprika for garnish (optional—skip it if you are using any of the Fork in the Road options)

1. Cut the eggs in half lengthwise. Carefully remove each yolk and place it in the bowl of a food processor (or a medium-size mixing bowl). Place the egg whites on a serving platter, cut side up.

2. Add the mayonnaise, shallot, Dijon mustard, hot sauce, and salt and pepper to the egg yolks. Pulse the mixture if you want it to be a bit coarse, let it run if you are looking for supersmooth. Or, if you prefer, mash the ingredients together in a bowl with a fork until smooth and well blended.

Yield

Makes 24 deviled egg halves

What the Kids Can Do

Mash up the filling, decide which seasonings to add, fill the eggs—piping in the filling is one of the best kid kitchen tasks ever.

Make Ahead

The hard-boiled eggs can be made up to 5 days ahead of time and stored, in their shells, in the fridge. Peeled eggs can be stored well covered for 2 days. Filled deviled eggs can be stored in the refrigerator, covered, for a day. Add final toppings just before serving.

Middle Eastern,
with za'atar
and cumin

Lemon,
capers,
and chives

Avocado
and
bacon

Goat cheese, chive,
and
jalapeño

Classic,
with a sprinkle
of paprika

3. You can continue with Step 4 or see the Fork in the Road for even more devilish eggs.

4. Fill a sturdy zipper-top bag with the filling and cut a little hole in one bottom corner. Squeeze the filling into the egg whites to make attractive mounds. Or simply scoop the filling into the egg whites with a spoon. Sprinkle the yolks with paprika for a final touch.

FORK IN THE ROAD

Four More Deviled Eggs

The amounts below are for flavoring the whole batch of 24 egg halves. You can also fill half the eggs with the plain filling mixture, and season the rest of the filling with half the amount of any of the following.

Avocado and Bacon Deviled Eggs
When you mash up the yolk-mayonnaise mixture, add 1 nice ripe avocado cut into chunks and a little squeeze of lemon or lime juice. Once filled, sprinkle some nice fat crumbles of crisp cooked bacon on top of the filling.

Goat Cheese and Chive Deviled Eggs
Use either soft or slightly crumbly goat cheese, ⅓ to ½ cup for a dozen eggs, depending on how pungent the cheese is. You can either blend the cheese right into the yolk filling, or sprinkle it on top of the mounded filling. A few chopped chives on top add color and additional flavor, or a sprinkle of minced jalapeños add "hey now!"

Middle Eastern Deviled Eggs
Za'atar is an amazing seasoning that is a somewhat grassy, nutty, and slightly tart blend of herbs that is used often in Middle Eastern cooking. It usually contains thyme, sumac, and sesame seeds, but blends might also include oregano, marjoram, cumin, or fennel seed. Mix 1 teaspoon za'atar and ¼ teaspoon cumin into the yolk filling. Sprinkle the filled egg halves with additional toasted sesame seeds if desired.

Deviled Eggs with Lemon, Capers, and Chives
These are bright and lively. Blend 1 teaspoon finely grated lemon zest, 2 tablespoons rinsed, drained, and chopped capers, and 2 tablespoons minced chives into the yolk filling.

Making Perfect Hard-Boiled Eggs

Place the eggs (this recipe calls for 12) in a large saucepan and add water to cover by at least an inch. Bring the water to a boil over high heat. Allow the water to boil for 30 seconds, then remove the pan from the heat and let the eggs sit in the water for 9 minutes. Drain and let sit in a bowl of very cold water for a few minutes.

Peeling the eggs while they're still slightly warm often makes it easier to remove the shells in big pieces, so you don't have to chip them off and mess up the eggs. Tap them lightly and give them a quick roll on the counter to crackle up the shells. Return them to the water because it often helps to peel the eggs while they are submerged, or under running water. Peel carefully. (See the Make Ahead tip if making the eggs in advance.)

Granola Bars

FORK IN THE ROAD: Extra granola bars can be turned into a delicious parfait.

The only reason there wasn't a recipe for a granola bar in my first book, *The Mom 100 Cookbook,* was because I never got the recipe just right. But if at first you don't succeed . . . and finally, a bar worthy of making again and again.

When I was growing up, there was always a jar of wheat germ in my house, which made its way into pancakes, breads, shakes, and anything else my chic-hippie mother could think of. It didn't exactly endear me to wheat germ, and as for many kids of the seventies, it has the tendency to trigger slight flashbacks. This recipe, however, has ensured that a jar of wheat germ has taken its rightful place in my home. The wheat germ just gives some bonus nutrition to the bars (see What Exactly Is Wheat Germ?, page 52) and adds a little bit more crunch and texture, too.

Unsalted butter or nonstick cooking spray for greasing the baking pan

2½ cups old-fashioned oatmeal

½ cup toasted wheat germ

½ cup honey

¼ cup packed light or dark brown sugar

3 tablespoons unsalted butter

1 teaspoon pure vanilla extract

½ teaspoon kosher or coarse salt

1 cup dried fruit, such as raisins, cherries, cranberries, or chopped dried apricots, dates, or plums

1. Preheat the oven to 350°F. Butter a 9-inch-square baking pan or spray it generously with nonstick spray.

Yield

Makes 12 bars

What the Kids Can Do

Measure the ingredients; pour and maybe stir (with supervision) at the stove. They can also press the mixture into the pan, using the back of a spoon.

Make Ahead

These will keep in an airtight container at room temperature for up to a week.

2. Spread the oatmeal on a rimmed baking sheet and bake for 10 minutes. Then add the wheat germ, give it a stir to combine with the oats, and toast until the oatmeal is golden brown, 5 minutes longer. Remove the oat mixture and reduce the heat to 300°F.

3. Meanwhile, melt the honey, sugar, and butter in a medium-size saucepan over medium heat until the mixture comes to a simmer. Simmer for a minute, then stir in the vanilla and salt.

4. Scoop the oatmeal and wheat germ into the pot, add the dried fruit, and stir vigorously until everything is well combined. Transfer the mixture to the prepared baking pan and press it carefully so that it fills the pan evenly, including the corners. (The mixture is hot; use a spoon or folded wax paper if you are using your fingers.)

5. Bake until golden brown (the mixture shouldn't be super hard, but will firm up as it cools), about 25 minutes. Cool in the pan on a wire rack for at least 3 hours before cutting into bars. Make one cut across the middle of the pan, then another across the middle going the other way, then slice each quarter into 3 rectangular bars.

FORK
IN THE
ROAD

Granola Parfaits

For each parfait, crumble 1 granola bar. Layer the crumbles in a glass, alternating them with 1 cup of vanilla yogurt (or the flavor of your choice).

What Exactly Is Wheat Germ?

Tiny little wheat germ grains pack a pretty powerful punch in terms of vitamins, minerals, and protein.

So, wheat germ (short for germination) is the part of wheat that sprouts and grows into a new plant. It's actually the most nutritious part of the wheat kernel, but it gets removed when wheat is processed into white flour, to keep the flour from being too coarse. The germ, interestingly, makes up a mere 2.5 percent of a grain of wheat. It takes over 50 pounds of wheat to make 1 pound of wheat germ. That gives one a little more respect for this sturdy little germ.

The crumbles go
to the baker.

SAVORY ZUCCHINI PUFF PASTRY TARTS, *page 67*

Whenever we have people over, it means appetizers are in the mix, which makes my guys very happy. When time is tight, I stop by the olive/antipasti bar at the local supermarket or specialty store, grab a cheese and some bread or crackers, and then maybe take five minutes to transform a container of peanuts into a fragrant bowl of fabulousness (see page 56). A bowl of sliced peppers and baby carrots never hurts either.

Appetizers

When I want the pre-dinner hour to feel more robust, I go for a hot dip, either vegetarian or lush with crab (page 59), or easy Prosciutto-Wrapped Shrimp or asparagus (page 65), or zucchini tarts using store-bought puff pastry (page 67).

And when I'm feeling really generous, a platter of lick-your-fingers chicken wings—maybe Buffalo (page 61), maybe glazed with honey garlic sauce (page 63), will always be greeted with good cheer and a certain hint of voracity—at least it will in my house. As my older son, Jack, said recently, "I hate to be that guy . . . but does anyone want the last chicken wing?"

Other smart options: the Hummus on page 41 and the various options for filled tortilla scoops on page 45.

Sweet and Spicy Peanuts

FORK IN THE ROAD: *A handful of spicy sweet nuts or a handful of savory herbed nuts.*

My family loves peanuts as much as we love popcorn, and that is saying a lot. We buy them in the shell in five-pound bags, and the crunch of a peanut shell underfoot in our house is not unusual. Saloonlike, yes, but not unusual.

Although peanuts—like popcorn, like lobster, like fresh corn, like many other pretty perfect foods—generally need no adornment, sometimes a little embellishment is fun and delicious. These nuts are a crazy combo of sweet with a slap of piquant—just pretty fantastic. And SO EASY.

2 tablespoons sugar

⅛ teaspoon cayenne

2 cups cocktail peanuts, preferably lightly salted

1 tablespoon water

1. Preheat the oven to 400°F.

2. Mix the sugar and cayenne together in a small bowl, or see the Fork in the Road for an herbed spiced alternative.

3. On a rimmed baking sheet, toss the peanuts with the sugar mixture, then sprinkle on the water and toss again. Bake, stirring once or twice during the baking time, until the nuts are glazed and just barely browned and smell fantastic, 6 to 8 minutes. Watch carefully because they start to burn quickly. Cool completely on the baking sheet before transferring to bowls for serving.

Yield

Serves 8 to 12

What the Kids Can Do

Measure and mix the ingredients and toss them on the baking sheet with the nuts. After baking, make sure the kids don't touch the nuts until they are really cool; the sugar makes them quite hot.

Make Ahead

You bet. Keep them in a container at room temperature for up to 5 days.

Herbed Spiced Nuts

An herbal note on nuts is often unexpected. I didn't really know if my kids would like these, and was happy when they did. A little bowl of them accompanying a cheese platter is such a nice and easy and special nosh to offer your guests, who will probably ask you for the recipe. The fact that they're so easy to make won't make them love you less.

Just toss the following ingredients together with the 2 cups of cocktail peanuts. Or use half of each of the main recipe ingredients and half of the below ingredients, and use each to season up 1 cup of peanuts. Put each type on one half of the baking sheet, and serve in separate bowls.

1 tablespoon light or dark brown sugar

1 teaspoon freshly minced garlic

1 teaspoon chopped fresh thyme

1 teaspoon chopped fresh rosemary

½ teaspoon smoked paprika (optional)

½ teaspoon freshly ground black pepper

Mix all the ingredients together in a small bowl, then toss them with the peanuts and sprinkle on the water, following Step 3 on page 56. Bake as above, watching carefully to make sure they don't burn. Cool as directed.

You could try the basic recipe with any kind of nuts from cashews to pecans.

Lemony Parmesan Artichoke Dip

FORK IN THE ROAD: This addictive dip can be made with crab instead of artichokes, or made with half the amount of each and baked in two smaller dishes.

Hot artichoke dips are not exactly revolutionary, but this one is lush with Parmesan cheese and a sparkly shot of lemon to make it more modern. Go for half crab and half artichoke if you are really celebrating, making both vegetarians and pescatarians feel indulged.

Serve this decadent dip with crackers or raw vegetables. You can also scoop it on crostini. And it would be very cool to serve it with leaves of steamed large artichokes.

1 package (8 ounces) cream cheese, regular or low-fat (Neufchâtel), at room temperature

2 tablespoons milk, half-and-half, or heavy (whipping) cream

1 red bell pepper, stemmed, seeded, and minced

½ cup freshly grated Parmesan

3 tablespoons minced fresh flat-leaf parsley

3 scallions, white and light green parts, minced

1 teaspoon finely grated lemon zest

1 tablespoon fresh lemon juice

Freshly ground black pepper, to taste

2 cans (7¾ ounces each) artichoke hearts, drained, rinsed, and chopped, ▬◀€ or see Fork in the Road for a crabmeat substitution

Kosher or coarse salt, to taste

Yield

Serves 8 to 12

What the Kids Can Do

Measure the ingredients, zest the lemons (if they can handle the grater), mix up the ingredients, spoon the dip into the baking dish.

Make Ahead

You can prepare the dip following Step 2 up to a day ahead and refrigerate, covered. Either bring to room temperature before placing in the oven, or add about 5 minutes to the baking time.

1. Preheat the oven to 400°F.

2. Stir together the cream cheese, milk, bell pepper, Parmesan, parsley, scallions, lemon zest, lemon juice, and black pepper in a medium-size bowl until well blended. Blend in the artichoke hearts. Taste and season with salt.

3. Transfer the mixture to a small shallow baking dish and bake until bubbly, 20 to 25 minutes. You may want to pass it under the broiler during the last few minutes to give it a beautiful golden top. Serve hot.

FORK IN THE ROAD

Lemony Parmesan Crab Dip

Swap out the artichoke hearts for 1 pound crabmeat (see Note, page 143). Or, for half artichoke and half crab, divide the cream cheese mixture in half, add 1 can of artichoke hearts (chopped) to one portion and ½ pound crabmeat to the other. Put each of them into a 2-cup shallow baking dish, and proceed with baking in Step 3, baking them until each is browned and bubbly, 15 to 20 minutes.

What Does "To Taste" Really Mean?

Throughout these and many other recipes you often see salt, pepper, or other ingredients without amounts given, but an indication to add "to taste." To whose taste? How do you know if your taste is the same as your kid's taste, or your guest's taste? What amount do you start with? And what happens when other ingredients get added later in the recipe; how will that affect what you did "to taste" earlier?

Through experience and tasting you'll get a better understanding of what that means to you and your family. A few things to keep in mind:

1. Season a bit as you go. This lets the flavors develop together, and ensures that you don't add too much all at once.

2. Consider other ingredients in the dish. Canned beans, tomatoes, cheeses, broths, and other packaged items sometimes pack in a lot of salt, especially if you're not using a reduced-sodium version. And, of course, things like anchovies, soy sauce, and capers are all super-salty.

3. You can always add seasoning at the end, and people can always season at the table. Too little salt and pepper is almost always preferable to too much.

Buffalo Chicken Wings

FORK IN THE ROAD: **What says "I love you" more than Buffalo wings? Buffalo wings *and* honey garlic wings!**

On the rare, indulgent occasion we find ourselves in the situation where we are ordering a bunch of good-crappy bar snacks in a group, and people are throwing out ideas ("Nachos? Spinach dip?"), I watch my husband casually waiting to see if someone is going to say "wings." And if no one does, he'll offer it up, but in this simulated, nonchalant voice, "Hey, how 'bout wings?" Like, "Hey!—it just occurred to me, and I don't really care one way or the other, but I'm just thinking of the good of the group."

Frank's RedHot Original hot sauce bills itself as the perfect blend of flavor and heat, and while you are welcome to experiment with all kinds of different hot sauces, you will probably find that it's Frank's RedHot that makes you feel like you are eating authentic, traditional Buffalo wings. It is, as they say on their website, the "secret ingredient used in the original Buffalo wings created in Buffalo, N.Y. in 1964." A fine year for wings. I'm a believer.

FOR THE WINGS

- Vegetable oil or nonstick cooking spray, for oiling the baking sheet
- 4 pounds chicken wings, whole or cut apart at the joints, wing tips discarded, if desired

FOR THE BLUE CHEESE DRESSING

- 1 cup crumbled blue cheese
- ½ cup sour cream
- ½ cup heavy (whipping) cream or half-and-half
- 1 tablespoon white wine vinegar or cider vinegar
- Kosher or coarse salt and freshly ground black pepper, to taste

- ⅔ cup Frank's RedHot pepper sauce, or to taste (see Note)
- Celery sticks for serving (optional, but recommended)

Yield

Serves 8

What the Kids Can Do

Measure ingredients, drizzle the sauce(s) over the wings. Mix up the blue cheese dressing.

Make Ahead

The blue cheese dressing and honey garlic sauce can be made up to 2 days ahead of time and stored in the fridge.

Note: The ⅔ cup of hot sauce makes for some pretty spicy wings. You can use less if you want.

1. Preheat the oven to 500°F (if your oven goes to 550°F, all the better, do that). Lightly oil a rimmed baking sheet, or spray it with nonstick spray. If you have an exhaust fan, turn it on.

2. Place the wings on the baking sheet, meaty side down. Bake the wings until quite crispy, 30 minutes, turning them after 15 minutes.

3. ━━◣ You can continue with Step 4 or see the Fork in the Road to make honey garlic wings.

4. Meanwhile, make the dressing. Mix together the blue cheese, sour cream, cream, vinegar, and salt and pepper in a small bowl. Set aside.

5. Remove the wings from the oven and sprinkle the hot sauce over them. Toss so the wings are coated with the sauce (use tongs if the wings are too hot). Serve on a platter with the blue cheese dressing for dipping, and the celery sticks, if desired.

Always Remember and Never Forget

1. Lots of napkins. Lots of them.

2. Bowls for the bones (to be emptied regularly—no one likes to keep track of how many wings she's eaten).

Honey Garlic Chicken Wings

NICELY STICKY, SLIGHTLY SWEET, a little peppery from the ginger, these first graced the cocktail table at Gary's birthday party/Academy Awards party, and let's just say I should have made more.

The amounts here are also for 4 pounds of wings. Or split the 4 pounds of wings into two batches, and make half the spicy hot version, half as follows (using half the ingredient amounts).

½ cup reduced-sodium soy sauce (or ⅓ cup regular soy sauce plus 3 tablespoons water)

⅓ cup honey

2 tablespoons minced fresh ginger

2 teaspoons minced garlic

2 teaspoons cornstarch

¾ cup water

1. Follow the steps on the facing page through Step 2.

2. While the wings are cooking, combine the soy sauce, honey, ginger, garlic, cornstarch, and water in a small saucepan and whisk until well combined. Bring to a simmer over medium-high heat and simmer until thickened slightly, about 5 minutes.

3. When the wings are cooked though, remove from the oven and reduce the oven temperature to 450°F.

4. Pour the honey-garlic sauce over the wings. Toss the wings so that they are coated with the sauce (you can use tongs if the wings are too hot), then return them to the oven. Bake until the sauce gets a nice glazed look, about 5 minutes. Serve the wings on a platter.

Skip the blue cheese dressing and hot sauce for this version, but keep the celery; what the hell.

Prosciutto-Wrapped Shrimp with Smoked Paprika

FORK IN THE ROAD: Try the asparagus version for a change or a contrast.

These are a huge hit in my house. You can make them with smaller shrimp (reduce the cooking time slightly), but the bigger the shrimp, the bigger the *wow* factor. It's really nice to do both the wrapped shrimp and wrapped asparagus, as the different shapes look pretty cool and festive together. You can also grill either version.

Make sure you have napkins on hand, and a little bowl (or two) for people to toss their shrimp tail shells into.

Nonstick cooking spray (optional)

1 tablespoon extra-virgin olive oil

1½ teaspoons smoked paprika

½ teaspoon freshly ground black pepper

1 pound jumbo shrimp (16 to 20 per pound), shelled (tails left on) and deveined, ▬◄ or see the Fork in the Road to use asparagus

4 ounces very thinly sliced prosciutto (see page 9), sliced lengthwise into ½-inch strips

1. Place the oven rack about 4 inches below the heat source and preheat the broiler. Spray a rimmed baking sheet with nonstick cooking spray, or line it with parchment paper.

2. Combine the olive oil, paprika, and pepper in a bowl. Add the shrimp and toss until they are coated with the seasoned oil.

3. Wrap each shrimp with a strip of prosciutto, spiraling it up the shrimp until the shrimp is encased. Place the shrimp on the prepared baking sheet.

Yield

Serves 6

What the Kids Can Do

Wrap the prosciutto around the shrimp or asparagus: It's a little bit of fine motor-skill work, but that's a good thing. And when cooked, any mistakes will probably not be visible and they sure won't harm the flavor.

Make Ahead

You can wrap the shrimp or asparagus up to a day ahead and leave them loosely covered in the refrigerator.

4. Broil until the tops are crispy, 3 minutes, then turn each shrimp and broil to crisp the other side, 3 minutes more. The shrimp will be cooked through.

5. Serve with the crispier side up.

FORK IN THE ROAD
Asparagus Wrapped in Prosciutto

Such a lovely way to kick off a spring meal. Try not to use the super pencil-thin asparagus, which don't have enough heft for this recipe—medium or fat ones are best. Just substitute 1 pound medium-thick asparagus (trimmed and bottoms peeled if the outer skin is thick) for the shrimp. Coat the asparagus with the seasoned oil, then wrap each stalk with the prosciutto, leaving the top and bottom of the stalk exposed. Broil for 2 to 3 minutes, turn the asparagus over, and broil another 2 to 3 minutes for crisp prosciutto and crisp-tender asparagus.

You can also use ½ pound shrimp and ½ pound asparagus, and divide the seasoned oil, placing half in a small bowl to toss with the shrimp. Drizzle the rest over the asparagus on a plate and toss carefully to coat the stalks.

Frankly, you could wrap a pencil in prosciutto and I might eat it.

Shrimp Come in All Sizes

Shrimp are sold by the quantity per pound, and then given corresponding names like medium or jumbo. However, the name attached to the quantity per pound varies from brand to brand, market to market. Here's a good scale to use, with the two numbers representing a range of how many shrimp per pound that size will yield. If a recipe provides a count per pound, that's usually a more reliable measure to go by than a name.

Small: 51/60 per pound

Medium: 41/40 per pound

Large: 31/35 per pound

Extra Large: 26/30 per pound

Jumbo: 16/20 per pound

Colossal: 13/15 per pound

Super Colossal: U-12 (meaning under 12 per pound)

Extra Colossal: U-10 (meaning under 10 per pound . . . also meaning invite me over for dinner)

Savory Zucchini Puff Pastry Tarts

FORK IN THE ROAD: Simple, or with a sprinkle of your favorite cheese.

I f I were a country music writer I would write a song to Pepperidge Farm. I want to thank them for making puff pastry accessible to all of us, and therefore turning all of us into skilled tart makers. It might go something like this:

Oh, frozen puff pastry, you're buttery and flaky.

I think of you when I don't want to bake-y.

Of all the things I could make from scratch

Puff pastry would put me in the booby hatch.

Shall I keep my day job? I believe that's what's called a rhetorical question.

A lot of puff pastry recipes require you to roll out the dough a bit; I don't find it's necessary, and I'm always looking for shortcuts.

2 sheets puff pastry (from a 17.3-ounce package)

1 tablespoon olive oil

2 small zucchini, thinly sliced

Kosher or coarse salt and freshly ground black pepper, to taste

1 teaspoon chopped fresh oregano

2 tablespoons Dijon mustard (optional; see Note)

1. Preheat the oven to 400°F. Remove the puff pastry from the freezer and thaw according to the package directions.

2. Unfold both of the puff pastry squares onto a clean surface and cut them into thirds (it will probably be very easy to

Yield

Serves 8 to 10

What the Kids Can Do

Unfold the puff pastry, spread on the mustard (if using), distribute the zucchini, and sprinkle the cheese if desired.

Make Ahead

This is best eaten on the day it's made, but it can keep at room temperature happily for several hours. If you made it a day or two ahead, wrap it in plastic wrap and keep it in the fridge. Bring to room temperature or gently reheat in a 325°F oven for about 4 minutes.

Note: I love the kick of Dijon as a base for the tarts, but if you think it might be too spicy for some in your family, skip it, or use 1 tablespoon and coat a few of the rectangles and leave the others bare under the zucchini.

Going, Going, Going . . .

Gone

cut along the folds). You will have 6 pieces. Place them onto 1 or 2 rimmed baking sheets—whatever will fit the pieces without them touching. Use a fork to prick holes all over the pastry, leaving a ¼-inch border unpricked on all sides (see the Cooking Tip).

3. You can continue with Step 4 to make the zucchini topping, or see the Fork in the Road for some other topping suggestions.

4. Heat the olive oil in a large skillet over medium-high heat. Add the zucchini, season with salt and pepper, and sauté until tender, about 5 minutes. Remove the skillet from the heat and stir in the oregano.

5. Spread each piece of pastry with 1 teaspoon of the Dijon mustard, if using, leaving the borders plain (again about ¼ inch on all sides). Spread the sautéed zucchini evenly over the mustard, still maintaining the border.

6. Bake until the border of the puff pastry is nicely browned and puffed, 20 to 25 minutes. Transfer the baking sheets to wire racks and let the pastries cool for a couple of minutes, before cutting each into pieces.

Cooking Tip

To create a more defined, puffed-up border on each tart, use a sharp knife to score all around the rectangle about ⅓ inch from the border.

Cut down no more than halfway through the thickness of the uncooked pastry. This will allow the edges to really rise, while the ingredient-covered middle section will remain flatter, though still flaky.

FORK IN THE ROAD

Savory Continued

You could also sprinkle grated Parmesan, Gruyère, or crumbled goat or blue cheese on top for the last couple of minutes of baking. Use about ¾ cup of cheese for the 6 rectangles.

And, you can use this as a blueprint recipe for about five million different tarts. It's that simple, and it's that flexible. Thaw puff pastry and cut the sheets into thirds, smear them with something delicious, like pesto or mayonnaise or a flavored aioli, layer on some quick-cooking, thinly sliced vegetables, and sprinkle or crumble something else on top, such as chopped nuts or pumpkin seeds.

Kale

Sprouts

There's life beyond romaine (not that we don't love our romaine)

Arugula

Red
leaf

Once upon a time, not too long ago, when someone said "salad," we all immediately envisioned a pile of lettuce with some dressing, maybe a few slices of tomato or carrot or cucumber. Now the word "salad" evokes a broad spectrum of possibilities—it's really become a kind of limitless category. Grains, proteins, vegetables, and fruits. Cooked and/or raw. Appetizer, main course, side dish. Warm, room temperature, cold. Pops of dried fruit, little elements of crunch, multiple textures playing off each other. What defines what a salad is? You do.

Salads

I love the notion of the flexible, convertible salad. A salad that can do double duty as a side dish and as a main dish (especially if there is a vegetarian in the house). Or a salad that can make use of last night's leftovers. Or a salad that might start off warm, and then the next day be a packed room-temperature lunch for your kid. And, of course, a Fork in the Road salad, with a flexible and customizable list of ingredients. The versatility of salad clearly gets my blood pumping.

Pickle-y Cucumber Salad

FORK IN THE ROAD: Tangy or creamy, your choice.

I grew up with various versions of this salad—sometimes homemade, sometimes from the deli—as part of the much anticipated bagels-and-smoked-salmon brunches we sometimes had at our house. The rich oily fish and the steaming bowl of savory scrambled eggs clearly inspired my mother to find something slightly green and slightly fresh to round out the menu. Though she clearly wasn't looking for something with no salt in it.

If you like a super-crispy salad, make this right before serving. But, if you like (as I do) a salad with some crunch but a slightly more pickle-y marinated quality, then make it a day ahead. My kids are fond of cucumbers, but they are nuts about pickles, so calling this Pickle-y Cucumber Salad makes this even more appetizing to them (see Bagels and Appetizing, page 74).

If you don't have the time to salt and drain the cucumbers and onion, you will still have a lovely, clean-tasting salad. But without salting first, the salad will get watery more quickly, so if you do skip that step, it's best to serve it within a day. And with that said, I am always happy to discover a container of leftover pickle-y salad in my fridge, even a few days later.

12 mini or baby cucumbers (see Note)

1 medium-size red onion, halved and very thinly sliced

1 tablespoon kosher or coarse salt

2 tablespoons white wine vinegar

2 tablespoons minced fresh dill (preferable), or
    2 teaspoons dried dill

1 teaspoon sugar

Freshly ground black pepper, to taste

Yield

Serves 6 as a side dish

What the Kids Can Do

Measure and combine the ingredients for either or both dressings, and toss the salad.

Make Ahead

This can be made ahead and refrigerated, covered, a few hours before you plan to serve it. Leftovers are fine, but the cucumbers will lose some crunch and the dressing might get a bit watery; you can drain off any excess liquid if you like.

Note: You can also use 2 seedless cucumbers, if you can't find the small ones. Slice the cucumbers in half lengthwise and scoop out the seeds using a teaspoon (see Seedless Cucumbers, facing page). Cut the cucumber halves into thin half-moon slices.

1. Thinly slice the cucumbers. Place the cucumber and onion slices in a colander and toss with the salt. Let sit in the sink or over a bowl for 30 to 40 minutes to catch the liquid that will drip out.

2. Rinse the cucumbers and onion in very cold water. Using your hands, squeeze the slices to remove as much water as possible.

3. ⊨ You can continue with Step 4 and make the vinaigrette, or see the Fork in the Road (page 74) for a creamy, corny alternative.

4. Stir together the vinegar, dill, sugar, and pepper in a serving bowl. Add the cucumber and onion and toss to combine. Serve immediately, or refrigerate for a day, knowing the salad will soften as it marinates.

Seedless Cucumbers

Yes, they're called seedless cucumbers, but, of course, there is still a nominal amount of seeds in them. Removing them gives the salad a nicer texture, without the slightly slimy consistency of the seeds, and helps reduce the amount of water in the salad. If you can find baby seedless cucumbers, just thinly slice them and don't bother cutting them into half moons.

Creamy Cucumber Salad with Corn

This has no Proustian history in my house, other than the time I realized I had two extra ears of cooked corn, and some sour cream, and that a creamy version of cucumber salad (available at the same kinds of delis that sell salmon and bagels; see Bagels and Appetizing, this page) would be lovely. However, this one should be made no more than a few hours before serving—it tends to get watery after that.

Salt the cucumbers and the onions, but instead of making the vinaigrette, make the chive dressing below. When you toss the dressing with the salad, add 1 cup of lightly cooked corn kernels (fresh or frozen) and toss well.

You can also make a half-recipe of both the chive dressing and the vinaigrette, then divide the cucumber mixture in half and add the creamy dressing and ½ cup corn to one portion and vinaigrette to the other, and let people choose.

Creamy Chive Dressing

½ cup sour cream

1 teaspoon finely grated lemon zest

1 tablespoon fresh lemon juice

2 tablespoons fresh dill

1 tablespoon minced fresh chives

Freshly ground black pepper, to taste

Mix together the sour cream, lemon zest, lemon juice, dill, and chives in a serving bowl. Add the salad ingredients (see above), season with pepper, toss, and serve.

Bagels and Appetizing

This is one of the oddest phrases in the Jewish culinary spectrum, in my modern opinion. *Appetizing* is an adjective, right? Yes, but it's also an old New York noun, and in this context it is defined as "the food one eats with bagels," and generally is understood to encompass the array of foods one finds on the Jewish brunch table: lox (or smoked salmon), whitefish, herring, cream cheese, pickled things. No nonfish meat products, however, because of kosher dietary laws. So, in Jewish parlance, an appetizing store is a place that sells fish and dairy products, whereas a kosher delicatessen sells meat.

So there you have it, but I can't imagine that the creators of this term ever thought there might be sun-dried tomato or blueberry cream cheese alongside the herring.

Light Green Crunchy Salad

FORK IN THE ROAD: For another layer of tart crunch, add some green apple slices to a portion or all of the salad.

This salad was so heartbreakingly pretty I wanted people to come over just to admire it. So I invited the neighbors. Not only did my kids love it, the two-year-old who used to live down the hall (and who is the cutest thing since sliced kohlrabi) also loved it, and she can't even say kohlrabi. It's just so clean and vibrant and refreshing, and we ate the hugest bowl in a matter of minutes.

It came about because I was writing an article about surprising salad add-ins and I decided to list shredded or slivered raw kohlrabi as one of the possibilities. Then I said to myself, "You are so full of it; you've never done that in your whole life." So I bought myself a kohlrabi and sliced it up, and really fell head over heels. It kind of reminded me of a daikon radish, crisp with just a hint of spiciness (see Kohlrabi: The UFO of Root Vegetables, page 77).

A handful of pea shoots on the top of the salad adds a fresh sweet pea-ness that's lovely, but don't skip the salad if pea shoots aren't on the immediate horizon.

1 small kohlrabi, trimmed and peeled (optional)

10 ribs celery

3 hearts romaine lettuce

3 tablespoons unseasoned rice vinegar

3 tablespoons extra-virgin olive oil

2 tablespoons Dijon mustard

Kosher or coarse salt and freshly ground black pepper, to taste

1 cup pea shoots (optional)

Yield

Serves 6 as a side dish

What the Kids Can Do

Slice the lettuce and celery with a kid-friendly knife, mix up the dressing, toss the salad.

Make Ahead

This salad can be made ahead and refrigerated for an hour. The longer it sits, the more melded the flavors will be, but the less crunch the vegetables will have, so it's a bit of a toss-up (ba dump bump). I've happily eaten it a day or two after it's been made. You can also make the vinaigrette a couple of days ahead and slice up the vegetables a day ahead, then toss right before serving.

Is this gorgeous or what?

1. If using the kohlrabi, cut it into manageable chunks then cut those chunks into thin planks, about ¼ inch thick. Then sliver up those planks into ¼-inch-thick matchsticks (this is what is known as a julienne cut). Don't worry if the slivers aren't neat and tidy.

2. Very thinly slice the celery crosswise, then do the same with the hearts of romaine so that you have thin ribbons of lettuce. Place it all in a serving bowl, along with the kohlrabi.

3. ━━━≣ You can continue with Step 4 or see the Fork in the Road for an apple add-in.

4. Whisk together the rice vinegar, olive oil, mustard, and salt and pepper in a small bowl (or shake it up in a small container with a lid). Toss the vegetables with the dressing and serve, topped with the pea shoots, if desired.

FORK IN THE ROAD

Crunchy Apple-y Salad

Quarter and core a Granny Smith apple and cut the quarters crosswise into thin slices. Add the slices to the vegetables before adding the dressing or add them to individual portions once the salad is tossed and served.

Kohlrabi: The UFO of Root Vegetables

Kohlrabi is a cruciferous vegetable from the Cruciferae family (broccoli, cabbage, and so on). It is about the size of an orange, with a bunch of stems sticking out and a thick skin that can range from pale green to purple-ish. The leaves, stems, and the bulb itself are all edible (but not the skin), and the smaller ones tend to be more tender and flavorful. Flavorwise, it gets compared to broccoli. Peel kohlrabi very thoroughly with a sharp knife—the skin is too thick for a vegetable peeler to have much effect—and slice, julienne, or grate it into your salad for a great crunch and a fresh but slightly spicy flavor. It can also be cooked: steamed, sautéed, stir-fried, or roasted.

There's always a green salad with dinner in our house, the crunchier the better. If I told you how many hearts of romaine we go through in a week you'd be unsettled.

Kale and Quinoa Salad with Dried Cherries

FORK IN THE ROAD: A brightly flavored whole grain salad, and the option of a plain kale-free quinoa side dish for the uninitiated.

If you haven't yet cooked quinoa (that's *KEEN-wah*) at home, you've probably thought about it, since it's been the "it girl" of the whole-grain food movement for some time (see What's This Quinoa Thing All About?, page 80). Try to find smaller tender kale or baby kale for this recipe since the kale isn't really cooked, just wilted from the heat of the quinoa. You can also use spinach instead.

This salad is very pretty, simple to make, elegant in its flavor balance (because isn't that what your kids are always asking for? Elegance in the flavor balance?), and very portable. Remember it when you have to sign up for a potluck. It's also seriously nutritious, what with the kale and the quinoa and the herbs.

½ teaspoon kosher or coarse salt, plus more to taste

1 cup quinoa

1½ cups fresh flat-leaf parsley leaves

¾ cup fresh mint leaves

3 scallions, white and light green parts, cut into 1-inch pieces

4 cups baby kale (preferable) or torn, stemmed kale leaves

1 tablespoon freshly squeezed lemon juice

2 tablespoons extra-virgin olive oil, or more to taste

Freshly ground black pepper, to taste

1 cup dried cherries

1. Bring 2 cups of water to a boil in a small pot over high heat. Add the salt and stir in the quinoa. Bring to a simmer, reduce the heat to medium-low, and simmer, covered, until all of the water is absorbed, 15 minutes.

Yield

Serves 6 to 8 as a side dish, 3 to 4 as a main

What the Kids Can Do

Measure the ingredients, pull the herb leaves from the stems, cut the scallions with a kid-friendly knife, tear the kale, juice and strain the lemon.

Make Ahead

This salad can be made ahead and refrigerated, covered, for up to 2 days, but it will lose some of its textural balance. But when you are packing a last-minute lunch, that's probably not a huge worry.

2. ━━┅ You can continue with Step 3 or see the Fork in the Road if you'd like to leave some of the grains plain.

3. Meanwhile, place the parsley, mint, and scallions in a food processor or blender and process until finely chopped. Add the kale and pulse until the kale is roughly chopped. Transfer the mixture to a large serving bowl.

4. When the quinoa is cooked (it will yield about 3 cups), add it to the bowl with the greens and stir to combine. Drizzle over the lemon juice and olive oil, season with salt and pepper, and toss. Let cool to room temperature. Mix in the dried cherries and serve.

VARIATIONS

Add some grilled chicken or grilled shrimp for a non-veggie salad. You can also add other dried fruit, such as cranberries or chopped dried apricots, or toss in other herbs, and maybe some chopped olives or shredded or crumbled cheese—this is a very fluid recipe.

FORK
IN THE
ROAD

Plain Old Quinoa

Need an ultra simple, unthreatening whole grain side? Or perhaps you think that introducing kale *and* quinoa to your family in the same dish is just asking for trouble? Before adding the quinoa to the greens, just spoon out some of the plain quinoa, give it a drizzle of olive oil, a sprinkle of lemon juice, and a bit of salt and pepper. Then dump the rest of the quinoa into the bowl with the chopped kale and herbs and finish up the recipe.

Quinoa (again, pronounced *KEEN-wah*) is actually a seed, but it's treated and cooked like a whole grain. Mild and delicious with a satisfying texture, it takes beautifully to all kinds of seasonings. It's got a crazy high protein count (8 grams of protein in a ½ cup of cooked quinoa), so it's a boon to vegetarians and vegans; it contains a nice dose of fiber; and it's gluten-free for those who have issues with gluten. It's quite popular these days, but actually it was a staple for the ancient Incas, because it could be grown in the high altitude of the Andes (this may or may not be of interest to your kids). It also cooks up much more quickly than most other whole grains, and any of us who have stood watching that pot of brown rice take its own sweet time will appreciate that.

Greek Tabbouleh Salad

FORK IN THE ROAD: A very lively version of tabbouleh, and a simpler version for those who aren't in the mood for lively.

So, this whole grain thing looks like it's here to stay. Now, how to get them onto the actual table, and into the actual mouths of our darling children (who are always open to new foods and experiences—*cough cough*).

This is a version of a very classic Middle Eastern bulgur wheat salad, with very approachable flavors. Great as a side dish, and you could even stuff a hollowed-out tomato with it if you're going for a luncheon presentation. I myself have served many lunches, but only a few luncheons, so I will think of this next time the opportunity arises.

Bulgur "cooks" by soaking in liquid, and in this recipe it absorbs the lemon juice along with the water, which really freshens up the earthy flavor (know going in that you need 2 hours to get the bulgur soft). Do make the tabbouleh frequently during the summer months when ripe tomatoes, cucumbers, and fat bunches of herbs are readily available.

1½ cups bulgur wheat

1¾ cups hot water

Finely grated zest and juice of 2 lemons

⅓ cup extra-virgin olive oil

½ cup finely chopped onion

1 clove garlic, finely minced

3 tablespoons finely minced fresh parsley leaves

3 tablespoons finely minced fresh mint leaves

1 teaspoon kosher or coarse salt

½ teaspoon freshly ground black pepper, to taste

1 seedless cucumber, diced (peeled or not, your choice)

1 pint cherry or grape tomatoes, halved

¾ cup crumbled feta

⅓ cup slivered Kalamata olives

2 tablespoons minced fresh oregano

Yield

Serves 6 to 8 as a side dish

What the Kids Can Do

Juice the lemon, chop the herbs, dice the cucumber, and halve the tomatoes with an age-appropriate knife. Crumble the feta and slice the pit-free olives (again, with an age-appropriate knife).

Make Ahead

The bulgur wheat can be made up to 3 days ahead of time and refrigerated. The complete salad can be made a day ahead of time and refrigerated, but it's best when served within 6 hours of making.

1. Pour the bulgur into a large bowl and add the hot water and lemon juice. Stir and cover. Let sit at room temperature for 2 hours, until the bulgur has absorbed all of the liquid, or place it in the fridge for at least 4 hours.

2. Add the lemon zest, olive oil, onion, garlic, parsley, mint, and salt and pepper to the bulgur and combine well. Stir in the cucumber and tomatoes. Add the feta, olives, and oregano and gently combine, ➤ or see the Fork in the Road to simplify things.

VARIATION
For a non-vegetarian main dish, add cubed cooked chicken or poached or grilled shrimp.

FORK IN THE ROAD

Not-Greek Tabbouleh Salad

Skip the feta, olives, and oregano for a simpler salad. Or, remove half of the salad after adding the cucumber and tomato and set aside for the plain folks. (Continue with the recipe, but reduce the amounts of the feta, olives, and oregano by about half, or to taste.)

Whole Grains: All the Rage . . .

I am not an all-or-nothing person, and find that to be an inconvenient and unsustainable way to think about food and dietary trends. Right now, whole grains are the talk of the town. But in some circles and cultures, they've been so much a part of a daily diet for so long, there's no need for a big discussion. The Incas weren't cultivating quinoa 4,000 years ago because they were trying to be trendy. In hyper food-conscious areas, ordering white bread toast at a diner is akin to lighting up a cigarette in an elementary school— almost too shocking for words. Well, I like a good white bread, I like white rice, and I also like quinoa, brown rice, couscous, and bulgur wheat. I am making more of an effort to get more whole grains on the table, and incorporate them into my kids' diets, but when I am having a slice of pizza it's a safe bet that there will be white flour in that crust.

Cobb Salad with Creamy Pesto Dressing

FORK IN THE ROAD: A beautiful salad that allows everyone to pick and choose their favorite ingredients—and the vegetarian version makes sure no one is left out.

Even kids who don't think they like salad will, hopefully, give this gorgeous salad tableau a shot. Cobb salads are most often served with the ingredients lined up in neat little rows, and then the diner tosses it all together, or not, as he or she desires. Try it with a creamy pesto-like dressing or a simple vinaigrette, or a drizzling of olive oil and vinegar is also just right.

6 cups slivered romaine lettuce (or a combination of iceberg and romaine, for more crunch)

8 slices bacon, cooked (see Cooking Tip 1) and roughly crumbled, ●━━◄€ or see the Vegetarian Fork in the Road

3 hard-boiled eggs (see Making Perfect Hard-Boiled Eggs, page 50), peeled and cut into large dice

2 medium-size tomatoes, seeded and cut into large dice

1½ cups cubed cooked chicken, ●━━◄€ or see the Vegetarian Fork in the Road

1 avocado, peeled and sliced

½ cup diced red onion

½ cup crumbled blue cheese

Kosher or coarse salt and freshly ground black pepper, to taste

Creamy Pesto Dressing (recipe follows)

1. Scatter the lettuce over a large serving platter.

2. Make nice neat rows over the lettuce of the crumbled bacon, diced eggs, tomatoes, chicken, avocado, onion, and blue cheese. Season with salt and pepper. You can drizzle Creamy Pesto Dressing over the salad, or serve it on the side.

What the Kids Can Do

Measure and mix the ingredients for the dressing, work the blender with supervision, crumble the blue cheese, line the platter with lettuce, and make rows of all the ingredients (this is a popular job).

Make Ahead

You can make the salad up to a day ahead and refrigerate it, covered. But don't dress it until you are just about to serve.

Creamy Pesto Dressing

Makes about 1 cup

I have also made this with half mint leaves and half basil, and it's even brighter.

½ cup mayonnaise

¼ cup buttermilk (see Cooking Tip 2)

1 cup fresh basil leaves

2 tablespoons finely grated Parmesan cheese

1 clove garlic, finely minced

Kosher or coarse salt and freshly ground black pepper, to taste

Blend together the mayonnaise, buttermilk, basil, Parmesan, garlic, and salt and pepper in a blender or food processor until everything is well combined. Transfer to a plastic container. Cover and refrigerate until ready to serve. It will last for up to 2 days in the refrigerator.

Vegetarian Cobb Salad

Substitute 2 cans (15.5 ounces each) of drained and rinsed chickpeas for the chicken for a delicious and equally substantial veggie Cobb. Just skip the bacon, or try 1 cup of something else: Think along the lines of salted sunflower seeds, pumpkin seeds, or pine nuts.

You can easily make two platters, one veggie and one not. Use 1 can chickpeas standing in for half the chicken, and use about ½ cup of any of the above mentioned seeds and nuts in place of the bacon.

The order of ingredients is of no consequence—whatever strikes you works.

Cooking Tip 1

You are welcome to cook bacon the old-fashioned way in a skillet on the stovetop, or you can bake it. (It's neater, less splattery, less hands on.) Arrange the strips on a wire rack placed on a rimmed baking sheet covered with aluminum foil, and bake in a 350°F oven until crispy, about 15 minutes.

Cooking Tip 2

If you don't have buttermilk on hand, just mix ¼ cup milk with 1 teaspoon lemon juice or white wine vinegar, and let it stand for 5 minutes. The results can be used in any recipe calling for buttermilk.

Other Ingredients to Consider When Devising a Cobb Salad

Shrimp

Crab

Apples

Pears

Ham

Goat cheese

Bell peppers

Cucumber

Salmon

Asparagus

Turkey

If you can line it up, it's fair game.

SHORTCUT CHICKEN UDON SOUP, *page 97*

When you don't think you have anything in the house for dinner, you probably still have the makings of soup—and likely a pretty great soup at that. My kids love soup, Charlie in particular, which frankly makes things hum along nicely during those pervasive, last-minute "What am I making tonight?" moments. If you can work the general notion of soup into your weekly meal rotation, your life will be easier. That much I know.

Soups & Stews

Every cuisine has a stake in the soup game. From the most ruggedly delicious bowl of peasant food to the silkiest puree, soup cuts across all cultures. But most important for us home cooks, on the whole, soups are easy. They can be quick (like the Shortcut Chicken Udon Soup—which can also be made with tofu), they can be robust (like the Sausage, White Bean, and Kale Soup—or for a vegetarian version, skip the sausage), they can be smooth (try the Butternut Squash Soup —plain or with warm Indian spices). Whatever the choice, they are always comforting. I pledge allegiance to soup.

Butternut Squash Soup

FORK IN THE ROAD: You choose: smooth and simple, or Indian-spiced.

Creamy, comforting, silky, gorgeous. The slightly sweet and rich flavor of butternut squash needs very little adornment. But having said that, of course, there is a twist for those seeking more flavor.

- 2 tablespoons unsalted butter
- 1 large onion, chopped
- 2 large carrots, peeled and sliced
- 1 large butternut squash, peeled, seeded, and cut into 1-inch cubes
- Kosher or coarse salt and freshly ground black pepper, to taste
- 5 to 6 cups chicken or vegetable broth, preferably low-sodium (see Note, page 89)
- ½ cup heavy (whipping) cream
- Sour cream or crème fraîche to serve (optional)

1. Melt the butter in a stockpot over medium heat. Add the onion, carrots, and squash and cook until the onion starts to soften, 5 minutes. Season with salt and pepper. Add 5 cups of the broth and bring to a simmer.

2. ◄═══ You can continue with Step 3 or see the Fork in the Road to add a bit of Indian spice.

Yield

Serves 6

What the Kids Can Do

Peel the carrots, measure the broth, stir the soup; maybe puree the soup with very attentive supervision; help decide how much of the Fork in the Road seasoning to include.

3. Simmer, partially covered, until the vegetables are all very soft, 25 to 30 minutes.

4. Working in batches, puree the soup in a blender or food processor, or use an immersion blender. (You could also run the mixture through a food mill, which offers a great kind of nubby texture.) Return the pureed soup to the pot. If the soup is too thick, add up to 1 cup more broth.

5. Add the cream, heat just until warmed through, and serve in bowls. Top with a dollop of sour cream or crème fraîche, if desired.

FORK IN THE ROAD

Indian-Spiced Butternut Squash–Carrot Soup

This is one of my favorite recipes in the book, and the friends that I've served it to use wonderful words like *sunny, earthy, layered,* and *warming.*

Make a half batch (2½ tablespoons) of the Tikka Masala Paste (page 125). Stir in 3 to 5 teaspoons of the paste as you simmer the squash and carrots in the broth in Step 3. After you puree everything, taste and stir in a bit more of the paste if you want a stronger flavor, and do keep in mind that the addition of the cream softens the punch of the spice a little bit.

You can also make the soup plain and serve a few bowls without any additional seasoning. Then stir the spice paste (about ½ teaspoon per serving) into the rest of the finished soup. Let the soup simmer as you add the spice paste slowly and taste as you go; it can sneak up on you.

Make Ahead

The soup can be made up to 4 days ahead and refrigerated. If made in advance without the cream, reheat and add the cream right before serving. If the cream was already added in, make sure you bring the soup only to a gentle simmer over medium-low heat so it doesn't curdle.

Note: This can easily be made as a vegetarian dish by using the vegetable broth instead of chicken.

Vegan Note: If you'd like a vegan soup, or if there is a dairy intolerance in your household, swap the butter out for olive oil, and skip the cream—you'll have a lighter, lactose-free, vegan soup.

I always coordinate my outfit to the bowls and napkins (yeah, right).

Carrot-Ginger Soup with Shrimp

FORK IN THE ROAD: This can be made as a fully vegetarian soup, with the shrimp added to individual portions.

My amazing friend Chris Styler has to be one of the finest and most comfortable-in-the-kitchen cooks I know. I love the food he makes and I love cooking with him. The fact that his partner, Joe, has what can only be described as a dishwashing/cleaning fetish . . . well, you can just imagine what lovely guests they are.

One day when I was in a bonkers-busy stretch of time, Chris dropped off this soup for us. "What's this soup called?" asked a ravenous Charlie sniffing suspiciously. "Oh, I'm not actually sure," says me. He takes a slurp and says, "I know what it's called. It's called *The Best Soup in the World!*" He did beat a hasty retreat after such effusive praise, issuing qualifiers, clearly remembering where his bread is buttered (or his soup is simmered) on any given day. But I think this is, in fact, one of the best soups in the world.

This can be a vegetarian soup, too (see the Fork in the Road), or even a vegan soup (see the Vegan Note).

1½ tablespoons unsalted butter

1½ tablespoons olive oil

2 tablespoons coarsely chopped peeled fresh ginger

3 medium-size leeks (see Note, page 92), white and light green parts only, well rinsed and roughly chopped

2 pounds carrots, peeled and roughly chopped

6 cups chicken or vegetable broth, preferably low-sodium

Kosher or coarse salt and freshly ground black pepper, to taste

1 pound large shrimp (31 to 35 per pound), peeled, deveined, and cut into bite-size pieces

1 package (5 ounces) baby spinach (about 3 cups)

Yield

Serves 4 to 6

What the Kids Can Do

Peel the ginger, carrots, and shrimp.

Make Ahead

The pureed carrot-leek soup base can be made ahead and refrigerated for up to 3 days or frozen for up to 3 months. Reheat over medium heat, and stir in the shrimp and spinach just before serving.

1. Melt the butter in the olive oil in a large stockpot over medium heat. Add the ginger and stir until fragrant, about 1 minute. Stir in the leeks and cook until slightly wilted, about 4 minutes. Stir in the carrots, reduce the heat to medium-low, cover, and cook, stirring often, until the carrots are softened just a little, about 8 minutes.

2. Pour in the broth, raise the heat to high, and bring to a boil. Lower the heat to medium-low so that the soup is just simmering and cover the pot. Cook until the vegetables are very tender, about 20 minutes.

3. Puree the soup in batches in a blender or food processor (be careful, it's hot!) until smooth and return to the pot. (Or use an immersion blender and puree it right in the pot.) Season with salt and pepper.

4. Bring the soup back to a simmer over medium-high heat.

5. ━━► You can continue with Step 6 or see the Fork in the Road to keep the soup vegetarian.

6. Stir in the shrimp and spinach. Cook just until the shrimp is pink throughout and the spinach is wilted, about 2 minutes.

Vegan Note: Use an additional 1½ tablespoons olive oil instead of the butter, use vegetable broth, and skip the shrimp.

Note: I'm a leek devotee, but you can certainly use a chopped onion in place of the leeks.

This soup takes the humble carrot and gives it bragging rights.

FORK IN THE ROAD

Vegetarian Carrot-Ginger Soup

If you've used vegetable broth, the soup is vegetarian until you add the shrimp, so just add the spinach and stir for a minute until the spinach is wilted.

To go halfsies, ladle out portions of the soup in its vegetarian incarnation, then add the shrimp to the rest of the soup, cooking until the shrimp is cooked through, 2 minutes more, and serve to the non-vegetarians.

Mexican Tortilla Chicken Soup

FORK IN THE ROAD: A couple of extra ingredients turns this freaking great soup into a freaking great stew.

Recipe inspiration strikes from many places, and in this case it was simply my friend Catherine Skobe saying, "I need you to come up with a recipe for Mexican tortilla soup, please." A friend in need—that counts as inspiration right? She did say "please" (she was brought up in the South and has lovely manners).

My version of tortilla soup is homey, comforting, and my family is nuts about it—as are the Skobes. And the real fun

Yield

Serves 4 to 6

What the Kids Can Do

Cut the tortillas into strips with an age-appropriate knife, shred the chicken if you let it cool enough, and help choose and prepare some of the soup toppings.

Make Ahead

You can make the soup ahead through adding the shredded chicken and keep it refrigerated for up to 4 days. Reheat, adding the lime juice when you are ready to serve (and, of course, don't fry the tortillas or prep the toppings until just before serving!). Same goes for the stew.

is in the garnishes, from the crispy tortillas to all of the other options listed below. This is a real-meal soup.

If you're making this soup in late summer, try using 3 seeded and chopped large fresh tomatoes in place of the canned. A brighter, lighter-tasting version of itself.

FOR THE SOUP

2 tablespoons extra-virgin olive oil

2 medium-size onions, chopped

2 cloves garlic, minced

1½ teaspoons ground cumin

1 teaspoon ground coriander

1 teaspoon pure chile powder

1 can (14.5 ounces) crushed tomatoes

6 cups chicken broth, preferably low-sodium

Kosher or coarse salt and freshly ground black pepper, to taste

3 skinless boneless chicken breasts, trimmed of fat (about 1½ pounds; see Note)

Canola or vegetable oil, for panfrying

6 corn tortillas, halved and cut crosswise into thin strips (see Cooking Tip 1)

Juice of 1 lime

TO SERVE (OPTIONAL, PICK AND CHOOSE)

1 or 2 avocados, peeled and diced

1 cup shredded Monterey jack cheese

½ cup coarsely chopped fresh cilantro leaves

Salsa or Pico de Gallo (page 222)

1 lime, cut into wedges

1. Heat the olive oil in a large stockpot over medium heat. Add the onions and garlic and sauté until tender and golden, 5 minutes. Stir in the cumin, coriander, and chile powder and cook until fragrant, 1 minute. Add the tomatoes and chicken broth, season with salt and pepper, and bring to a simmer over high heat. Add the chicken breasts and lower the heat to medium-low (see Cooking Tip 2). Simmer uncovered (don't let the soup come to a boil), stirring

Cooking Tip 1

Is this slicing and frying the tortillas an added step, and maybe a little bit of a pain in the butt? Why, yes it is. But it's not a *big* pain in the butt. However, if it's going to keep you from making this soup on any given night, then skip the tortillas or take this shortcut: Grab a bag of tortilla chips, lightly crush a few handfuls, and use those instead. It is highly unlikely you will receive any complaints from the peanut gallery.

Cooking Tip 2

When making a broth or a soup with chicken, I am a big fan of cooking the chicken in already-prepared chicken broth. The theory being that the broth flavors the chicken while it cooks, and the chicken enriches the broth: win-win. Chicken simmered in water is fine, but the chicken itself tends to lose a lot of its flavor to the liquid.

occasionally, until the chicken is just barely cooked through, about 12 minutes. Remove the chicken to a plate and let sit until cool enough to handle. Keep the soup gently simmering over medium-low heat.

2. Meanwhile, pour the canola oil to a depth of 1 inch into a medium-size skillet and heat over medium-high heat. Line a plate with a couple of paper towels. When the oil is hot (see Cooking Tip 3), add the tortilla strips in batches and fry, stirring often, until they are crisp and lightly colored, about 2 minutes. Remove with a slotted spoon to the plate and sprinkle lightly with salt while they are still hot.

3. Shred the slightly cooled chicken, and stir it and the lime juice into the soup.

4. ⟍⟍⟍ You can continue with Step 5 or see the Fork in the Road for add-ins that will make a heartier stew.

5. Ladle the soup into soup bowls and top with the fried tortilla strips, along with your choice of diced avocado, cheese, cilantro, salsa, and lime wedges.

Cooking Tip 3

You can tell if the oil is hot enough to fry the tortilla strips by adding a couple to the pan. If they sizzle gently, you're good to go. Fry the strips in a couple of batches so that you don't crowd the pan, thereby lowering the temperature of the oil and merely poaching those tortillas. You want them to have space to move around and crisp up nicely.

Note: If you have leftover roast chicken, use it instead of poaching your own. Shred up about 2 cups of chicken and add it to the soup after the tomatoes and spices have cooked for about 10 minutes.

FORK IN THE ROAD

Black Bean, Corn & Chicken Tortilla Stew

When you add the shredded chicken and lime juice to the soup in Step 3, add 2 cans (15.5 ounces each) black beans (rinsed and drained) and 2 cups fresh or frozen corn kernels. Simmer until everything is hot, about 5 minutes.

If you want to serve half of the soup now and enjoy a stew later in the week, at the end of Step 1, divide the soup in half and refrigerate one portion for stew later. When ready for stew, add 1 can of black beans and 1 cup of corn kernels. Reheat at a simmer and top with the tortilla strips and other toppings as desired.

Is this a happy
kid or what?

Shortcut Chicken Udon Soup

FORK IN THE ROAD: Use tofu for a vegetarian version.

There is an honesty and a simplicity and a satisfyingness (is that a word? I may have made it up; if you're reading it, it means my editor let me keep it) to recipes that are born of necessity. This recipe was birthed one night when we were just settling back into our house after some minor construction, and when I say the cupboard and the fridge were bare, I mean they were almost bare-naked. I threw together the few ingredients I could scrape together, and my family has been requesting the soup ever since.

So, I first made this soup with a few cups of leftover roasted chicken which I just shredded and added to the broth, and which you can certainly do (hello, supermarket roast chicken, you lovely item). But I usually start with uncooked chicken. And note: This starts with a lot of broth because the udon is cooked right in the soup (one-pot wonder), and some of that broth gets absorbed by the noodles as they cook.

Use a light hand with the hot sauce if you have heat-sensitive dinner companions, and you may need to sprinkle the scallions over individual portions if they are a deal breaker for your kids.

10 cups chicken or vegetable broth, preferably low-sodium

3 skinless boneless chicken breasts or thighs (about 1½ pounds), trimmed of fat, ➤ or see the Fork in the Road for a tofu sub to make a vegetarian soup

Kosher or coarse salt, to taste

6 ounces dried udon noodles (see Note)

1 teaspoon sriracha, or to taste

1 tablespoon toasted sesame oil, or to taste

4 scallions, white and light green parts, thinly sliced

Yield

Serves 4

What the Kids Can Do

If you cook the chicken ahead of time and let it cool a bit more, they can shred the chicken. They can and should participate in seeing how much sesame oil and sriracha should be added to the broth. They can slice scallions with an age-appropriate knife.

Make Ahead

If using chicken, you can poach and shred it in advance. Transfer the broth to a covered container. Place the chicken in a sealed plastic bag or plastic container. Both will keep for up to 3 days in the refrigerator. When ready to serve, continue with Step 2.

1. Pour the broth into a large stockpot and bring it to a simmer over high heat. Add the chicken and salt, and lower the heat to medium-low. Cover the pot and simmer gently until the chicken is cooked through, about 10 minutes. Turn off the heat, remove the chicken with a slotted spoon, and let cool on a plate for about 10 minutes.

2. Return the broth to a simmer over medium heat and add the udon and sriracha. Cook according to package directions, stirring frequently, until the noodles are just soft but not mushy, about 7 minutes.

3. Meanwhile, shred the chicken using your fingers (or two forks if you prefer), as fine or as chunky as you like. Add the shredded chicken to the soup as you shred it. As soon as the noodles are tender, stir in the sesame oil and turn off the heat.

4. Taste the soup and season it with additional sriracha or sesame oil if desired; stir in the scallions. Serve the soup hot.

Note: Dried udon noodles are featured in Japanese cuisine and are made from wheat flour. When cooked, they are thick, chewy, and soft. The noodles are available in many supermarkets in the Asian foods section. They are often sold bundled in packages— use 2 of the 3-noodle bundles in a 10-ounce package, and 2 of the 4-noodle bundles in a 12.8-ounce package.

FORK IN THE ROAD

Vegetarian Udon Soup

Use vegetable broth instead of chicken broth. Instead of poaching chicken, use tofu, and skip the poaching step. Add 1½ pounds medium-soft tofu, cut into cubes, to the broth in Step 2 when the noodles begin to soften (after a minute or two).

You could easily have two soups simmering side by side, if both versions are in order. If you don't want to double the recipe, use vegetable broth, divide it into 2 small pots, and add ¾ pound chicken for one and ¾ pound tofu to the other. Divide the remaining ingredients between the two.

Sausage, White Bean, and Kale Soup

FORK IN THE ROAD: You can make half of this with sausage and keep the other half vegetarian.

This is the type of recipe that turns writers into cliché machines, spewing phrases like "warms you from the inside out," and is "stick-to-your-ribs comfort food." I won't do it. But, you know, it's quite warming . . . and comforting. . . .

1 pound sweet Italian pork or turkey sausage, ◄━══ or see the Vegetarian Fork in the Road

2 tablespoons olive oil

1 onion, chopped

1 teaspoon finely minced garlic

2 large carrots, peeled and chopped

2 ribs celery, chopped

2 cans (15.5 ounces each) white beans, such as cannellini or navy

8 cups chicken or vegetable broth, preferably low-sodium

1 large all-purpose potato, peeled and diced

8 cups thinly sliced or chopped kale (tough stems discarded)

2 tablespoons tomato paste

1 teaspoon dried thyme

1 teaspoon crushed dried rosemary

2 dried bay leaves

Kosher or coarse salt and freshly ground black pepper, to taste

Grated Parmesan (see Note), for serving (optional)

1. Heat a stockpot or Dutch oven over medium-high heat. Squeeze the sausage from its casing, add it to the pot, and cook, breaking it up with a spoon, until it is crumbly and browned. Remove the sausage to paper towels to drain.

Yield

Serves 8

What the Kids Can Do

Drain and rinse the beans, squeeze out the sausage, maybe chop the kale with an age-appropriate knife.

Make Ahead

A perfect soup to make up to 4 days ahead (it's even better after the first day). You can also freeze it for up to 3 months.

2. Pour off any remaining fat and return the pan to the heat without cleaning it. Add the olive oil and heat over medium heat. Add the onion, garlic, carrots, and celery and sauté until the vegetables are tender and starting to turn golden brown, 5 minutes. Stir in the beans, broth, potato, kale, tomato paste, thyme, rosemary, and bay leaves. Season with salt and pepper. Bring to a simmer over medium-high heat, then reduce the heat to medium and continue to simmer until the potato and kale are tender, about 15 minutes. Add the sausage and simmer to heat through, 2 minutes more. Fish out the bay leaves, sprinkle the soup with Parmesan if desired, and serve.

Note: If you have a rind of Parmesan lurking in the fridge this is the perfect soup to throw it into for extra flavor. This is a classic Italian trick—saving the rind from a piece of Parmesan, which is too tough to eat on its own, and adding it to a soup (or stew) to get that wonderful, slightly salty flavor to permeate the soup. A good reason to grate your own Parmesan, at least on occasion. Waste not, want not.

FORK IN THE ROAD

Vegetarian Bean & Kale Soup

You can make this soup vegetarian by using vegetable broth and a meat-free sausage, or skipping the sausage altogether. If making the soup without any type of sausage, just start with the olive oil (in a clean pan) in Step 2.

You can also make half with meat, half without: Brown ½ pound sausage meat in a large saucepan. Set it aside while you cook the vegetables in a separate pan in Step 2. To the sausage, add half of the vegetables and 4 cups of chicken broth. To the remaining vegetables, add 4 cups of vegetable broth (and crumbled meat-free sausage, if using).

A pot of this in the fridge is like an internal high-five you can give yourself all day long.

SPANISH PORK CHOPS, *page 109*

My kids and husband are unabashed carnivores. They are certainly happy with vegetarian options, but they are *really* happy when there's meat on the table. I often pick a cut that can be cooked very simply, and served with a sauce on the side so that everyone can keep their options open. Tender pork loin can get a dollop of mustard-maple sauce, lamb can be gilded with a choice of salsa verde or a creamy yogurt-mint sauce, and thinly sliced skirt steak can meet up with a vibrant and flavorful chimichurri sauce.

Meat

The other options are tangy Asian Spareribs, which can be made spicy or on the sweeter side (or—as you surely know by now—both!), and Spanish Pork Chops, which can be rubbed with as much or as little seasoning blend as each person likes.

You might also check out the carnitas tacos or enchiladas (pages 220 and 223), Spanish–Style Beef Pot Roast (page 235), and the dish my husband would trade me for, One-Skillet Beefy Enchilada Noodle Casserole (page 239).

CHAPTER 7

Skirt Steak
with Chimichurri

FORK IN THE ROAD: Divide the sauce into two batches: one milder, one with more heat (and cilantro if you like).

Chimichurri is a magical sauce that has become a fridge staple for us. It's Argentinean in origin, and since I have an Argentinean sister-in-law whom I love, I am predisposed to like anything that hails from that neck of the woods. It's a very common partner to steak, and since steak appears to be the main food group in Argentina, it is ubiquitous.

While chimichurri is a traditional accompaniment to grilled steak, and sometimes also a marinade, it's also just fantastic with fish, seafood, and chicken, and if you have it on hand, remember to pass it at the table when fish tacos are on the menu (see page 214)—it really works. The skirt steak cut of beef is a suggestion—a great, flavorful steak with nice, chewy texture. Chefs and beef lovers often name skirt steak as their favorite cut. However, choose your favorite cut, and just cook it accordingly (see Other Steak Suggestions, facing page).

Dial the amount of garlic up or down. Sometimes other vinegars, or lemon or lime juice, are used instead of white wine vinegar; play with what you have around. And of course, check out the Fork in the Road. I almost always make two batches, one for my cilantro-hating husband and Jack, and one for Charlie, me, and other people with more evolved palates (kidding, of course).

Leftover steak is great sliced over a salad or slivered into soft tortillas, with a drizzle of the sauce on top, or maybe piled on a bed of Creamy Coleslaw (page 281) or the Cauliflower Puree (page 278).

Yield

Serves 4 to 6 (and if you want to grill extra steaks, leftovers are always useful)

What the Kids Can Do

Even very little kids can pull the leaves off the parsley, oregano, and cilantro stems. They can measure ingredients and dump them into the food processor, and run the machine with supervision. They can season the steaks and/or fish.

Make Ahead

The sauce will keep in the refrigerator for up to a week, though it will lose its nice bright green color after a day or so.

2 pounds skirt steaks (also called New York skirt steak) or other steak (see Other Steak Suggestions), cut into 8 pieces

2 cups fresh flat-leaf parsley leaves

5 cloves garlic, peeled

¼ cup chopped onion

3 tablespoons white wine vinegar

2 teaspoons fresh oregano or ¾ teaspoon dried oregano

½ teaspoon red pepper flakes

Kosher or coarse salt

¾ cup extra-virgin olive oil, plus 2 tablespoons (or as needed) for searing the steak

Freshly ground black pepper, to taste

1. Bring the steaks to room temperature, letting them sit out for 20 to 30 minutes.

Other Steak Suggestions

2 bone-in rib-eye steaks (1¼ inches thick, 1½ pounds each): These will take 6 to 7 minutes per side in a cast-iron skillet, a grill pan, or over a medium-high fire for medium-rare, 8 to 9 minutes per side for medium-well. Let the steaks rest for 10 minutes. Cut the steak off the bone, slice across the grain, and serve. Serves 4 to 6.

2 New York strip steaks (1¼ inches thick, 12 to 14 ounces each): These will take about 7 minutes per side in a cast-iron skillet, a grill pan, or over a medium-high grill fire for medium-rare, or 8 to 9 minutes per side for medium. Let the steaks rest for 5 minutes, slice across the grain, and serve. Serves 4 to 6.

2. Combine the parsley, garlic, onion, vinegar, oregano, red pepper flakes, and ¾ teaspoon salt in a food processor and puree. Drizzle in the ¾ cup olive oil through the feed tube with the motor running until everything is well combined. Taste and adjust the salt and add ½ teaspoon black pepper, or to taste.

3. ━━◄ You can continue with Step 4 or see the Fork in the Road to make a more pungent sauce.

4. Set the chimichurri aside. Generously salt and pepper the steaks. Heat 1 or 2 large skillets, preferably cast-iron, over high heat (or preheat a grill; see Note). When hot, add enough olive oil to coat the bottom(s) of the pan(s). When the oil just begins to smoke, add the steak pieces in a single layer, without crowding them. Sear them in batches, if you have just one pan. Cook, without disturbing, until well browned, turning them only once (see Cooking Tip), 5 minutes or so per side for medium-rare.

5. Let them sit for at least 5 minutes for the meat to reabsorb the juices before slicing thinly across the grain. Drizzle the chimichurri over the meat, or pass it on the side if you prefer.

Cooking Tip

If the pan is at the right temperature, which is to say pretty hot, the meat will release itself from the bottom once the exterior is cooked. Meaning, it will stick at first if you try to move it, and that's why you just need to leave it alone. Let it get that great sear for the best flavor and texture, and then flip it over.

Note: To grill the steak, season it with salt and pepper as directed, and preheat a grill to medium-high. Grill to desired doneness, about 5 minutes per side for medium-rare. Transfer to a cutting board; let rest at least 5 minutes before slicing.

FORK IN THE ROAD

Spicy Cilantro Chimichurri

After pureeing the chimichurri in Step 2, pour half into one container or pitcher. To the sauce remaining in the food processor, add ½ cup fresh cilantro leaves and/or ½ minced jalapeño pepper and puree. Transfer to another pitcher, choosing one that is easily distinguishable from the other.

Mustard and Maple–Glazed Pork Loin

FORK IN THE ROAD: The pork loin with its nice glaze is great on its own, or pass a side of punched-up mayonnaise for more flavor.

Pork loin is one of the most brilliant dinnertime solutions in the world. It is inexpensive, readily available, takes well to almost any flavoring, and is quick and easy to prepare. Leftovers make great sandwiches and it can also make itself right at home later in the week in stir-fried rice, quesadillas, casseroles, and so on.

The flavors used to season the pork are echoed in the sauce, which is the optional twist here. Should you brine the pork? If you have the time, great; if not, let it sit in the marinade for an hour or so if possible (see To Brine or Not to Brine, page 246). And if not, just roast that sucker.

1 boneless pork loin (3½ to 4 pounds)

1 tablespoon plus 2 teaspoons extra-virgin olive oil

¼ cup Dijon mustard, coarse or smooth

3 tablespoons pure maple syrup

2 teaspoons minced fresh rosemary or 1 teaspoon crumbled dried rosemary

3 cloves garlic, minced

Kosher or coarse salt (optional) and freshly ground black pepper, to taste

1. Brine the pork loin, if desired (see Basic Brine, page 108).

2. Preheat the oven to 375°F.

3. Mix together the 1 tablespoon olive oil, Dijon mustard, maple syrup, rosemary, garlic, salt (skip the

Yield

Serves 8 to 10

What the Kids Can Do

Mix up the brine, if brining. Measure and mix up the marinade and sauce, if making. Rub the marinade on the pork (with clean hands, see page xi).

Make Ahead

Obviously the pork can and should be brined ahead, and the Mustard-Maple Sauce can be made up to 3 days ahead.

salt if you brined the pork), and pepper in a small bowl until well blended. Smear the mixture all over the pork.

4. Heat the remaining 2 teaspoons olive oil in a large ovenproof skillet over medium-high heat until almost smoking. Place the coated pork in the hot pan. Brown on each side for 2 minutes, turning so that the entire outside gets nicely seared, about 10 minutes in total. Transfer the pan to the oven and roast until an instant-read thermometer inserted into the center of the pork registers 140°F, anywhere from 25 to 40 minutes (depending on the thickness of the loin). Let rest for 10 to 15 minutes before slicing.

5. Serve plain, or see the Fork in the Road for a Mustard-Maple Sauce.

Mustard-Maple Sauce

Makes about ½ cup

ADDING A BIT OF seasoning to mayonnaise is a good quick trick for making an easy sauce. Citrus juice, honey, mustards of all kinds, maple syrup, hot sauces, horseradish, wasabi powder, fresh herbs—many ingredients can be used to turn a small amount of mayo into a great spread or dipping sauce.

½ cup mayonnaise

2 tablespoons Dijon mustard

1 tablespoon pure maple syrup

Kosher or coarse salt and freshly ground black pepper, to taste

½ teaspoon minced fresh rosemary (optional)

Combine the mayonnaise, Dijon, maple syrup, and salt and pepper in a small bowl. Stir in the rosemary if using.

Basic Brine

1 cup very hot water

½ cup kosher or coarse salt

⅓ cup sugar (or brown sugar, honey, or pure maple syrup)

OPTIONAL INGREDIENTS:

2 tablespoons black peppercorns

4 dried bay leaves and/or 2 branches fresh rosemary

7 cups ice water

Pour the very hot water into a large container. Stir in the salt and sugar, then add any of the optional ingredients you are using. Stir until the sugar and salt are pretty well dissolved. Add the ice water and stir to combine. Submerge the pork loin completely in the mixture. Refrigerate for 4 to 8 hours, but not longer, or the texture will start to change and it will become too salty. Remove the pork loin from the brine and pat dry with paper towels. Discard the brine.

Spanish Pork Chops

FORK IN THE ROAD: **This is the ideal trick for introducing new flavors to kids in manageable doses—use a more restrained amount of the rub on their chops.**

I am a total pork convert. That whole "the other white meat"—I'm buying it hook, line, and sinker.

This recipe was originally inspired by a tapas kebab recipe in David Tanis's wonderful cookbook *One Good Dish*. His food is just so pleasingly simple, and so uncluttered. I am always filled with gratitude toward a recipe writer who reminds me that the key to fine home cooking is simplicity, and that the temptation to over-adorn our dishes is where things get sloppy.

The sliced lemons on the pork chop thing is quite pretty, but not necessary.

1 teaspoon minced garlic

1 teaspoon paprika or pimentón, sweet, spicy, or smoked (see page 236)

1 teaspoon ground cumin

1 teaspoon ground coriander

1 teaspoon dried oregano

1 teaspoon minced fresh thyme (optional)

Pinch of cayenne pepper

½ teaspoon kosher or coarse salt, or to taste

Freshly ground black pepper, to taste

1 tablespoon extra-virgin olive oil, plus more for cooking the chops

1 teaspoon red wine vinegar or sherry vinegar

4 pork chops (each 1-inch thick, about 2½ pounds total)

4 thin slices lemon (optional)

Chopped fresh flat-leaf parsley, extra paprika, and/or lemon wedges, for garnish

Yield

Serves 4 (maybe more if you're slicing up the chops to serve)

What the Kids Can Do

Measure and blend up the spice paste, and rub it on the chops (washing their hands well before and after; see page xi).

Make Ahead

You can make the paste up to 2 days ahead and store it, covered, in the refrigerator. You can also smear the chops with the paste and refrigerate them, covered, for a day before cooking.

Sliced lemons caramelize during
the sautéing, and provide a beautiful citrusy
pop of color and flavor.

1. Combine the garlic, paprika, cumin, coriander, oregano, thyme, if using, cayenne, salt, and pepper in a small bowl. Add the olive oil and vinegar and stir to make a paste. Smear the paste on both sides of the pork chops and place a lemon slice on top of each (➤━━◀ see the Fork in the Road if you'd like milder chops). Let the chops sit in the fridge for 30 to 45 minutes, or longer (or skip the fridge if you don't have the time).

2. Heat a large skillet over medium-high heat until very hot. Add a couple of teaspoons of olive oil and when the oil just starts to smoke, add the pork chops, lemon slice side down. You may have to do this in 2 batches, using a bit more olive oil if the pan is crowded. Let the chops sear without moving them until nicely browned on the bottom, about 4 minutes. Turn the chops, keep the lemon slices in place, and sear the other side, again without moving them, for another 4 minutes or so, until nicely browned on the underside and a meat thermometer inserted into the middle of a chop registers 150°F (the meat will continue to cook after it leaves the pan).

3. Transfer the chops to a serving plate or cutting board and let sit for 4 or 5 minutes before serving whole, or in slices. Sprinkle with parsley or additional paprika if desired, and serve with lemon wedges for squeezing over the pork.

FORK IN THE ROAD
Milder Spanish Pork Chops

The recipe makes a shy ¼ cup of rub, and if you divide it evenly among all of the pork chops, you'll have 4 robustly flavored chops. But if you think a more delicately seasoned chop will hold more allure for some of your brood, then simply rub 1 or 2 of the ribs with only 1 teaspoon of the rub each. Great flavor? Yes. Too much flavor? Nope. If you end up with leftover rub, toss it with some cubed Yukon Gold potatoes and some olive oil, and roast those potatoes at 425°F for 30 to 40 minutes to go with your pork.

A Couple of Other Quick Paste Rubs

All these amounts are enough for 4 pork chops (or chicken breasts, for that matter).

Italian

1 tablespoon olive oil

1 teaspoon minced garlic

1 teaspoon dried oregano

½ teaspoon crushed fennel seeds

Salt and freshly ground black pepper, to taste

Asian

1 tablespoon vegetable or canola oil

1 tablespoon brown sugar

1 tablespoon paprika

1 teaspoon mustard powder

1 teaspoon ground ginger

½ teaspoon ground allspice

Pinch of red pepper flakes

For either of the above rubs, just combine all of the ingredients and smear on the meat of your choice.

Asian Spareribs

FORK IN THE ROAD: Slightly sweet or slightly spicy—or some of each!

I came up with this recipe as my Father's Day gift to my husband, Gary, who loves ribs more than anyone else I know, with the exception of my own father. My kids are no slouch in the rib-loving department either. I have a photo of Jack when he was about 1½, eating his first rib. In it he looks simultaneously surprised and perplexed and ecstatic, and maybe a little drunk. In my mind the caption for this photo is, "For the love of God, where have you people been hiding the pork?"

If you have a food processor, small or large, this marinade comes together in a flash. If you are a cutting-board-and-knife kind of a cook, then it will take a tiny bit longer, but it's still an extraordinarily simple and flavorful sauce.

I almost feel like paper napkins should be listed in the actual ingredients list, since they are so critical to the enjoyment of this dish. These are great eaten outside, with no white clothes or tablecloths or cushions in sight.

3 cloves garlic, peeled

3 scallions, trimmed

¾ cup hoisin sauce

½ cup ketchup

½ cup reduced-sodium soy sauce (or ⅓ cup regular soy sauce plus 2 tablespoons water)

½ cup honey

¼ cup rice wine vinegar or cider vinegar

¼ cup mirin or 2 tablespoons dry sherry

1 rack (about 5 pounds) St. Louis–style pork ribs (see Sidebar, page 115)

Yield

Serves 4

What the Kids Can Do

Measure and dump the marinade ingredients into the food processor or bowl; with supervision, press the buttons to run the food processor.

Make Ahead

The ribs can be marinated for up to 2 days, or made through the initial baking and then refrigerated for up to 3 days. Bring them to room temperature and then give them the final grilling or baking at the higher temperature for ½ hour or so. Leftover fully cooked ribs can also be reheated in a 300°F oven for 15 minutes.

Note: Say you didn't have the time to marinate the ribs for the full 4 hours. You are still going to make some fine ribs. The flavors won't penetrate the meat so deeply, but that's okay.

1. Finely mince the garlic and scallions in a food processor or blender. Add the hoisin, ketchup, soy sauce, honey, vinegar, and mirin and process until well blended.

2. ➤ You can continue with Step 3 if you want all of the ribs to be on the milder, sweeter side, or see the Fork in the Road to make the ribs spicier.

3. Pour the sauce into a plastic container with a lid, one large enough to hold the ribs (you can cut the ribs into 2 pieces if that makes life easier). Add the ribs to the marinade and turn them so they are well-coated. Or, place the marinade and ribs in a large heavy-duty zipper-top bag and seal.

4. Marinate the ribs in the fridge for at least 4 hours (see Note on page 112) or up to a day.

5. Preheat the oven to 300°F. Line two rimmed baking sheets with aluminum foil (do not be tempted to skip this step).

6. Place the ribs, meaty side up, on the prepared baking sheets, and pour any remaining marinade over them. Bake the ribs for 1½ hours. (To finish the ribs in the oven, see Cooking Tip 1.)

7. To finish the ribs on the grill, shortly before the baking time is up, preheat the grill to medium (see Cooking Tip 2). Once finished baking, arrange the ribs on the grill, meatier side down, and grill, turning the ribs frequently so they won't burn and basting them as you go with any marinade that remains on the baking sheets. Don't wander away. Grill until the outsides have a nicely browned and slightly crusty exterior, about 10 minutes.

8. Let the ribs sit for 5 or 10 minutes before slicing them. Serve hot or warm.

Cooking Tip 1

To cook the ribs completely in the oven, simply crank the heat up to 400°F at the end of the 1½ hours and let them go for another 20 to 25 minutes, giving them a good baste or two toward the end and watching carefully to see that they don't burn.

Cooking Tip 2

SAUCY VS. JUICY

If you like your ribs juicier, work with the whole racks, and cut them after they are completely cooked. But if you like a rib that is well coated with sauce on all sides, and somewhat crisper and chewier, then you can cut the racks into segments of two ribs each after the initial baking (let them sit for a few minutes first), and give them a very good basting on the cut ends right before you put them on the grill or back in the oven.

FORK IN THE ROAD

Spicy Asian Spareribs

ADD THE FOLLOWING TO the marinade in the food processor and process to blend for more intensely flavored ribs:

2 tablespoons minced fresh ginger
2 teaspoons sriracha (or other Asian chili-garlic sauce), or to taste
1 teaspoon five spice powder
Additional 2 to 3 cloves garlic

Or, to divide and conquer, pour half the marinade into a container. Then add half of the above ingredients to the marinade still in the food processor and process until everything is well combined. Pour this marinade into another container. Marinate one rack in each of the marinades and proceed with the cooking directions.

This recipe makes me wish I had invested in moist towelettes.

St. Louis–Style Ribs

These are racks that have been trimmed, resulting in a nice narrow rack of ribs that walks a perfect line between the diminutive baby back ribs (which are usually quite pricey and tend to be quite lean), and those behemoth Fred Flintstone slabs of ribs that can be very fatty and just plain cumbersome. However, any rib will take well to this marinade, so pick the type you like best (baby backs take only an hour for the first cooking phase, regular ribs at least 2 hours).

Roast Leg of Lamb with Two Sauces

FORK IN THE ROAD: One or both of the sauces make this spectacular . . . but the lamb itself is some pretty fine fare.

This is a gorgeous, make-an-impression main course. So when you get lucky enough to see a beautiful boneless or semiboneless leg of lamb on sale, grab it, roast it, and consider yourself indulged. It's actually a very simple cut of meat to prepare, and leftovers are fabulous as is or piled in sandwiches.

Lamb is one of those meats that people have very particular opinions about how well done it should be. My friend Ted likes it super well-done, my friend Kelly likes to say, "just let it lean up against the radiator for a few minutes." Ted gets the ends; Kelly gets the middle slices. If you've been procrastinating buying an instant-read thermometer, this is a good moment to get that task off the list.

Olive oil or nonstick cooking spray for coating the baking sheet

4 cloves garlic, peeled

1 tablespoon fresh rosemary leaves

2 tablespoons olive oil

Kosher or coarse salt and freshly ground black pepper, to taste

1 boneless or semiboneless leg of lamb (3½ to 4 pounds), trimmed and tied (you can buy it this way or a butcher can do it for you)

Salsa Verde or Lemon Mint Cream (━━◀ see the Fork in the Road for recipes), optional

1. Lightly coat a rimmed baking sheet with olive oil or cooking spray.

Yield

Serves 8 to 10

What the Kids Can Do

Make the garlic-rosemary paste in the food processor with supervision; rub the lamb with the paste (see Make Ahead, page 118); measure the ingredients for and mix up the Lemon Mint Cream or the Salsa Verde, if making.

2. Combine the garlic, rosemary, olive oil, and salt and pepper in a food processor and puree to a paste. Place the lamb on the prepared baking sheet and rub it all over with the garlic-rosemary paste. Let it sit for 30 minutes to come to room temperature and for the marinade to penetrate a bit.

3. Place the oven rack in the lower third of the oven and preheat the oven to 425°F. Roast the lamb until the temperature is 135°F (rare), 140°F (medium-rare), or 145°F (medium) when an instant-read thermometer is inserted into the thickest part of the meat, about 50 minutes for rare, 1 hour for medium-rare, and 1 hour and 10 minutes for medium. Transfer the lamb to a carving board and allow it to rest for about 20 minutes to reabsorb its juices. Slice and serve, either on its own, or with the Lemon Mint Cream or the Salsa Verde.

Make Ahead

The paste can be made ahead of time and refrigerated for 2 days. In fact, the lamb can be rubbed with the paste and refrigerated, covered, for up to 2 days before roasting. The cream sauce should be made no more than 6 hours ahead, but the salsa verde can be made a day ahead. Cover and refrigerate both sauces until just before serving.

Serving a simple cut of meat with a sauce or two for dipping is a nice way to entertain a crowd of adults and kids.

Two Sauces for Lamb

The lamb on its own needs no adornment for those who like their meat plain, but either of these sauces turns it into a celebratory dinner. Charlie pronounced the combination of the two sauces "delicious" as well.

Salsa Verde

Makes about 1 cup

2 cups fresh flat-leaf parsley leaves

½ cup extra-virgin olive oil

3 tablespoons capers, drained and rinsed

2 anchovies, rinsed

2 cloves garlic, chopped

Zest of 1 lemon

Pinch of red pepper flakes

Freshly ground black pepper, to taste

Place the parsley, olive oil, capers, anchovies, garlic, lemon zest, red pepper flakes, and black pepper in a food processor and pulse or puree to the desired texture. You can also finely mince everything by hand and combine it in a small bowl.

Lemon Mint Cream

Makes about 1 cup

⅔ cup sour cream or Greek yogurt (preferably full-fat)

3 tablespoons heavy (whipping) cream

Finely grated zest and juice of 1 lemon

2 tablespoons minced fresh parsley leaves

2 tablespoons minced fresh mint leaves

Kosher or coarse salt and freshly ground black pepper, to taste

Combine the sour cream, heavy cream, lemon zest and juice, parsley, mint, and salt and pepper in a small bowl.

Fresh with loads of parsley, and a bit tangy and salty.

Lemony, minty, spring-y.

You can dial the heat up or down for this Jerk Chicken.

JERK CHICKEN, *page 127*

Many of us have a love-sigh relationship with chicken. We love it for its versatility, its affordability, its availability, its popularity. But we get bored with it. But wait a minute—it's really not chicken we're bored with; it's the furrow we tend to fall into when preparing it.

Chicken

These five recipes should shake things up a little (but not enough to scare the kids—that's not what we're looking for here). Two of the recipes—Chicken Tikka Masala-ish and Chicken in Orange Sauce—can also be made in vegetarian versions so no one misses out. And then there's Jerk Chicken; Bacon, Sage, and Provolone Chicken Rolls (which gets drizzled with marsala sauce for those who like it); and Chicken in Mushroom Cream Sauce (mushrooms optional). Boring? Not hardly.

Chicken Tikka Masala-ish

FORK IN THE ROAD: Instead of all chicken, you can use half the marinade for a cauliflower version.

I rarely talk about my food allergies, because I like to make them take a back seat to everything that I love about food and cooking and entertaining. So, other than dealing with them in as careful a way as I can, I won't let them be the boss of me.

But because I am allergic to various spices (cardamom, nutmeg, mace) and all tree nuts, one of the cuisines that is the most problematic for me is Indian. I walk by Indian food carts and restaurants, taunted by the delicious smells emanating from them, and know that it ain't gonna happen.

But, wait! *I* like to cook!

So, while most of the Indian-inspired food that comes out of my kitchen is just that . . . inspired, it does satisfy my cravings, and my family doesn't seem to mind that lack of überauthenticity. Chicken Tikka Masala is one of the most popular dishes on Indian menus in this country, loved for its combination of bright, warm spices and cooling yogurt. The word *savory* may have been invented for this dish. It needs to marinate for a number of hours or overnight, so plan for that.

3 pounds skinless, boneless chicken thighs, trimmed, ⬤━◢ or see the Vegetarian Fork in the Road for a cauliflower substitute

Kosher or coarse salt and freshly ground black pepper, to taste

1 cup plain yogurt

Tikka Masala Paste (recipe follows)

2 tablespoons canola or vegetable oil, plus more oiling for the baking sheet

1 onion, minced

1 can (35 ounces) crushed tomatoes in puree

½ cup heavy (whipping) cream

¼ cup roughly chopped fresh cilantro leaves, for serving (optional)

Yield

Serves 6 to 8

What the Kids Can Do

Measure the components and mix up the spice blend and the marinade. Peel the ginger with a spoon (see Cooking Tip, page 124).

Make Ahead

The spice mix can be made up to 4 days ahead of time. The chicken and cauliflower can be marinated for up to 2 days. The entire recipe can also be made ahead up to 3 days in advance and warmed gently on the stove.

With
cauliflower
instead

Chicken
version

1. Cut the chicken into 2-inch or so pieces (no need to make the pieces neat). Season them with salt and pepper.

2. Combine the yogurt and 2 tablespoons of the spice paste in a large glass or nonreactive bowl and stir to combine well. Add the chicken, toss to coat the pieces with the marinade, and cover the bowl with plastic wrap. Marinate in the refrigerator for at least 8 hours, or overnight. Cover the rest of the spice blend and refrigerate that, too.

3. Preheat the broiler and lightly oil a rimmed baking sheet.

4. Remove the chicken from the marinade and place the pieces in a single layer on the baking sheet. Broil until lightly browned, about 5 minutes per side.

5. Meanwhile, heat the oil in a large heavy pot over medium-high heat. Add the onion and sauté until tender and slightly golden, 4 minutes. Add the remaining spice paste (if you want a milder version, just add 1 tablespoon of the paste), and stir until you can really smell all the seasonings, about 1 minute. Add the tomatoes and bring to a simmer. Reduce the heat and simmer for 10 minutes more. Add the chicken along with the cream and bring back to a gentle simmer. Let simmer for 5 minutes to blend the flavors and finish cooking the chicken. Serve, passing the cilantro on the side, if using.

Cooking Tip

A great kitchen trick to know is that you can peel ginger with a spoon. The skin is very thin, so if you just scrape the edge of the spoon against the skin with a bit of pressure, the skin will come right off. This is especially useful when navigating those twists and bumps, and also allows your kids to help out without the risk of a sharp peeler or knife.

This gets a 10 in the "what smells so great in here?" department.

Tikka Masala Paste

If you don't use all of this paste, add what's left over to the Butternut Squash Soup on page 88. It creates an amazingly flavorful version.

2 tablespoons fresh ginger, peeled and minced
1 tablespoon minced garlic
1 tablespoon ground coriander
1 tablespoon ground cumin
½ teaspoon ground cinnamon
½ teaspoon ground cayenne pepper
¼ teaspoon turmeric (see What Is Turmeric?)
Pinch of ground cloves
1 teaspoon salt
½ teaspoon black pepper

Combine the ginger, garlic, coriander, cumin, cinnamon, cayenne, turmeric, cloves, salt, and pepper in a small bowl. Use immediately or cover and refrigerate for up to 2 days.

Paste Yield

**Makes a generous
5 tablespoons of paste**

What Is Turmeric?

Turmeric is a spice used frequently in South Asian and Middle Eastern cooking—a key ingredient in curries. It's a rhizome, part of the ginger family. Although it has an earthy flavor, its main contribution is the bright gold color it imparts to whatever dish it's added to. It is usually used in small amounts in savory dishes, but occasionally it's added to sweet ones. Turmeric can be used fresh, but for the most part it's available in powder form.

VEGETARIAN

FORK
IN THE
ROAD

Cauliflower Tikka Masala

For a fully vegetarian tikka masala, you can roast cauliflower instead of broiling the chicken: Remove any leaves and the thick core from 2 large heads of cauliflower and cut into florets. Toss the florets with the seasoned yogurt marinade, and let sit for a couple of hours at room temperature. Spread the florets evenly on the oiled baking sheet and roast in a preheated 450°F oven until tender, 15 to 18 minutes. Continue with Step 5.

You can also make both versions at the same time using 1½ pounds of chicken thighs and 1 head of cauliflower. Just divide the yogurt marinade between the two of them, and marinate and cook accordingly. Make all the sauce in one pot, and then pour half into a second medium-size pot. Use one pot of sauce to finish cooking the chicken, and one for the cauliflower. Add half the cream with each main ingredient when it goes into the sauce for the final cooking.

This is the anti-boring chicken dish.

Jerk Chicken

FORK IN THE ROAD: A pleasantly spicy, Jamaican-inspired chicken, with a jerkier version for those looking for a slow, more intense burn.

In my first book there was a recipe for pulled pork, and one of the bonuses when making the dish was the fact that kids can say "pork butt" several times—a lovely perk, or so it went in my house. And now, *jerk* chicken! The ability to use another word usually frowned upon! Does the fun never end?

Make sure you have time to marinate the chicken (at least 6 hours). Serve with rice—or the starch of your choice—as a buffer to the seasonings. Creamy Coleslaw (page 281) is a great accompaniment, as is a simple mixed salad.

1 medium-size onion, coarsely chopped

2 cloves garlic, peeled

4 scallions, white and light green parts, cut into pieces

1 piece (1½ inches) fresh ginger, peeled and sliced

1 jalapeño pepper, stemmed, seeded, and cut into chunks

2 tablespoons soy sauce

1 tablespoon canola or vegetable oil, plus more for the baking sheet

Juice of 2 limes

1 tablespoon ground allspice

1 teaspoon dried thyme

1 teaspoon sugar

½ teaspoon ground cinnamon

1 teaspoon kosher or coarse salt

½ teaspoon freshly ground black pepper

6 pounds skin-on, bone-in chicken parts (your choice of thighs, breasts, and/or drumsticks)

Hot cooked rice, for serving

Yield

Serves 6

What the Kids Can Do

Measure and blend the ingredients for the marinade, using the food processor with supervision. Juice the limes. Repeat the word *jerk* as many times as possible before their parents snap.

Make Ahead

The marinade can be stored in the refrigerator for a week before using. The cooked chicken lasts up to 4 days in the refrigerator, and can be eaten cold, at room temperature, or reheated in a 350°F oven for about 15 minutes until warm (bring the chicken to room temperature before reheating).

1. Place the onion, garlic, scallions, ginger, jalapeño, soy sauce, oil, lime juice, allspice, thyme, sugar, cinnamon, and salt and pepper in a food processor or blender. Process until very well combined, about 1 minute (scrape down the sides of the mixer partway through).

2. 🍴 You can continue with Step 3 or see the Fork in the Road to make a hotter jerk paste.

3. If using chicken breasts, cut any large pieces in half. Place the chicken pieces on a baking sheet and rub them all over with the jerk paste (yes, it's a bit messy), then transfer to a big bowl and cover (or place in a zipper-top bag). Refrigerate the chicken for at least 6 hours, or preferably overnight— it can marinate for up to 2 days; the flavors will deepen over time.

4. Preheat the oven to 375°F. Lightly oil a rimmed baking sheet.

5. Place the chicken pieces on the baking sheet and rub any marinade remaining in the bowl over them. Bake until the chicken is cooked through and the outside is nicely browned, about 50 minutes. Serve with plenty of hot rice.

FORK IN THE ROAD

Bring It Jerk Chicken

Some people like their jerk chicken to make them sweat. If you are one of those people, you can divide the marinade in half and keep one half just as it is (nicely spicy but not hot-hot). After whirling up the marinade in Step 1, divide it between two bowls. In the food processor, mince up 1 seeded habanero or Scotch bonnet pepper, 2 additional garlic cloves, and an additional 1-inch piece of peeled ginger. Add this fiery little blend to one of the bowls, and marinate half the chicken in this really jerky mixture while you marinate the remaining chicken in the tamer, original marinade. Bake as directed.

What Exactly Is Jerk Chicken?

Hailing from Jamaica (with its roots in Africa), *jerk* denotes both a spice blend and a style of cooking. Pork and chicken are the two most commonly *jerked* meats, but now jerk seasoning and cooking methods are applied to everything from tofu to beef. Allspice and peppers, specifically Scotch bonnets (see the Fork in the Road), are the two most integral ingredients in a jerk paste, which can be either dry or wet.

Traditional jerk cooking involves smoking, though now grilling is a commonly used cooking method, and in this indoor version, the good old oven is employed. If weather allows, grilling is a great option.

Bacon, Sage, and Provolone Chicken Rolls with Marsala Sauce

FORK IN THE ROAD: You can hold back on the marsala sauce for those looking for a plainer dish.

This is the kind of leftover I would like to have waiting in the fridge for me for lunch. Or, thinking about it, breakfast. Grown-ups and hungry kids might eat two of these for dinner. My husband, Gary, might eat three.

In addition to the plain-Jane Fork in the Road option, know that if the sage isn't going to appeal to anyone at your table, you can skip it. Nubby little noodles like tubetti are nice with this.

8 (about 1 pound) thinly sliced chicken cutlets (see Note)
Kosher or coarse salt and freshly ground black pepper, to taste
4 slices provolone cheese, halved
8 fresh sage leaves (optional, or as desired)
8 slices bacon
1 teaspoon garlic, minced
½ cup marsala wine
½ cup chicken broth, preferably low-sodium

1. Preheat the oven to 350°F. Create a large clean workspace—it's easier to roll up all of the chicken breasts at the same time, assembly-line fashion; you may want to line the counter space with wax or parchment paper (or use a huge cutting board).

2. Lay the chicken breasts on the work space and season them lightly with salt and pepper. Place a piece of provolone

Yield

Serves 4 to 6

What the Kids Can Do

If you are pounding chicken breasts (see Note), they would love to help with that. They can also layer the ingredients and roll up the chicken bundles, and skewer them with toothpicks.

Note: Thinly sliced chicken breast cutlets are pretty readily available, but if they aren't at your market, just place regular chicken breasts (4 breasts of 4 or 5 ounces each will do it) between two pieces of wax or parchment paper and gently pound them with a meat mallet (if you have one) or a rolling pin, or a bottle of wine until they are uniformly thin, about ⅓-inch-thick all over. They will be quite large at this point, so cut them in half before proceeding, which will give you 8 pieces.

on each cutlet (trim it so it doesn't extend over the edges of the chicken), and a sage leaf if desired. Roll up each breast, and then wrap a slice of bacon around the middle, trimming the bacon so that the ends just overlap to seal the rolls (see the Cooking Tip). Skewer each with a toothpick to keep it closed.

3. Heat a large, ovenproof skillet over medium-high heat. Add the bacon-wrapped chicken and brown on all sides, turning the rolls with tongs so they hold their shape, about 8 minutes in all.

4. Transfer the skillet to the preheated oven and bake until the rolls are cooked through, 8 to 10 minutes. A little cheese will probably melt out; that's okay. Transfer the chicken to a serving dish, remove the toothpicks, and keep warm while preparing the sauce. ━━◀ Or forgo the sauce—see the Fork in the Road.

5. There should be just a couple of teaspoons of fat left in the skillet; pour off any more than that. (The skillet will be very hot. Remember to use pot holders while preparing the sauce.) Heat the pan over medium-high heat. Add the garlic and stir for a few seconds until it starts to color, then add the marsala and stir to scrape up any bits from the bottom of the pan to flavor the sauce. Add the broth, allow the sauce to come to a simmer, and simmer until the mixture is slightly reduced, about 3 minutes.

6. Serve the hot chicken rolls with the sauce, either spooned over or passed at the table.

 ## Super-Plain Chicken Rolls

For the sauce-phobic, serve the rolls plain, maybe with a last little drizzle of olive oil just before serving.

Make Ahead

You can roll and wrap the chicken parcels up to a day ahead of time and keep them in the refrigerator. Leftovers can be heated in a 325°F oven for 10 minutes.

Cooking Tip

Any leftover extra-small pieces of uncooked bacon should be crisped up in the pan next to the rolls, and either snacked on, or saved for another recipe—sprinkle them on pasta or a baked potato (page 259), or use them as a reason to make Cobb Salad (page 83) later in the week.

You can also serve the rolls in the pan with the sauce.

If mushrooms are a no-go, it's easy to skip them.

Serve with Honey-Glazed Carrots (page 276) and Simple Sautéed Spinach (page 287)

Move mushrooms for you.

Chicken in Mushroom Cream Sauce

FORK IN THE ROAD: Your kids don't like mushrooms? They get chicken in plain cream sauce and you get the extra mushrooms.

This is a slightly decadent, creamy sauce that really enrobes the chicken in the most appealing way. It's elegant enough for company, but easy enough for a weeknight. It goes with so many sides, though you'll probably want some color on the plate. Try Honey-Glazed Carrots (page 276), Warm Brussels Sprouts with Bacon and Mustard Vinaigrette (page 288), or Simple Sautéed Spinach (page 287). My husband also enjoys a Lactaid on the side. Sorry if that's TMI.

4 teaspoons olive oil

1 teaspoon minced garlic

8 ounces mushrooms (any assortment), cleaned and sliced

4 large skinless, boneless chicken breasts (about 2½ pounds)

Kosher or coarse salt and freshly ground black pepper, to taste

1 onion, minced

¾ cup dry white wine

¾ cup heavy (whipping) or light cream

2 tablespoons minced fresh flat-leaf parsley, tarragon, or basil leaves (optional)

Hot cooked quinoa or rice, for serving

1. Heat 2 teaspoons of the olive oil in a large skillet over medium heat. Add the garlic and stir until fragrant, 1 minute. Add the mushrooms and turn up the heat to medium-high. Cook until the mushrooms are tender, have released all of their liquid (see Cooking Tip, page 134), and are golden brown, about 8 minutes. Transfer the mushroom mixture to a plate or bowl and set aside.

2. Heat the remaining 2 teaspoons olive oil in the same skillet over medium-high heat. Season the chicken with salt and pepper and add to the skillet. Sear until the chicken is browned and almost cooked through, but not quite, 4 to 5 minutes on each side. Place the chicken on top of the mushrooms.

3. Return the skillet to the heat without cleaning it, add the onion, and sauté until slightly tender, about 4 minutes. Pour in the white wine and scrape up any bits stuck to the bottom of the pan. Allow the wine to reduce by half, about 4 minutes, then add the cream and bring to a simmer.

4. ▬◀═ You can continue with Step 5 or see the Fork in the Road for a plain sauce.

5. Return the chicken and mushrooms to the pan, along with the herbs. Simmer until the chicken is fully cooked and the sauce has thickened, about 3 minutes.

6. Remove the chicken from the sauce and let it sit to reabsorb its juices for 2 minutes. Then slice it up and return it to the sauce so that it becomes nicely coated with sauce, and serve everything over the quinoa or rice.

Cooking Tip

SAUTÉING MUSHROOMS: Perfect sautéed mushrooms—instead of limp, soggy ones—are not a mystery. Here's how. First, never submerge your mushrooms in water; they already contain quite a bit and are very porous, so they soak up water like a sponge, making them (let's say it together) sponge-y. Wipe any dirt off your mushrooms with a slightly damp paper towel just before cooking them. Then, sauté the mushrooms, whether they are sliced or chopped, at high heat, so that they release their liquid. After the liquid evaporates in the pan, they will start to caramelize and brown, giving them great flavor and texture. Wait for this to happen and you will be rewarded with lovely caramelized, sautéed mushrooms.

FORK IN THE ROAD

Chicken in Plain Cream Sauce

In Step 5, return just the chicken to the sauce (without the mushrooms) and simmer until it is cooked through, 2 to 3 minutes. Remove the chicken from the sauce and let cool for a couple of minutes before slicing. Set aside some chicken to serve mushroom-free, topping it with some of the cream sauce, with or without the herbs stirred in. Return the remaining chicken to the skillet, add the mushrooms and herbs if they have not yet been added, and heat through for another minute or so.

Chicken in Orange Sauce

FORK IN THE ROAD: Chicken or tofu, or both, get a slick of delicious tangy-sweet glaze.

This is one of those dishes that makes you feel quite pleased with yourself. Fast, easy, with fairly universally appealing flavors, and healthier and more delicious than its Chinese takeout inspiration. There's plenty of sauce, too, to spoon over hot rice or quinoa. Serve with broccoli, broccoli rabe, or another hearty green to balance flavor, color, and texture.

When you're feeding a group that includes one or more vegetarians, this kind of recipe makes life so much easier. Essentially you sauté some chicken in one pan, some tofu in another pan, then divide up a simple sauce between the two.

3 cloves garlic, minced

3 tablespoons honey

1 teaspoon finely grated orange zest

¾ cup orange juice, preferably fresh but not necessary

⅓ cup reduced-sodium soy sauce, or ¼ cup regular soy sauce plus 2 tablespoons water

3 tablespoons rice vinegar

3 tablespoons cornstarch

1 tablespoon finely minced peeled fresh ginger

Freshly ground black pepper, to taste

2 pounds skinless, boneless chicken breasts or thighs, cut into ¾-inch pieces, ◀━◀ or see the Vegetarian Fork in the Road for a tofu alternative

Kosher or coarse salt

2 tablespoons canola or vegetable oil

4 scallions, white and light green parts, sliced

Hot cooked rice (brown or white) or quinoa, for serving

Toasted sesame seeds (see page 286), for serving (optional)

Yield

Serves 6

What the Kids Can Do

Zest the orange and juice it (if you are using fresh juice). Kids of the right age can cut up the chicken (younger ones can tackle the tofu) with an age-appropriate knife.

Make Ahead

The chicken or tofu can be cut up a couple of days ahead of time, and the sauce can be combined a couple of days ahead, and refrigerated, too.

1. Whisk together the garlic, honey, orange zest and juice, soy sauce, rice vinegar, cornstarch, ginger, and pepper in a small bowl. Set the sauce aside.

2. Season the chicken lightly with salt and pepper. Heat the oil in a very large skillet or a wok over high heat. Add the chicken and sauté until it starts to turn white, 3 minutes. Add the sauce and scallions and cook until the sauce thickens and the chicken is cooked through, 3 to 4 minutes more.

3. Serve over hot rice or quinoa, with the sesame seeds sprinkled over if desired.

Tofu in Orange Sauce

Replace the chicken with 2 pounds extra-firm tofu, blotted dry and cut into ¾-inch cubes. To get the tofu nicely browned, in Step 2, heat the oil in the skillet over high heat, and when very hot, add the cubes, which should sizzle and sear (watch for splattering). Cook the tofu, *not* moving it for at least 3 minutes, so it has a chance to brown on the bottom. Flip the cubes using a thin metal spatula (and knowing some cubes will break) and continue to cook to brown the bottoms, 3 minutes more. Add the sauce and scallions and continue with the recipe.

If you want to make the dish half chicken and half tofu, use a pound of each, sauté them separately in two large skillets with a tablespoon of oil in each, and divide the sauce and scallions evenly between the pans. The cooking times are the same.

The sweetness in the sauce makes this a dish that most picky eaters will lean into.

CAESAR-ROASTED SALMON, *page 151*

CHAPTER 9

The mere fact that you've flipped to this chapter, AND are spending time reading the introduction means that you are a game person, an experimenter, a person who's up for a challenge. Take a moment. Feel good about this. Making fish at home is probably a cooking task that makes you, like most people, nervous. Not to mention the notion of feeding fish to your kids.

Fish & Seafood

WAIT—COME BACK—I DIDN'T MEAN TO SCARE YOU!

1. Cooking fish is easy. It really is.

2. You are going to get your kids to like fish. You really, really are. Maybe not all fish, but something in the fish and seafood family. I cannot offer a money-back guarantee on this, but these five recipes have been tested on many kids, including my own, and the results have been very encouraging.

Quick Caesar dressing perks up a piece of salmon, mild halibut is wonderful enrobed in a salty piece of prosciutto (sauce optional), and the cornmeal-crusted tilapia is a firm favorite with my kids. Plump shrimp star in a simple stir-fry, and you will be delighted to find out how easy crab cakes are to make at home.

Crab Cakes

FORK IN THE ROAD: Vegetarians who thought they would never have the pleasure of crab cakes again will be fully cheered by the hearts of palm version.

If you have kids, you are probably overly familiar with the show *SpongeBob SquarePants*. Can you imagine the meeting where the show was first pitched? "See, there's this guy, but he's actually a sponge. And he lives in a pineapple under the sea. And his best friend is a starfish. And SpongeBob works in an underwater burger joint, where they sell burgers, which are actually called Krabby Patties. . . ." It took a more evolved mind than mine to see the potential in this.

The point being that if your kids know the show, they have heard of a Krabby Patty, and are probably interested to know what the fuss is all about. Tell them that this is the secret recipe (gloss over the fact that in the show the burgers are probably beef patties), and that they can join their favorite cartoon characters in experiencing one of the finest foods in the underwater realm.

1 pound cooked crabmeat (see Note, page 143), ➤🍴 or
  see the Vegetarian Fork in the Road for a meat-free substitute

2 large eggs

1 sleeve saltines (see Cooking Tip 2, page 142), finely crushed

¼ cup mayonnaise

3 tablespoons minced red onion

3 tablespoons chopped fresh parsley or cilantro leaves

2 teaspoons Dijon mustard

1½ teaspoons Worcestershire sauce

¼ teaspoon cayenne pepper, or more to taste

Freshly ground black pepper, to taste

3 tablespoons canola or vegetable oil

Lemon wedges, for serving

Rémoulade Sauce (recipe follows), for serving (optional)

Yield

Serves 4 to 6 (see Cooking Tip 1)

What the Kids Can Do

The crushing of the saltines is total fun (see Cooking Tip 2), and there is plenty of measuring and stirring to do for both the crab cake mixture and the optional sauce. And let them form the mixture into cakes and dredge them in the crushed saltines. Irregular crabcake shapes? Part of their charm.

1. Pick over the crabmeat, removing any stray shell pieces or bits of cartilage. Pat dry with paper towels and let drain on the towels for a few minutes.

2. Beat the eggs in a medium-size bowl and add ½ cup of the saltine crumbs, the mayonnaise, onion, parsley, mustard, Worcestershire, cayenne, and black pepper and stir to blend well. Add the crabmeat and stir to combine.

3. Divide the mixture into 6 portions and shape each into a patty ¾-inch thick, using your hand to make the rounds nice and neat. Place the remaining saltine crumbs on a plate. Dredge the patties in the crumbs to cover completely.

4. Line a clean plate with paper towels. Heat half of the oil in a large skillet over medium-high heat. Sauté 3 of the patties until golden brown on both sides, 4 to 5 minutes per side. Drain briefly on the paper towel–lined plate. Repeat with the remaining patties. Serve with lemon wedges, and Rémoulade Sauce if desired.

VEGETARIAN

FORK IN THE ROAD

Hearts of Palm Cakes

Interestingly, though the taste is different, hearts of palm have a somewhat similar texture to crabmeat, and they work amazingly well as a substitute in this recipe. Drain 2 cans (14 ounces each) hearts of palm and pulse in a food processor until roughly chopped (or do it by hand), then blot up some of the moisture with paper towels. Use instead of the crabmeat in the recipe, but note that hearts of palm have less flavor than crabmeat, so you may want to slightly bump up the amounts of Worcestershire, mustard, and cayenne.

If you want to make the patties half and half, combine the egg/crumb mixture up to the point where you add the crab. Divide it into 2 bowls, then add ½ pound crab to 1 bowl and 1 can of chopped hearts of palm (with a bit of additional seasoning if desired) to the other and gently fold in. Proceed with the recipe, but they might look a lot alike, so keep the two batches straight! Both are great with Rémoulade Sauce.

Cooking Tip 1

This recipe makes 6 dinner-size patties. You can make little 1½-inch patties for appetizers, too; you will get about 15 per recipe. Cook them for 3 to 4 minutes per side.

Cooking Tip 2

You can crush saltines in a food processor, or, more satisfyingly, do it yourself: Place them in a sturdy zipper-top bag, press out the air, seal the bag, and smash the crackers with a rolling pin or meat mallet or a can of beans or anything that won't break and that you can use to beat the stuffing out of those saltines. Don't pulverize them into dust; you still want a little texture.

This recipe doesn't call for salt because the finely crushed saltines have salt in them, but if you happen to use unsalted saltines (which, to me, defeats the purpose and the name), then you may want to add a ½ teaspoon kosher or coarse salt.

Rémoulade Sauce

Makes ¾ cup

Try to get fresh tarragon for this. However, if you don't feel like making a homemade sauce, do remember that you can buy commercial rémoulade sauce, or use tartar sauce instead, or any kind of flavored mayo: Now's the time to use that leftover half jar of spicy mango aioli—or whatever is in the fridge door.

½ cup mayonnaise

1 tablespoon Dijon mustard

1 tablespoon minced shallots

2 teaspoons chopped fresh tarragon or 1 teaspoon dried

2 teaspoons chopped fresh flat-leaf parsley

2 teaspoons drained capers, minced

2 teaspoons white wine vinegar

¼ teaspoon cayenne pepper

Combine the mayonnaise, mustard, shallots, tarragon, parsley, capers, vinegar, and cayenne in a small bowl. Refrigerate, covered, until ready to serve. The sauce will keep in the refrigerator, covered, for 2 days.

Mr. Krabs would be proud.

Make Ahead

All ingredients can be prepped a day or two ahead, and you can also form the patties a day ahead, but don't dredge them in the remaining crumbs until just before sautéing so that they get that nice outer crust. As noted, the Rémoulade Sauce will keep in the fridge for 2 days.

Note: Jumbo lump crabmeat has gorgeous fat pieces and is the most expensive, claw meat is quite flaky and the least pricey, and there are various grades in between. These crab cakes work beautifully with whatever crab your budget allows for.

Stir-Fried Shrimp and Scallions

FORK IN THE ROAD: Add a slap of flavor with some black bean sauce and jalapeño.

This is a total weeknight dish, a dinner to fall in love with preparation-wise (fast and easy) and flavor-wise (simply delicious)—and if you wanted to make it (or half of it) with cubed boneless chicken, that's an easy swap.

If you have a really big wok, you could do this in one batch, but the secret to great stir-frying (and lots of other cooking methods, like frying and sautéing) is not to crowd the pan. Give the individual pieces of food a chance to come into direct contact with the hot pan on a continuous basis— that's the difference between nicely browned pieces and a pile of steamed food. So, cook it in two batches: The cooking process is super-quick, made quicker when the batches of food are small, so it takes only a handful of extra minutes.

And yeah, a picky kid might pick around the scallions . . . there's no helping that, but they still add nice flavor to the whole dish.

2 tablespoons reduced-sodium soy sauce

2 tablespoons dry sherry

2 teaspoons cornstarch

1 teaspoon sugar

4 tablespoons vegetable or canola oil

1 tablespoon minced fresh ginger

2 bunches scallions, trimmed, white and all the green parts, cut into 1-inch pieces

2 pounds extra large (26 to 30 per pound) shrimp, peeled and deveined

¾ cup chicken broth, preferably low-sodium

Hot cooked rice, for serving

Yield

Serves 6

What the Kids Can Do

Measure and mix the sauce ingredients, peel the ginger with a spoon (see Cooking Tip, page 124), peel the shrimp, cut scallions with an age-appropriate knife.

1. Mix together the soy sauce, sherry, cornstarch, and sugar in a small bowl. Set aside.

2. Heat 2 tablespoons of the oil in a large skillet or wok over high heat. Add half the ginger and stir until you can smell it cooking, 1 minute. Add half the scallions and half the shrimp and sauté until the shrimp start to turn pink and the scallions start to soften, about 2 minutes. Transfer the shrimp and scallions to a serving bowl.

3. Repeat with the remaining oil, ginger, scallions, and shrimp, and when the shrimp starts turning pink, return the first batch of shrimp and scallions to the pan, along with any juices that have accumulated.

4. ⊱═ You can continue with Step 5 or see the Fork in the Road if you want to kick up the shrimp a notch.

5. Add the soy sauce mixture to the wok and stir to coat the shrimp. Add the chicken broth, bring to a simmer, and allow the sauce to thicken while the shrimp finishes cooking, about 2 minutes. Serve right away with the hot cooked rice.

Make Ahead

This is best made right before serving (but in fact we are always delighted to have reheated leftovers the next day).

VARIATION

You can use cubed chicken instead of the shrimp if you prefer.

FORK IN THE ROAD

Black Bean–Garlic Shrimp

This becomes a smack-your-mouth dish when you spike up the shrimp with black bean–garlic sauce and minced jalapeño. Add 3 tablespoons of store-bought black bean–garlic sauce and 1 teaspoon minced jalapeño at the end of Step 3, after returning the first batch of shrimp and scallions to the pan. Then proceed with the soy sauce mixture and then the broth.

If you want to keep half the mixture simple, when you are cooking the first batch of shrimp and scallions, proceed with adding half the soy sauce mixture, then half the broth and finish the first batch completely. For the second batch, add 1 heaping tablespoon black bean–garlic sauce and ½ teaspoon minced jalapeño before you add the remaining soy sauce mixture and broth.

Cornmeal-Crusted Tilapia with Shallot, Tomatoes, and Mustard Sauce

FORK IN THE ROAD: Just skip the sauce and shallot-tomato topping, and it's an easy gateway fish dinner.

The first time I made this for dinner, Charlie put down his fork, looked at me, and said, "Congratulations, Mom. You've finally found a way to make fish taste like chicken." Stop, stop, you're embarrassing me. But it's true: There's a very good chance that kids who don't think they like fish will like this fish prepared in this way.

The ease of making this fish recipe cannot be overstated, and tilapia is possibly one of the most available, sustainable, inexpensive, and unthreatening fish out there, so it's a star on many levels.

1 cup cornmeal

1 tablespoon sweet paprika

Kosher or coarse salt and freshly ground black pepper, to taste

4 fillets tilapia (8 ounces each)

3 tablespoons olive oil

4 shallots, thinly sliced

2 ripe tomatoes, seeded and diced

½ cup chicken broth, preferably low-sodium

2 tablespoons Dijon mustard, coarse or smooth

1. Combine the cornmeal, paprika, 1 teaspoon salt, and ½ teaspoon pepper in a shallow bowl. Cut each fillet down the middle (you will see a dividing line). Dredge each piece in the cornmeal mixture, making sure each piece is completely coated. Set aside.

Yield

Serves 4 to 6, assuming some people will have 1 piece, some 2

What the Kids Can Do

Make the cornmeal mixture, dredge the fish, and slice the tomatoes with an age-appropriate knife.

Make Ahead

Not much, but you can certainly prep the ingredients a day or so ahead of time, and prepare the cornmeal mixture and keep it in a sealed container for a few days.

2. Heat 1 tablespoon of the olive oil in a large skillet over medium-high heat. Add the shallots and cook until soft and golden, 5 minutes. Stir in the tomatoes and season with salt and pepper. Let cook until heated through, 1 to 2 minutes. Transfer to a bowl and set aside. Wipe out the pan.

3. Add 1 tablespoon of the olive oil to the skillet and heat over medium-high heat. Place half the coated fillets in the pan, making sure they are not touching. Cook until each side is golden brown, and the fish is cooked through, 5 to 8 minutes in total, depending on the thickness of each piece (when you cut them in half you'll see one side is thinner than the other). Transfer the fish to a plate and tent the plate with aluminum foil to keep the pieces warm. Wipe out any dallying crumbs from the skillet, add the remaining 1 tablespoon olive oil, and cook the remaining fish, transferring it all to the plate as it is finished cooking.

4. When you're finished cooking the fish, keep the pan over the heat and add the chicken broth, scraping up any brown bits from the bottom of the pan. When the broth begins to simmer, whisk in the mustard.

5. Serve the fish with mustard sauce drizzled over each piece and a scoop of the tomato-shallot mixture, ●━━◄ or see the Fork in the Road and serve some of the pieces plain.

The simple fish will keep your kids happy, and the easy—but sophisticated—topping will make you feel like a 4-star chef.

FORK IN THE ROAD

Simple Cornmeal-Crusted Tilapia

This one's quite easy: Skip the sauce or skip the tomato mixture, or skip both, and your kids (or whoever is not interested in the adornments) can enjoy a piece of simply prepared fish while you enjoy a restaurant-esque, interesting meal.

A photo of a
teenage boy eating fish—
not a mirage . . .

Caesar-Roasted Salmon

FORK IN THE ROAD: This simple Caesar dressing would also make a great marinade for boneless, skinless chicken breasts (see ▬◀═ the Fork in the Road.)

This recipe should be filed under N for "Necessity is the mother of all invention"—one of the most important life and cooking lessons, and a concept I validate daily in my kitchen.

Dressing left over from Caesar salad (one of the boys' favorite dishes ever; it's in *The Mom 100 Cookbook*) plus salmon fillets (the best-loved fish in our house) plus the realization that friends were coming over for dinner in an hour (and I had grossly underestimated how much time I would need to collect the laundry from the floor and sweep up what I can only hope was a chewed dog biscuit) . . . and this equals? Caesar-Roasted Salmon. Now this kind of math I love. (By the way, if I had skinless boneless chicken breasts instead of salmon, they would have worked, too. Next time.)

This made its first appearance with the Warm Roasted Tomato, Couscous, and Chickpea Salad (page 271), and even if I had more time (Ha!) a prettier, springier meal would have been hard to come by. You can also serve it with a simply cooked vegetable, like asparagus or broccoli, and some rice, quinoa (page 80), or roasted or mashed potatoes. Another great side would be the Warm Brussels Sprouts with Bacon and Mustard Vinaigrette (page 288).

Yield

Serves 6

What the Kids Can Do

Measure the ingredients for the dressing and shake it up in the container. Smear the dressing on the fish. If you want to give older kids a substantial and interesting cooking task, let them help separate the roasted fish from the skin.

2 tablespoons extra-virgin olive oil, plus more for oiling the
  baking sheet

2 tablespoons mayonnaise

1 tablespoon fresh lemon juice

1 tablespoon Dijon mustard

1 teaspoon Worcestershire sauce

½ teaspoon finely minced garlic

1 finely minced anchovy fillet or ¼ teaspoon anchovy paste (optional)

Kosher or coarse salt and freshly ground black pepper, to taste

¼ cup finely grated Parmesan

6 skin-on salmon fillets (7 to 8 ounces each)

Make Ahead

The dressing can be made up
to a week ahead of time. It will
keep in a covered container in
the refrigerator. Give it a good
shake before using. Roast the
fish just before serving.

1. Preheat the oven to 450°F. Lightly oil a rimmed baking
sheet with olive oil.

2. Place the olive oil, mayonnaise, lemon juice, Dijon,
Worcestershire sauce, garlic, anchovy (if using), and salt
and pepper in a container with a lid. Cover tightly and
shake to combine well. Add the Parmesan and shake again
to combine. The mixture should be fairly thick.

3. Place the salmon fillets skin side down on the baking
sheet. Evenly smear all of the Caesar dressing over the tops
and sides of all of the fish.

4. Roast the fish until it is done to your liking, 8 to 10 minutes.
Check during the last few minutes, and if you like a more
browned top, switch to the broiler for the last minute or two
of cooking. Slide a metal spatula under each fillet, leaving the
skin on the baking sheet if possible, and serve hot or warm.

FORK IN THE ROAD

Caesar-Roasted Chicken Breasts

**Substitute boneless skinless chicken breasts for any amount of the salmon
fillets. The chicken may need a few more minutes to cook through.**

Prosciutto-Wrapped Halibut Piccata

FORK IN THE ROAD: Are some people a little less interested in sauce? That's just fine.

My whole family loves chicken piccata, with its fresh-tasting, lemony sauce. Clearly those flavors (garlic, capers, herbs, citrus) are also good friends with fish, so that inspired this dish, that and the prosciutto left over from Prosciutto-Wrapped Shrimp (page 65).

The prosciutto does not have to be wrapped neatly around the fish—it will look and taste just fine even if you don't do a very artistic job.

Olive oil or nonstick cooking spray, for oiling the baking sheet

1 pound halibut fillets, cut into 6 to 8 pieces, each piece about 2 x 3 inches

Kosher or coarse salt and freshly ground black pepper, to taste

6 to 8 very thin slices prosciutto (about 2 ounces; speck or serrano ham may be substituted; see Bacon, Prosciutto & Other Pork Cousins, page 9)

1 tablespoon olive oil

½ teaspoon minced garlic

2 tablespoons minced shallots or ¼ cup minced onion

½ cup dry white wine

½ cup chicken broth, preferably low-sodium

2 tablespoons fresh lemon juice

1 tablespoon chopped drained capers (optional)

2 teaspoons unsalted butter

1. Preheat the oven to 450°F. Lightly oil a rimmed baking sheet or spray with nonstick cooking spray.

2. Season the fish with salt (very lightly, the prosciutto is

Yield

Serves 4

What the Kids Can Do

Wrap the fish in the prosciutto, juice the lemon, measure the ingredients.

Make Ahead

Not such a great make-ahead dish, but you can wrap the fish in prosciutto a day ahead and keep it covered in the refrigerator.

salty) and black pepper and wrap a slice of prosciutto around each piece, making sure the prosciutto goes all the way around and trimming it as needed. Place the fish prosciutto-seam side down on the prepared baking sheet. Bake until the prosciutto is crisp, about 12 minutes.

3. ━━◀ You can continue with Step 4 or see the Fork in the Road if you're happy as is.

4 . As the fish bakes, heat the olive oil in a medium-size skillet over medium heat. Add the garlic and shallots and sauté until translucent and tender, about 2 minutes. Add the wine, increase the heat to medium-high and bring to a simmer. Add the chicken broth, return to a simmer, and cook until the liquid reduces by half, 2 to 3 minutes more. Add the lemon juice, capers, if using, and butter and stir until the butter is melted. Taste the sauce and season with salt and pepper. Place the cooked fish on a serving platter and spoon the sauce over.

FORK IN THE ROAD

Prosciutto-Wrapped Halibut (The End)

After baking the fish, stop right there and call it a day if you like. This is still a lovely main course, and a fish dish that may well win over the pesca-phobic people in your house.

A great example of the easy sauce-or-no-sauce Fork-in-the-Road technique—one meal and everyone gets it the way they want.

These five flexible recipes will have you knocking it out of the park, or at least getting on base. If that sports analogy either excited you or confused you, please don't think too much about it—it's probably the only one I'll make.

SOUTHWESTERN VEGETARIAN BLACK BEAN BURGERS, *page 166*

It's hard to go wrong with a burger or a plate of meatballs in the feed-the-family department. And yet, it's easy to get stuck in a rut in the burger and meatball department.

CHAPTER 10

Burgers & Meatballs

Here, beef burgers can be sizzled up plain and simple or given a Cajun kick. Southwestern black bean burgers are the answer to vegetarian burgers at home. And for a real change of pace, Japanese salmon burgers bring fish into Burgerville, and the light Asian seasonings are a surprising twist. (Do I pretend these are my kids' very favorite burgers? No, I do not. But they are mine, and sometimes Mom gets to pick.)

Over in the realm of meatballs, the chicken Parmesan meatballs feature an optional gooey chunk of melted mozzarella in the center, and pork meatballs can be made in a spicy barbecued version or a slightly sweet maple edition, or ... both! One recipe, any number of happy people: That's what the book is all about.

Cajun Burgers

FORK IN THE ROAD: A burger pumped up with Cajun seasonings, or just plain and simple—you choose. Try them with ground turkey as well.

Yield

Makes 6 burgers

Whoo-wee, we love our burgers. They're grilled summertime bliss, and as long as the weather is cooperating, there will be patties sizzling on the grill. And when it isn't, there will be burgers sizzling on the stove or under the broiler.

Avocado, tomato, and Lime Crema (page 348)

Just plain old ketchup—let's hear it for the purists

Tomato, red onion slices, avocado, and Avocado Crema (page 348)

But after one or two straight-up burger dinners, many of us crave a little more something—a little more pizzazz, a little more flavor. Luckily, burgers are a perfect Fork-in-the-Road dish. The spicy Cajun version is for those who want more bang for their burger, the plain are for the less spice-inclined. And, you can certainly use a smaller amount of the spice mix in some of the burgers—maybe half a teaspoon or so per patty, so that the burgers have more interest, but aren't so interesting that they cause kids to grimace. The cooking instructions are for grilling, but they can easily be broiled or pan seared as well.

Piled high with Creamy Coleslaw (page 281) and avocado slices

Butter lettuce, tomato, and melted sharp cheddar

Sprouts, red onion, lettuce, and Chipotle Mayonnaise (page 355)

1 tablespoon chili powder

2 teaspoons paprika

1 teaspoon dry mustard

1 teaspoon ground cumin

1 teaspoon ground coriander

1 teaspoon dried oregano

1 teaspoon kosher or coarse salt

¼ teaspoon freshly ground black pepper

¼ teaspoon cayenne pepper

1½ pounds ground beef chuck, ━━◀ or see the first Fork in the Road for a turkey version

Sliced cheddar, Monterey jack or provolone cheese (optional)

6 hamburger buns for serving, toasted if desired

Toppings (optional): ketchup, mustard, relish, sliced tomatoes, sliced onions, sliced avocados, lettuce, Lime Crema (page 348), Avocado Crema (page 348), and Chipotle Mayonnaise (page 355)

Make Ahead

You can keep the seasoned meat mixture (in the bowl or shaped into patties) covered, in the fridge, for up to a day before grilling. Uncooked patties can also be frozen, well wrapped, for up to 2 months. Defrost before cooking.

1. Preheat a grill to medium high.

2. Combine the chili powder, paprika, dry mustard, cumin, coriander, oregano, salt, pepper, and cayenne in a small bowl.

3. ━━◀ You can continue with Step 4 or see the second Fork in the Road for another option.

4. Place the meat in a large bowl, add the spice mix, and use your hands to combine it very well so that the spices are fully incorporated.

5. Form the meat into 6 patties, using your fingers to make an indentation in the top of each. This will help the burgers end up relatively flat, as they will swell in the middle when cooked.

6. Grill the patties until they are cooked through (160°F on an instant read thermometer), 6 or 7 minutes per side. If you want cheeseburgers, place a slice of cheese on the burgers

and cover the grill to melt the cheese for the last minute of cooking. Place each burger on a bun, pass the condiments, and let everyone top their own.

1. Cajun Turkey Burgers

Instead of ground chuck, use 1½ pounds ground turkey (preferably dark meat or a mixture of dark and white meat ground together—available from the butcher and sometimes packaged at the supermarket). Add 1 large beaten egg and ¼ cup chicken broth and mix in before you add the spice blend. Or make both turkey and beef burgers dividing the spice mixture between the meats (plus ½ beaten egg and 2 tablespoons broth for ¾ pound turkey). Or double the recipe, as it's always nice to serve a combo when you are grilling for a crowd.

2. Plain & Simple Burgers

If you want to reserve some meat for plain beef or turkey burgers, mix the amount you want to be spiceless with salt and pepper to taste in a smaller bowl, using your hands. Keep in mind that you'll be making a total of six burgers. For each burger that's going spice-free, remove about 1¾ teaspoons of the seasoning mix from the bowl, and save it in a small sealed container or zipper-top bag for another time. (It's nice to have on hand. Toss some cubes of beef, pork, or chicken with the spice blend and kebab them up, or just rub it on any of the meats and roast or grill it. You could also use it to season a simple vegetable soup.)

Keep the unseasoned burgers to one side of the grill so you don't confuse them with the spicy ones.

Deciding how to top a burger is a highly personal matter.

Pickled ginger, sliced radishes,
and Avocado Wasabi Crema (page 165)
top my favorite burger in the book.

Japanese Salmon Burgers with Avocado Wasabi Crema

FORK IN THE ROAD: Just skip the ginger and sesame oil and make plain salmon burgers instead.

Several years ago I read a recipe for a Japanese-seasoned burger in the *New York Times* and thought, "Well, that's clever." Despite my love of cooking, my all-time favorite food is actually sushi, the least cooked food around. And my favorite kind of sushi is salmon. But what I really love besides the fish are the flavors of wasabi, soy, and ginger. So then, why not snap up those flavors to spike a salmon burger? And by the way, if salmon isn't your thing, you can totally use the same flavors in a beef or turkey burger as well.

The simpler version of these burgers is quite plain, with nice flavor from the soy sauce and onion, but the more glittery version also has fresh ginger and sesame oil. Either way, know that the patties will be soft and need to be handled with care. And note that if you have 30 to 45 minutes to let the mixture chill in the fridge, you will have an easier time flipping them. The Avocado Wasabi Crema (or Soy Wasabi Ketchup) is by no means necessary, but it's fun and pretty flavorful.

You can also broil the patties, but be sure to chill them first and that your broiler pan is clean and well oiled.

Yield

Makes 4 burgers

What the Kids Can Do

Mix up the Soy Wasabi Ketchup, mix the salmon patty mixture, and form the burgers. Older kids can flip the patties with supervision.

Make Ahead

You can make the salmon mixture up to a day ahead of time, if your fish is quite fresh, and keep it covered in the fridge, either in the bowl or in patty form.

FOR THE SALMON BURGERS

⅔ cup panko, or other dried bread crumbs

1 tablespoon milk

¼ cup finely minced onion

1 tablespoon soy sauce

Kosher or coarse salt and freshly ground black pepper, to taste

1 pound skinless fresh salmon fillet, checked for bones and finely chopped (see if the fish monger can do this for you, or see the Cooking Tip)

1 teaspoon sesame oil

2 teaspoons finely minced fresh ginger

1 tablespoon canola or vegetable oil

FOR SERVING (OPTIONAL)

4 hamburger rolls

Sliced radishes

Pickled ginger (see Note, page 165)

Avocado slices

Avocado Wasabi Crema or Soy Wasabi Ketchup (recipes follow)

1. Make the burgers: Place the panko and milk in a bowl and combine well. Add the onion, soy sauce, and salt and pepper and stir to combine. Add the salmon and, using your hands, gently mix everything together until well combined.

2. ▬◀ You can continue with Step 3 or see the Fork in the Road for another option.

3. Gently mix in the sesame oil and fresh ginger. Form the salmon mixture into 4 patties. If you have time, let them sit in the fridge for 30 minutes or so to firm up.

4. Heat the oil in a heavy skillet, preferably cast-iron, over medium-high heat. Add the patties and cook, turning them only once, until they are cooked the way you like them, about 4 minutes on each side for medium-rare. Flip them carefully; salmon burgers are a bit more delicate than their beefy cousins.

Cooking Tip

Chopping the salmon with a large sharp knife on a cutting board gives you more control over the texture, and doesn't take all that much time. If you'd prefer to use the processor, make sure the salmon is well chilled, then cut it into 1-inch chunks. Place in the processor. Pulse in *very* short bursts just until the salmon is chopped and not pureed.

If you have time (either chopping by hand or—more important—if you are using the food processor), put the salmon pieces in the freezer for 30 to 45 minutes, which will firm them up and make them easier to chop. (Don't let them totally freeze.)

5. If you like, serve the patties on rolls with radishes, pickled ginger, avocado, and/or Avocado Wasabi Crema or Soy Wasabi Ketchup (or plain ketchup) on the side.

Avocado Wasabi Crema

So easy—just stir 1 tablespoon (or more to taste) of wasabi paste into the recipe for Avocado Crema (page 348).

Soy Wasabi Ketchup

Makes ½ cup

- ½ cup ketchup
- 1 tablespoon soy sauce
- 1 tablespoon wasabi paste (see Note)

Combine the ketchup, soy sauce, and wasabi paste in a small bowl.

Plain Salmon Burgers

For plain salmon burgers, skip the sesame oil and ginger.

Or, to make two plain burgers and two with more pronounced Asian flavors, separate out half of the plain mixture, and then mix ½ teaspoon sesame oil and 1 teaspoon minced fresh ginger into the remaining mixture, and make two more patties.

Note: Wasabi paste and pickled ginger are readily available online, in Asian and other specialty food stores, and in many well-stocked supermarkets. You can also buy wasabi powder and make it into a paste following package instructions. Wasabi powder keeps for months at room temperature, wasabi paste keeps for ages in the fridge (and is a fun condiment to have on hand). After opening, jarred pickled ginger will last for a few months in the fridge.

Southwestern Vegetarian Black Bean Burgers

FORK IN THE ROAD: This fork is about the toppings. Three sexy sauce possibilities—and maybe some slaw—make these veggie burgers into an eye-popper of a meal.

The world is populated with veggie burgers these days. Most of them . . . *bleh,* pretty disappointing, right? My sister is a die-hard vegetarian who has been raising her girls vegetarian and could probably write a book called *Veggie Burgers U.S.A.,* chronicling their exploration of various vegetarian burgers around the country. Lizzie and the girls gave these a thumbs up, as did my vegetarian mother and various other meat-free friends.

These burgers are flavorful, not dry, and have a lot of character. That's what seems to be largely missing in the world of vegetarian burgers.

3 tablespoons olive oil

¾ cup chopped onions

1 teaspoon minced garlic

2 teaspoons ground cumin

1 teaspoon chili power

½ teaspoon ground coriander

½ teaspoon kosher or coarse salt

½ teaspoon freshly ground black pepper

2 cans (15.5 ounces each) black beans, rinsed and drained

2 tablespoons tomato paste or ketchup

¾ cup quick cooking oats

1 cup corn kernels, fresh or thawed frozen

4 to 6 hamburger buns, toasted if desired

Toppings (●━━◀ and see the Fork in the Road for sauce and slaw options): ketchup, mustard, lettuce, sliced tomatoes, sliced onions, sliced avocado, bean sprouts

Yield

Makes 4 to 6 burgers

What the Kids Can Do

Measure and mix the ingredients and shape the mixture into patties.

Make Ahead

The patties may be prepared and shaped ahead of time, and held for up to 3 days, well wrapped, in the refrigerator. Cooked burgers can be reheated in the microwave or the oven.

1. Heat 2 tablespoons of the oil in a large skillet over medium heat. Add the onions and garlic and sauté until the onions are tender, 5 minutes. Stir in the cumin, chili powder, coriander, salt, and pepper. Add the beans and tomato paste and stir to blend.

2. Place the oats in a food processor, add the black bean mixture, and pulse until everything is combined; the mixture should still have some texture, but be quite nicely blended. Remove the processor blade and stir in the corn with a spoon.

3. Shape the mixture into 4 large or 6 smaller patties. Place them on a plate and chill for about 30 minutes, if you have time. If you don't, don't—they'll just be a bit more delicate to flip.

4. Wipe out the skillet and heat the remaining 1 tablespoon olive oil over medium-high heat. Add the patties and cook without moving them until well browned on the bottoms, about 5 minutes, then flip them carefully and cook on the second side until nicely browned, 5 minutes more (see Cooking Tip).

5. Serve the burgers on buns with the toppings of your choice.

Cooking Tip

Definitely let the burgers get a nice crust on the exterior. The interior will be fairly soft, so the relationship between the slight crunch of the exterior and the tender interior really makes the burger. You can also bake these in a 350°F oven for 30 to 40 minutes, flipping them once after 20 minutes, until they are crusty.

More Burger Toppings

You simply must try these with the Chipotle Mayonnaise on page 355 or the Lime Crema or Avocado Crema on page 348. You must, you must, and if you can get the rest of your family to try one, too, you will be sharing a magical moment. Also, pile on some of the Creamy Coleslaw from page 281, with or without one of the sauces. If you're not interested in making one more thing, there are also some good chipotle ketchups on the market, and these burgers are a good reason to buy one.

Maple-Barbecue Pork Meatballs

FORK IN THE ROAD: When you want a change of pace this recipe turns into Spicy Pork Meatballs—so choose between nicely sweet and comforting, or a bit more of a kick.

With a sweetness from apples and maple syrup, these meatballs are ridiculously kid-friendly (and the barbecue sauce doesn't hurt much in that arena either). You could pile them on rice or couscous or quinoa with a few extra spoonfuls of barbecue sauce for an easy and different weeknight dinner.

Yield

Serves 6 (makes about 42 small meatballs)

Canola or vegetable oil, for oiling the pan

¾ cup panko bread crumbs

½ cup barbecue sauce, plus more for dipping if you like

½ cup grated peeled apple

⅓ cup minced onion

1 large egg, lightly beaten

Kosher or coarse salt, to taste

1 tablespoon maple syrup, or see the Fork in the Road for a spicy swap-in

1½ pounds ground pork

What the Kids Can Do

Measure the ingredients, maybe peel and grate the apple, blend everything up, and form the meatballs.

Make Ahead

The baked meatballs can be refrigerated, covered, for up to 3 days. Reheat briefly in the microwave, or in a 300°F oven for 10 minutes.

1. Preheat the oven to 375°F. Lightly oil a rimmed baking sheet.

2. Combine the bread crumbs, barbecue sauce, apple, onion, egg, and salt in a large bowl. Add the maple syrup and stir to blend. Add the pork and combine well using your hands, but try not to squeeze the mixture too much. Form 1-inch-round meatballs and place them on the baking sheet.

3. Bake the meatballs until cooked through, 16 to 20 minutes. Serve hot, with extra barbecue sauce on the side.

FORK IN THE ROAD

Spicy Pork Meatballs

Instead of the maple syrup, add 2 teaspoons chili powder and a pinch of cayenne pepper to the apple mixture. Add the pork, combine, and bake as directed.

To go half sweet and half spicy, divide the panko mixture at the beginning of Step 2 into 2 bowls. Add 1½ teaspoons maple syrup and half the pork to one bowl, and 1 teaspoon chili powder, a small pinch of cayenne, and the other half of the pork to the other bowl. Blend, form, and bake as directed (be sure to separate the spicy and nonspicy meatballs on the baking sheet).

Easy, Cheesy Chicken Parmesan Meatballs

FORK IN THE ROAD: Not interested in the cheesy mozzarella part? Plain chicken Parm meatballs are even easier.

Rarely has the title of a recipe made me so happy, and I'm hoping you feel the same way. So here's what it means: The great flavors of chicken Parmesan are packaged in a tidy little meatball, with a chunk of mozzarella that melts inside and is just so satisfying and exciting.

You can serve the meatballs atop a heap of spaghetti with a generous dose of sauce and more Parmesan, *or* you can pile them onto a nice crusty roll topped with the aforementioned sauce and Parmesan to create a meatball sub to remember.

Or just serve them plain, with some homemade or jarred sauce on the side for dipping.

Nonstick cooking spray or vegetable oil, for oiling the baking sheet

½ cup milk, preferably whole

1 large egg

½ cup panko bread crumbs

½ cup freshly grated Parmesan, plus more for serving

⅓ cup minced fresh flat-leaf parsley

2 tablespoons minced shallots, or ¼ cup minced onion

1 teaspoon finely minced garlic

1½ teaspoons dried oregano

Kosher or coarse salt and freshly ground black pepper, to taste

2 pounds ground chicken (preferably a mix of white and dark meats)

½ pound mozzarella, cut into ½-inch cubes (28 cubes)

Super Simple Tomato Sauce (see page 347)

Slivered fresh basil (optional)

Yield

Serves 6 to 8 (makes 24 to 28 meatballs)

What the Kids Can Do

Measure the ingredients, blend the mixture, and form the meatballs. Tuck in the mozzarella cubes.

Make Ahead

The meatball mixture or the shaped meatballs can be made up to 2 days ahead of time and stored, well sealed, in the refrigerator. Cooked meatballs can be refrigerated for up to 3 days, then reheated in a 325°F oven for 10 minutes, or better still you can reheat them in a pot of simmering tomato sauce over medium heat for 5 minutes or so.

1. Preheat the oven to 375°F. Spray a rimmed baking sheet with nonstick spray or coat lightly with vegetable oil.

2. Mix together the milk and egg in a large bowl, then stir in the bread crumbs. Add the Parmesan, parsley, shallots, garlic, oregano, and salt and pepper and stir to combine well. Add the chicken, and use your hands to mix everything until very well blended, trying not to squish the mixture too much.

3. ━━◀ You can continue with Step 4 or see the the Fork in the Road for a simpler meatball.

4. Form the mixture into 1½-inch meatballs, tucking a cube of mozzarella into the middle of each one, then sealing it in with the chicken mixture.

5. Place the meatballs on the baking sheet. Bake until cooked through and the cheese inside is all melty, 16 to 20 minutes (cut one open to test; that one is yours).

6. Serve with the tomato sauce and additional Parmesan, sprinkling with fresh basil if desired.

FORK IN THE ROAD

Easy Italian Chicken Meatballs

Skip the mozzarella, and just bake the meatballs as is for the same amount of time.

Once I made 12 pounds of these for Jack's football team. With the mozzarella cubes. If that's not love, I don't know what is.

CHICKEN VEGETABLE POTPIE CASSEROLE, *page 183*

One of the prettiest phrases in the English language, the words "one-dish meal," assures the cook that it's all going to be just fine, there will be dinner on the table, and a minimum of components to think about and pots to wash. Might you want to make a salad, too? You might, but you have full permission to skip it with all of the recipes in this chapter; all of the food groups are covered (*muted sounds of cheering in background*).

CHAPTER 11

One-Dish Meals

Thai Chicken Stir-Fry has zippy flavors, and tofu is the Fork in the Road option. Chicken, potatoes, and broccoli are roasted all on one baking sheet, a chicken potpie casserole is jammed with vegetables (and you can skip the chicken, if desired). Grabbing onto the concept of a make-your-own Asian rice bowl is one of the more fun and interactive one-bowl dinners you can put together. Baked Shrimp and Grits with Caramelized Fennel and Leeks is as close as I get to Southern sophistication. If you skip the fennel and leeks, toss a few carrot sticks in a bowl. (Even if you fall back on the carrots we can still count this recipe as one pot, right? Okay, thanks.)

Thai Chicken Stir-Fry

FORK IN THE ROAD: Chicken for those who like it, tofu for those who don't—bright Thai flavors all around.

Ask Gary what he'd like for dinner any day of the year, and stir-fry will be the first words to come out of his mouth (unless it's one of the beefy noodle dishes, like the recipe on page 239). Hey, easier than duck confit, right? (He would not get duck confit.)

Cookbook writers will fill you in on the same few things about stir-fries, but here's the reality: The best way to get good at making stir-fries is to read through the recipe before starting (no news there), then giving it a go. No amount of studying will make you a better stir-fryer than making a couple.

The small amount of cornstarch in this recipe gives the sauce just a bit of thickening for some nice texture and body.

⅓ cup chicken or vegetable broth, preferably low-sodium

2 tablespoons fish sauce (see Sidebar, page 178)

1 teaspoon sugar

1 teaspoon cornstarch

2 tablespoons canola or vegetable oil

1 bell pepper, any color, stemmed, seeded, and cut into slivers

2 cups sugar snap or snow peas, destringed

4 scallions, white and light green parts, cut into 1-inch pieces

1½ pounds skinless boneless chicken breasts or thighs, diced or thinly sliced (see Cooking Tip), ▬◉ or see the Vegetarian Fork in the Road for a tofu substitute

2 cloves garlic, minced

½ cup thinly sliced basil leaves (regular or Thai basil)

1 jalapeño, halved lengthwise, seeded, and cut into the thinnest slices you can manage (optional)

Juice of ½ lime

Hot rice (jasmine is nice), for serving if desired

Yield

Serves 4 to 6

What the Kids Can Do

They can measure the ingredients and mix up the sauce. If you're using tofu, they can cut that up. They might be able to slice the scallions, peppers, and basil using an age-appropriate knife.

Make Ahead

You can cut up all of the ingredients a day or two ahead to make life easier when you pull out that pan at 6:47 P.M. Or maybe I'm just projecting.

Cooking Tip

When you need to cut meat very thin, or even to finely chop it, it's helpful to first wrap it in plastic wrap and put it in the freezer for 20 minutes. This firms up the meat so it's easier to get super-thin slices, but it will lose its chill as you cut it, so no need to worry about additional cooking time. This works for steak, fish, lamb, pork—pretty much everything.

One version with chicken

A vegetarian version with tofu instead

1. Whisk together the broth, fish sauce, and sugar in a small bowl. Whisk in the cornstarch. Set the sauce aside.

2. Heat 1 tablespoon of the oil in a wok or a very large skillet over high heat. Add the bell pepper, sugar snap peas, and scallions and stir-fry until just starting to become tender, 2 minutes. Transfer to a serving bowl.

3. ━━◄ You can continue with Step 4 or see the Fork in the Road for a vegetarian option.

4. Heat the remaining 1 tablespoon oil in the pan, add the chicken and garlic, and stir-fry until the chicken is almost cooked through, about 3 minutes (dark meat may take 4 or 5 minutes). Return the vegetables to the skillet, add the basil, and jalapeño, if using, and stir to blend. Re-whisk the sauce, add it to the pan, and stir for 1 to 2 minutes more to allow it to thicken up a bit. Serve over rice if desired, with the lime juice squeezed on top.

FORK IN THE ROAD

Thai Tofu Stir-Fry

Instead of the chicken, use 1 pound firm or extra-firm tofu, cut into ½-inch dice. It will fall apart a little during the stir-fry process but that's a-okay. Use vegetable broth, and either vegetarian fish sauce (see Sidebar) or soy sauce instead of the regular fish sauce.

If you want to do half veg and half meat, use ½ pound thinly sliced chicken and ½ pound diced tofu. Make the sauce with vegetarian fish sauce or soy sauce. Sauté the vegetables as stated in the recipe. Divide the oil and garlic between two skillets and sauté the tofu in one and the chicken in the other. Divide the vegetables, sauce, basil, and jalapeños, if using, between the two pans. And apologies—this is no longer a one-dish meal.

Fish Sauce

Fish sauce, or *nam pla* in Thai, is one of the basic ingredients in Thai and Vietnamese cuisine. It has a pungent odor that may take you by surprise, but when used in cooking the flavor is much milder than that big sniff that you took from the bottle. It is used in marinades, stir-fries, and condiments, and it adds a wonderful tangy, "umami" quality (see Umami?, page 258) to many dishes. It's actually made from the liquid given off by anchovies that have been salted or fermented. This is the kind of thing you might want to keep to yourself until your kids have eaten and enjoyed fish sauce in a recipe.

Fish sauce is available in Asian food stores and well-stocked supermarkets. Vegetarian fish sauces—which have a soy base—are also available. And you are more than welcome to use soy sauce in its place, though the fish sauce is the main ingredient that makes this stir-fry Thai-inspired.

One-Sheet Middle Eastern-ish Chicken Dinner

FORK IN THE ROAD: Skip the spices for those who like their chicken plain.

T he concept of one-pot cooking, which has been around for ages, is loved for its ease, its simplicity, and in many cases its hands-off appeal. The slow cooker is marvelously popular for the same reasons. But a rimmed baking sheet can fill those same desires and needs, *and* invites a mix of textures, crispiness, and caramelization. A very smart cookbook called *Sheet Pan Suppers* by Molly Gilbert made me realize I was under-exploring the notion of a whole meal on one sheet pan, and I am forever grateful.

This recipe doubles easily for bigger groups or leftovers . . . and for that, yes, two sheet pans are needed. You can put the chicken on one pan, in that case, and the vegetables on the other.

Serve this right out of the pan if you're in casual family-style mode (warn everyone not to touch the hot pan), or transfer it to a serving platter or plates.

One pan, one dinner, one genius (you).

Yield

Serves 4

What the Kids Can Do

Measure the ingredients for the spice rub and mix it up. Rub the chicken with the spice mix. Toss the vegetables with the olive oil and season with salt and pepper.

Olive oil or nonstick cooking spray for oiling the baking sheet

1 teaspoon dried oregano

1 teaspoon ground allspice

¾ teaspoon ground cinnamon

1 teaspoon kosher or coarse salt, plus more to taste

¼ teaspoon freshly ground black pepper, plus
   more to taste

3 tablespoons olive oil

2 pounds skin-on, bone-in chicken breast halves,
   each cut in half

1 small head broccoli, cut into about 8 long stalks
   (see Cooking Tip)

2 large Yukon Gold potatoes, washed, each cut into eighths

¼ cup chopped fresh mint leaves

¼ cup chopped fresh flat-leaf parsley leaves

1 tablespoon white wine vinegar or lemon juice

1. Preheat the oven to 425°F. Lightly oil a rimmed baking sheet, or spray it with nonstick cooking spray.

2. ▬◣ You can continue with Step 3 or see the Fork in the Road for plain chicken.

3. Mix together the oregano, allspice, cinnamon, the 1 teaspoon salt, and the ¼ teaspoon pepper with 1 tablespoon of the olive oil in a small bowl. Rub the mixture all over the chicken breasts and place them on the baking sheet.

4. Toss the broccoli and potatoes with the remaining 2 tablespoons olive oil and spread them out on the baking sheet. Season the vegetables with salt and pepper.

Make Ahead

You can place the chicken and the broccoli on the sheet pan a day ahead of time, cover it with plastic wrap, and stick it in the fridge. Cut up the potatoes and add them to the baking sheet right before cooking so they don't discolor. Cooked leftovers can be reheated in a 325°F-ish oven for about 12 minutes until warm.

Cooking Tip

Because you want to time it so that everything comes out perfectly cooked at the same time, you'll want to think about the ingredient with the longest needed cooking time—in this case the chicken. So, while small pieces of broccoli could be roasted in less time, here you will want to cut it into substantial pieces so that the cooking paces itself with the chicken, which is cut in half to shorten its own cooking time. And the potatoes are cut to meet both in the middle.

5. Roast the chicken and vegetables until the chicken is cooked through, the skin is crispy, and the vegetables are tender and nicely browned, 35 to 40 minutes (see Cooking Tip). Sprinkle the mint and parsley over the chicken right on the sheet pan and sprinkle with the vinegar or juice (leave off the herbs and the vinegar or lemon juice from some of the pieces, if some chicken eaters will object).

FORK IN THE ROAD

One-Sheet Simple Chicken Dinner

Very uncomplicated: Skip the spice mixture on the chicken—just toss the pieces with a little olive oil and salt and pepper and you have a super simple but delicious sheet-pan dinner that will still hit the spot. Or leave a couple of the pieces of chicken spice-free, and spice up the others: best of both worlds. Same with the herbs and vinegar—leave them off of some pieces if desired.

A handful of ingredients goes into the oven on a sheet pan . . . and dinner comes out.

What a perfect example of cold-weather comfort food.
This recipe could have also found itself in the
"I Need a Big Fat Hug" chapter.

Chicken Vegetable Potpie Casserole

FORK IN THE ROAD: A big happy pan of old-fashioned comfort food and a meatless option as well.

This recipe was developed by riffing on my sister's notes on how she puts together a vegetarian potpie (see Vegetarian Fork in the Road) for her family on a regular basis. It's a true hodgepodge of ingredients, in the best possible sense, enveloped in an only slightly creamy sauce that brings it together into a kind-of-rich-and-kind-of-light-at-the-same-time filling. There are a lot of vegetables, even in the chicken version.

Also, this isn't made as a pie, but as a casserole, because I like to make everything in copious amounts, as you may have noticed by now. Cut the recipe in half and make it in a deep-dish pie pan if you don't have a big crowd or a desire for leftovers. The corn is optional, mostly because my son Jack doesn't like corn (I know . . . what?!), and so is the parsley for those who have kids who panic at the sight of green flecks.

Yield

Serves 10 to 12

What the Kids Can Do

Help choose the vegetables; peel the carrots and slice the mushrooms; measure ingredients; unroll the refrigerated pie crust, brush it with egg, and cut slits in it.

Make Ahead

The unbaked casserole can be refrigerated for up to a day. Put the crust on just before baking. The baked casserole can be refrigerated for up to 3 days and reheated in a 350°F oven for about 15 minutes until hot. Bring it to room temperature for about 30 minutes before reheating.

When you have a random assortment of vegetables in the fridge, it's time to make this casserole.

3 tablespoons extra-virgin olive oil

1 tablespoon minced garlic

8 scallions or 1 large leek, white and light green parts, chopped

2 cups diced red or white potatoes

1 cup sliced carrots

½ cup thinly sliced celery

4 cups roughly chopped broccoli florets and stems

Kosher or coarse salt and freshly ground black pepper, to taste

4 cups chicken or vegetable broth, preferably low-sodium

1 cup fresh or frozen peas

1 cup fresh or frozen corn kernels (optional)

1½ cups (an 8-ounce package) sliced mushrooms

1 tablespoon minced fresh rosemary or 1 teaspoon crumbled dried rosemary

3 tablespoons unsalted butter

⅔ cup all-purpose flour

½ cup heavy (whipping) cream or half-and-half

½ cup chopped fresh flat-leaf parsley (optional)

4 cups cubed raw chicken or turkey, ▬◀═ or see the Vegetarian Fork in the Road for a tofu substitute

1 refrigerated pie crust (half of a 15-ounce package)

1 large egg, beaten

1. Preheat the oven to 375°F.

2. Heat 1 tablespoon of the olive oil in a very large skillet, Dutch oven, or wok over medium-high heat. Add the garlic, scallions, potatoes, carrots, and celery and sauté to soften for 4 minutes. Add the broccoli, season with salt and pepper, and sauté until the vegetables are coated with the onion mixture, 1 minute. Add ½ cup of the broth, stir, and cover. Simmer until all of the vegetables are crisp-tender and the liquid is mostly evaporated, about 3 minutes. Stir in the peas and the corn if using. Transfer the entire mixture to a shallow 4-quart casserole or a second very large deep, ovenproof skillet and set aside. Return the first skillet to the stove.

3. Heat another 1 tablespoon olive oil in the pan over medium-

A Potpie for All Seasons

The potpie recipe is one you would make during the colder weather during the fall and winter seasons. Diced winter squash and/or sweet potatoes and cauliflower are other options. Then, try switching up the vegetables as the weather changes, for the perfect potpie all year round. Swap out any of the above vegetables for the following:

SPRING: asparagus, artichoke hearts (fresh, frozen, or canned and drained), fresh peas, spinach and other greens

SUMMER: zucchini, yellow summer squash, eggplant, tomatoes

high heat. Add the mushrooms and rosemary and sauté until the mushrooms are golden brown, 5 minutes. Add them to the vegetable mixture and return the pan to the stove.

4. Melt the butter in the pan over medium heat. Whisk in the flour and whisk occasionally until it turns blond in color, about 3 minutes. Add the remaining 3½ cups broth and bring to a simmer over high heat. Lower the heat back to medium and simmer, whisking occasionally, until the sauce has thickened, about 3 minutes. Season with salt and pepper, stir in the cream and the parsley, if using, and cook for 3 minutes more. Pour the sauce over the vegetable mixture and stir.

5. ✦ You can continue with Step 6 or see the Fork in the Road for a vegetarian option.

6. Wipe out the skillet, add the remaining tablespoon of oil, and heat it over medium-high heat. Season the chicken with salt and pepper and sauté until the insides are still a little pink, 4 minutes. Toss with the vegetables.

7. Center the pie crust over the filling. Brush the top of the pastry with the egg and use a sharp knife to make several slits in the crust. Bake until the crust is golden brown and the filling is bubbly, about 30 minutes. Spoon the casserole onto plates, making sure each serving has a piece of crust.

FORK IN THE ROAD

Vegetable Potpie

Use vegetable broth, and 2 or 3 cups of diced extra-firm tofu in place of the chicken, or just increase the amount of vegetables by a few cups.

If you want to make two smaller pies—one with chicken and one without, use two 9- or 10-inch deep-dish pie pans. You'll need both crusts that come in a 15-ounce pie crust package. Make the vegetable mixture using only vegetable broth, then divide it between the two pans. Stir 1½ cups of cubed chicken into the vegetables in one pan and 1½ cups diced tofu into the other, then place one pie crust on top of each pan, brush with egg, and make slits as instructed. The baking time for both should be about 25 minutes.

Dried Herbs vs. Fresh

When should you use one versus the other? And how much of one equals the flavor potency of the other? Dried herbs are almost always more potent than fresh, and the typical ratio is three times the amount of a fresh herb to the quantity of a dried one. Fresh herbs usually should be added toward the end of the cooking process—or used in uncooked dishes like salads—to maintain their fresh flavor. Dried herbs can be used in some uncooked recipes (I love a little dried oregano in a Greek salad dressing, for example), but usually they are added earlier in the cooking process so they have time to better season the dish. Dried herbs should be stored in a cool, dry, dark place. Resist the temptation to store them near or over the stove.

Common wisdom says to toss dried herbs after 6 months—you should also use your nose. Do the herbs smell herb-y? If not, treat yourself to a new jar. Sturdier herbs like oregano, rosemary, and thyme tend to last a little longer.

Baked Shrimp and Grits with Caramelized Fennel and Leeks

FORK IN THE ROAD: A plainer shrimp and grits, with no caramelized vegetables, is some fine Southern comfort food.

This classic Southern dish gets an (optional) flavor upgrade with the modern addition of caramelized leeks and fresh anise-y fennel. The shrimp cook in the grits right in the oven, so that's one step eliminated. Even though this tastes decadent, it's a rather lightened-up version of old-school shrimp and grits, which is often laden with heavy doses of butter and cream. I'm not saying this is just as virtuous as eating a half a cantaloupe filled with cottage cheese, but it's worth every single bite.

2 tablespoons olive oil, plus more for oiling the baking dish

1 large bulb fennel, trimmed, quartered, and very thinly sliced

2 large leeks, trimmed, well rinsed, white and light green parts thinly sliced

Kosher or coarse salt and freshly ground black pepper, to taste

2 cups 2% milk

4 cups chicken broth, preferably low-sodium

1 cup grits or coarse ground cornmeal (see Cornmeal vs. Polenta vs. Grits, page 188)

½ cup freshly grated Parmesan

⅓ cup heavy (whipping) cream

2 tablespoons unsalted butter

¼ cup chopped fresh flat-leaf parsley, plus more for optional garnish

1 pound large shrimp (31 to 35 per pound), peeled, deveined, and halved crosswise

Hot pepper sauce (optional)

Yield

Serves 6

What the Kids Can Do

Measure ingredients, add things to the pot and stir (with supervision), cut the shrimp in half, chop the parsley with an age-appropriate knife.

Make Ahead

This is best made right before serving and served hot. But true confessions, this might be one of my favorite leftovers to hoard and heat in the microwave.

Vegetarian Note: Skip the shrimp and use vegetable broth for a pretty terrific vegetarian side dish—cheesy, creamy grits.

1. Preheat the oven to 375°F. Lightly oil a shallow 2-quart baking dish.

2. Heat the olive oil in a large skillet over medium-high heat. Add the fennel and leeks, season with salt and pepper, and cook, stirring occasionally, until soft and lightly browned, 12 to 15 minutes. ◄══ Or skip the vegetables—see the Fork in the Road.

3. Meanwhile, combine the milk and broth in a large saucepan and bring to a simmer over medium-high heat. Gradually sprinkle the grits into the pot, whisking until they are all added. Reduce the heat to medium and simmer, whisking frequently, until the mixture has thickened, 5 minutes.

4. Add the Parmesan, cream, butter, the ¼ cup parsley, and the shrimp to the grits, along with the sautéed fennel and leeks. Stir until well combined and the butter is melted. Transfer the shrimp and grits to the prepared baking dish.

5. Bake until bubbly and lightly browned on the top, 20 minutes. Serve hot, sprinkled with the extra parsley if desired. Pass the hot sauce to those who want it.

FORK IN THE ROAD

Simple Baked Shrimp & Grits

Don't think caramelized fennel and leeks are going to delight everyone at the table? Skip them, or maybe just skip the fennel.

Or sauté 1 small fennel bulb with 1 leek, and make half the grits with vegetables and half without: Lightly oil or spray two 1-quart baking dishes with nonstick spray. After adding the shrimp to the grits, stir, and transfer half of the mixture to one of the baking dishes. Add the fennel and leeks to the remaining mixture in the pot and stir. Transfer the fennel-and-leek grits to the second baking dish. Bake both dishes for 15 to 20 minutes.

Polenta vs. Grits vs. Cornmeal

What we call stone-ground cornmeal pretty much has to do with geography and the kind of cooking we're doing. Both polenta and grits are actually stone-ground cornmeal, dried corn that's ground into coarse grainlike pieces. Finely ground cornmeal has a less nubby texture, and is used more in baking.

Italians call their stone-ground cornmeal *polenta* (and usually it's a yellow corn variety), American Southerners call it *grits* (and grits are most often made from white corn).

There are other subtle differences, but in short sometimes you will see a package that is labeled *polenta,* and sometimes you will see a package that is labeled *grits,* and often you will see a package that is labeled *coarse ground* or *medium-coarse ground cornmeal.* Inside each of these packages is coarse stone-ground cornmeal. For the purposes of most recipes, including this one, you can use any of these named products interchangeably, and you will achieve similar, lovely results.

Asian Rice Bowl Many Ways

FORK IN THE ROAD: The ability to customize your own rice bowl, and then choose one of two sauces to top it with, means that everyone is creating their ideal meal.

Asian flavors and dishes pepper this book wildly, because they pepper our dining table weekly. And the idea of taking an Asian dish and giving it an American twist is too good to resist.

This is a boilerplate recipe and an excellent reason to have extra cooked rice in the fridge. And a seriously unshabby way to turn leftovers into a brand-new meal, which I have been trying to make an Olympic sport for years. Damn IOC, so narrow-minded.

You can put out a variety of toppings and let everyone assemble their own rice bowls (fun), or make executive choices in the kitchen based on what you have and what your various family members like.

Yield

Serves 4

What the Kids Can Do

This is a perfect recipe to engage kids of all ages. Hunt through the fridge and pantry with them, deciding what would be attractive components to put in the bowls. Let them help prep whatever you choose, set up a little rice bowl buffet, and absolutely let them assemble their own creation.

Make Ahead

Not so much.

Shredded chicken, carrots, sautéed snow peas, Ginger Scallion Sauce (page 353)

Shrimp seaweed strips, bamboo shoots

Carrots, sautéed spinach (page 287), sprouts, sriracha sauce, peanuts

Sautéed mushrooms (page 134), cubed avocado, scallions, fried egg

A bowl
of steaming rice—
white, brown, jasmine,
basmati, Texmati—
whichever you like

And an eclectic
assortment of vegetables,
leftovers, sauces,
crunchy things—
DINNER!

4 cups hot cooked rice (such as brown, white, or jasmine)

VEGETABLE TOPPINGS

Sautéed greens such as spinach, kale, broccoli rabe, or Swiss chard (see Korean Spinach, page 284)

Sautéed snow peas

Sliced hearts of palm

Cubed or sliced avocados

Shredded lettuce

Shredded carrots

Sautéed or roasted mushrooms

Bean sprouts

PROTEIN TOPPINGS

Cooked fish or seafood

Cooked chicken, steak, or pork (see Note)

Fried or poached eggs

Steamed or sautéed tofu

CONDIMENTS, DRIZZLES, SPRINKLES, AND SAUCES

Hoisin sauce

Toasted sesame oil

Soy sauce, preferably reduced-sodium

Lemon, lime, or orange wedges

Sriracha, gochujang (see Sidebar), or other hot sauce

Cayenne pepper

Chopped peanuts

Sesame seeds

Crumbled dried seaweed

Cilantro Lime Sauce or Ginger Scallion Sauce (page 353), optional

1. Place a serving bowl with the rice in the center of the table. Surround the bowl with bowls or dishes of a selection of vegetables, protein, and condiments, and either of the sauces, if desired.

2. Spoon 1 cup of rice into each of 4 dinner bowls.

3. Let everyone customize their rice as they choose.

Note: Leftover takeout Asian food or homemade stir-fries are a great reason to think Asian Rice Bowl. Remember this recipe when you have extra Thai Chicken Stir-Fry (page 176), Korean Sesame Tofu and Mushrooms (page 263), or Stir-Fried Shrimp and Scallions (page 145).

Vegetarian Note: Rice bowls lend themselves to an endless array of vegetarian meals.

Gochujang

Sometimes called Korean red pepper paste, gochujang is a dark red, concentrated condiment made from chilies, glutinous rice, fermented soybeans, salt, and sometimes a bit of sweetener. It's featured in Korean cooking, and adds wonderful flavor and heat to various dishes. It lasts for months in the fridge.

When pasta was created (when and by whom is the subject of much discussion, though not just now) I wonder if the inventors knew that they had just created a food that would be the saving grace of families everywhere forevermore. But while it is one of the best lifelines come dinnertime, it can also become a bit of a crutch, especially if you have one of those kids who thinks noodles with butter should be the center of every meal.

Pasta & Sauces

Here's the thing: If your kids like pasta, it becomes a fabulous opportunity to introduce new ingredients and flavors. The familiar pasta serves as a friendly way to expand everyone's horizons. I have seen people large and small inhale portions of Vegetable Lo Mein at a startling clip; Bolognese sauce (meaty or vegetarian) turns pasta into a hearty meal; and Fettuccine with Shrimp and Asparagus is a blueprint recipe that shows how to create night after night of simple, satisfying dinners. Simple One-Skillet Chicken (or Shrimp) Alfredo Pasta is creamy and warm and just a little bit elegant, and finally there's the recipe with the clearest title in the book: Stupid Easy Chicken and Broccoli Pasta, which has saved many a night in our house.

Quick Bolognese Sauce with Linguine

FORK IN THE ROAD: Vegetarians will be happily surprised by the meatless version of this hearty Italian sauce.

I want to start off by telling you to double this recipe. Originally, the recipe was twice the amount that you see here, but because not everyone feels the need to hoard pasta sauce, restraint was exercised, and you see before you a recipe designed to make enough sauce for 1 pound of pasta, the amount that six normal people are most often looking for. (*Psst* . . . double this recipe. Invite over a lot of people, or freeze half.)

The definition of true Bolognese sauce, like all Italian pasta sauces, is a matter of opinion. My family's opinion is that this sauce is pretty terrific, and my opinion is that it is very easy and quick, and that it's a great make-ahead dish. Traditional Bolognese usually involves a much longer cooking period, and sometimes includes a pork product, but this is a quick weeknight version. The sauce is very thick, truly a ragu, and intended to be that way.

This is the kind of food I think of as snow-day food—wonderful to make and scent your house on a snowy day and amazing to come home to after a day of sledding or shoveling or skiing. And when extra kids trail into your house with their wet boots, just make more pasta, then maybe add some more tomato puree or sauce to the pot and watch the sauce magically expand.

Yield

Serves 6 (enough sauce for 1 pound of pasta)

What the Kids Can Do

Peel the carrots, measure ingredients, stir the sauce with supervision. Crumble the tempeh if you're making the vegetarian version. My older son, Jack, made this entire sauce from start to finish when he was 14, with me just hanging out working and advising a little in the background; he felt pretty pleased about it.

Make Ahead

You can make the entire dish up to 4 days ahead of time, and the flavor gets even deeper. Refrigerate, covered, until ready to use. Leftovers heat up beautifully in a pot over low heat—you may want to add a bit of chicken broth or even a bit of water to loosen up the sauce, which will thicken even further. You can also freeze the sauce—vegetarian or meat version—after Step 2 (before adding the milk) for 4 months, and then defrost it, heat it, and add the milk and cheese when you are ready to serve.

2 tablespoons olive oil

1½ pounds ground sirloin (see Note),  or see the Vegetarian Fork in the Road for a tempeh substitute

1 large onion, finely chopped

2 carrots, finely chopped

2 ribs celery, finely chopped

3 cloves garlic, minced

Kosher or coarse salt and freshly ground black pepper, to taste

1 cup dry red wine

1 can (35 ounces) tomato puree

3 tablespoons tomato paste

2 teaspoons dried oregano

Generous pinch of red pepper flakes (optional)

¾ cup whole milk

½ cup freshly grated Parmesan, plus extra for serving

1 package (1 pound) linguine

½ cup slivered fresh basil leaves, for serving (optional)

Note: Using a tender and flavorful cut of ground beef like sirloin means that the sauce will require less cooking time. If you'd like to make it with half ground beef and half ground pork, that's also a classic Bolognese meat sauce combo.

1. Heat 1 tablespoon of the olive oil in a large stockpot or Dutch oven over medium heat. Add the ground beef and sauté, crumbling it with a wooden spoon, until it is browned all over, 6 to 8 minutes. Drain in a colander and set aside.

2. Heat the remaining 1 tablespoon olive oil in the same pot, then add the onions, carrots, and celery and cook until tender and lightly browned, 5 minutes. Add the garlic and cook until you can smell the garlic, 1 minute more. Season with salt and pepper, add the red wine, and stir and scrape any bits from the bottom. Add the tomato puree, tomato paste, oregano, and red pepper flakes, if using. Return the browned beef to the pot and simmer the sauce for 20 minutes, until nicely thickened.

3. Add the milk and Parmesan and cook until the sauce is creamy and thick, another 10 minutes.

4. Meanwhile, bring a large pot of water to a boil. Salt the water generously and add the pasta. Return the water to a boil and cook the pasta according to the package directions. Drain the pasta, and return it to the pot.

5. Add the Bolognese sauce to the pasta and stir to coat the pasta well with the sauce. Serve hot, sprinkled with fresh basil, if desired. Pass additional Parmesan at the table.

FORK IN THE ROAD

Tempeh Bolognese

Make the bolognese with tempeh for a vegetarian sauce (but not vegan, because of the milk and cheese). Use 1 pound tempeh, crumbled into tiny bits, and skip the sautéing step—no need to sauté—just crumble the tempeh into the pot in Step 2 when you would have added the browned meat into the sauce. Tossing in about ½ teaspoon of smoked paprika along with the tempeh adds a bit more depth of flavor. Everything else is the same.

If you want to make the sauce half vegetarian and half meat, brown ¾ pound of beef in Step 1. Use a different pot to make the sauce. At the end of Step 2, pour half of the sauce into the pot you used to brown the beef. Return the beef to that pot. Add ½ pound of crumbled tempeh and a pinch of smoked paprika (optional) to the other pot of sauce. Divide the Parmesan, milk, and cooked pasta between the pots and toss. Garnish with basil, if using.

What Is Tempeh?

Most of us—even us non-vegetarians—have encountered tofu (been curd, ranging from very soft to quite firm) at some time or another. But tempeh may be less familiar. Tempeh is a very firm and dense soy product, made from cooked and slightly fermented whole soybeans which have been formed into a flat patty. It may be combined with some whole grains as well, and has a significant amount of protein, calcium, fiber, and vitamins, and is very welcome in vegetarian and vegan diets. Unlike tofu, which has almost no flavor, tempeh has a nutty and earthy flavor, sometimes enhanced by seasonings. It should be thinly sliced, diced, or crumbled before using in recipes because it's so concentrated in texture. It's a great ground meat substitute.

Simple One-Skillet Chicken Alfredo Pasta

FORK IN THE ROAD: Slightly decadent, more than a little comforting, and with some great add-in options to elevate it above the usual.

One of the reasons I like to cook mostly healthy food is so I can justify the occasional dish like this one. In between an evening featuring Kale and Quinoa Salad (page 78), and another dinner starring Cornmeal-Crusted Tilapia (page 147), I can rationalize this warm hug of a meal. Plus, any one-skillet meal where the pasta cooks right in the sauce is a gift with purchase, in my book.

1½ pounds skinless, boneless chicken breasts

Kosher or coarse salt and freshly ground black pepper, to taste

2 tablespoons unsalted butter

1 teaspoon minced garlic

4 cups chicken broth, preferably low-sodium

1 package (1 pound) penne rigate or ziti (see Note, page 199)

1½ cups heavy (whipping) cream or half-and-half, warmed

1 cup freshly grated Parmesan, plus more for serving

¼ cup chopped fresh flat-leaf parsley (optional)

1. Cut the chicken breasts into 1-inch pieces. Season with salt and pepper.

2. Melt the butter in a very large skillet over medium-high heat. Add the chicken, in batches if necessary, and sauté until nicely browned on the outside, but still a bit pink inside, about 4 minutes (the pieces don't have to be browned on all sides; two sides is fine). Remove the chicken and set aside on a plate.

3. Do not clean the pan! Those brown bits on the bottom of the pan are going to add flavor to the sauce. Add the garlic

---

Yield

Serves 6 to 8

What the Kids Can Do

Measure ingredients, pick add-ins, stir with supervision.

You can also use 1½ pounds of extra-large or jumbo shrimp instead of the chicken, and switch up the pasta to linguine, or another shape—see the cover photo!

to the pan and sauté over medium heat until you can smell it, 30 seconds. Turn the heat to high, add the chicken broth, and scrape the bottom of the pan to loosen up all of those delicious caramelized bits. Bring to a simmer, lower to medium heat, and simmer for 5 minutes. Add the pasta, stir well, and simmer until the pasta starts to soften, about 8 minutes. Stir in the warm cream and the browned chicken with any juices that have accumulated on the plate. Cover and simmer, stirring occasionally, until the pasta is tender, most of the liquid has been absorbed, and the chicken is cooked through, about 4 minutes more.

4. Stir in the Parmesan until well incorporated, and adjust the seasonings.

5. ➤—◄ You can continue with Step 6 or see the Fork in the Road for add-in suggestions.

6. Transfer the mixture to a serving bowl and sprinkle with the parsley, if desired. Serve hot and pass extra Parmesan at the table.

Make Ahead

While it's certainly reasonable to thrill over a meal of reheated leftover Alfredo pasta, either warmed on the stovetop or in the microwave, this dish is best when it's made just before serving.

Note: What does *rigate* mean? Ridges. And those ridges are what lets the pasta grab onto that sauce and hold it tight. Tighter than a preschooler hangs on to his mom who is about leave him at school for the first time, or maybe even a month or so into the school year, even though he *knows* she is coming back, because when has she ever not? (Can you tell I still have scars?)

FORK IN THE ROAD

Alfredo Add-Ins

When you add the Parmesan in Step 4, you can add any of the following to the pot, alone or in combination; stir over medium heat for another minute or two.

1 cup slivered sun-dried tomatoes or ¼ cup sun-dried tomato pesto (see page 351)

1 tablespoon pureed chipotles in adobo sauce (see page 355)

4 cups sliced mushrooms, sautéed (see page 134)

3 cups lightly cooked tiny broccoli florets

2 tablespoons fresh herbs, such as oregano, thyme, or parsely

Or, you can serve up portions of Chicken Alfredo Pasta for those who like it plain and simple, and add proportionate amounts of any of the add-ins to the pot.

Simple One-Skillet Chicken Alfredo Pasta

Broccoli for an all-in-one meal

Pureed chipotles in adobo sauce

You can add any of these ingredients alone or in combination.

Sautéed mushrooms

Slivered sun-dried tomatoes

Stupid Easy Chicken and Broccoli Pasta

FORK IN THE ROAD: Try the ramped-up version with pesto (and/or skip the chicken for a vegetarian dish).

The title of this recipe may not make your mouth water, but the actual dish will. All of us need those dinners that require little thought, little time, and a little collection of on-hand ingredients. I have no compunctions about opening up a jar of good sauce, pouring it over pasta, and calling it dinner . . . but this feels much more like a real meal.

Think of the recipe as a template (as with so many of these recipes), and swap ingredients in and out as you like. Check out some of the combos on page 208, and more importantly, check out what's in your fridge, in season, or on sale.

Yield

Serves 8

What the Kids Can Do

If your kids are comfortable with a knife and raw chicken, they may cut the chicken with supervision. They may be able to grate the Parmesan, and they can snap the broccoli into little florets. If you are making pesto, the kids can help work the food processor or blender.

Kosher or coarse salt

1 package (1 pound) linguine or other long, thin pasta

2 tablespoons olive oil

2 teaspoons finely minced garlic

2 pounds skinless, boneless chicken breasts, cut into
   1-inch pieces

1 tablespoon chopped fresh oregano leaves or
   1 teaspoon dried oregano

Freshly ground black pepper, to taste

½ cup dry white wine

2 cups chicken broth, preferably low-sodium

4 cups (about 4 large stems) small broccoli florets

¼ teaspoon red pepper flakes, or to taste

1 tablespoon unsalted butter

½ cup freshly grated Parmesan, plus more for serving

Make Ahead

This is best made just before serving, though leftovers heated in the microwave or on the stove over low heat are quite delicious. Add a little more broth to loosen everything up.

Vegetarian Note: Skip the chicken, use vegetable broth. Stupid Easy Broccoli Pasta!

1. Bring a large pot of water to a boil. Salt the water generously and add the pasta. Return the water to a boil and cook the pasta according to the package directions, but stop when it is very al dente, about 2 minutes before it's done. Reserve 1 cup of the cooking water and drain the pasta.

2. Meanwhile, heat the olive oil in a very large skillet over medium-high heat. Add the garlic, chicken, oregano, and salt and pepper and sauté until the chicken is just lightly browned on the outside, but not cooked through, about 3 minutes (see So What Does Sauté Mean, Anyway?, page 204).

3. Increase the heat to high, add the white wine, and cook and stir until the wine is reduced by half, about 1 minute. Add the chicken broth, ½ cup of the reserved pasta water, and the broccoli florets.

4. ━━◄ You can continue with the recipe or see the Fork in the Road to amp up the flavor with pesto.

We all need some stupid easy pasta recipes in our arsenal.

5. Cover the skillet and bring to a simmer. Add the drained almost-cooked pasta to the skillet, as well as the red pepper flakes and butter and stir well. Reduce the heat to medium, cover the pot, and simmer until the pasta and broccoli are just tender, about 2 minutes; add additional pasta cooking water if the amount of liquid seems too skimpy—you want it a little saucy. Stir in the Parmesan, add additional salt and pepper if needed, and serve, passing additional Parmesan on the side.

FORK IN THE ROAD

Stupid Easy Chicken, Broccoli, and Pesto Pasta

Add ⅓ cup or so of Basil Pesto (page 350) or storebought pesto when you add the broccoli in Step 3. You can also just serve up some portions of the pasta as prepared in the recipe and then stir some pesto into the remaining pasta at the very end. Think about 2 teaspoons per serving, but know that it's really to taste.

So What Does Sauté Mean, Anyway?

The word *sauté* comes from French, literally translating to "jump"—meaning that the food should jump in the pan as it is being cooked. The keys are a small amount of fat, food cut into small pieces, a shallow pan, and fairly high heat. That, and not crowding the food in the pan. You want to stir or flip the food frequently but not too frequently—not too often so it has a chance to brown nicely on the exterior, but often enough so that all sides get their chance to turn golden before the interior becomes overcooked.

Sometimes a recipe will talk about sautéing a larger piece of meat or fish, which really should be referred to as panfrying, because, technically, *sautéing* refers to smaller pieces of quickly cooked ingredients.

Fettuccine with Shrimp and Asparagus

FORK IN THE ROAD: Another boilerplate recipe that is just the beginning in terms of how you can mix and match ingredients and create an infinite number of quick and easy pasta dinners.

L et's take a full-on moment to appreciate pasta, a year-round dinnertime mainstay in most homes. It's an amazing food: inexpensive, available everywhere, easy to prepare. And there are so many ways to use it season to season, dish to dish—no wonder it's one of those items we all have on hand, even when the pantry is looking a little sparse.

This is the kind of pasta I like to make in the spring, when we've had our fill of the rugged Bolognese sauce (page 195) or the rich Alfredo sauce (page 198). Now it's time for light and fresh, an easy sort of blueprint for recurring weeknight pasta meals. (✦≡ See the Fork in the Road for more easy combinations.) And feel free to finish the dish with a a tablespoon or two of chopped fresh herbs, such as basil or oregano.

- Kosher or coarse salt, to taste
- 1 package (1 pound) fettuccine
- 2 tablespoons olive oil
- 3 shallots, halved and thinly sliced
- 1 pound large shrimp (31 to 35 per pound), peeled and deveined, tails on or off as you please
- 2 pounds medium-thick asparagus, trimmed and cut into 1½-inch pieces
- ½ teaspoon red pepper flakes, or to taste
- Finely grated zest and juice of 1 large lemon
- ½ cup heavy (whipping) or light cream, or half-and-half (optional)
- Freshly ground black pepper, to taste
- 2 tablespoons unsalted butter, cut into small pieces

Yield

Serves 6

What the Kids Can Do

Peel the shrimp; trim and cut the asparagus with an age-appropriate knife; zest and juice the lemon; cut up the butter.

Make Ahead

This is best made right before serving, but you can certainly prep the ingredients ahead of time, and then it comes together very quickly.

Cooking Tip

The addition of that little bit of butter at the end is one of those cooking techniques that will just make you a better cook. Yes, it adds a little bit of fat, but it also adds silkiness, flavor, and texture, and pulls together a dish in sophisticated and delicious ways like few other things can. And oh, by the way, that tablespoon or so of butter (divided six ways) is not going to be the reason your jeans are hard to button. C'mon, we know that.

Simple ingredients in a light, lemony sauce—that's a weeknight dinner.

1. Bring a large pot of water to a boil. Salt the water generously and add the pasta. Return the water to a boil and cook the pasta according to the package directions. Reserve 1 cup of the cooking water, drain the pasta, and return it to the pot.

2. As soon as you start the water on the stove, heat 1 tablespoon of the olive oil in a very large skillet over medium-high heat. Add the shallots and sauté until soft and lightly browned, 3 to 4 minutes. Add the shrimp and sauté until pink and almost cooked through, about 3 minutes. Transfer to a bowl.

3. Return the pan to the heat and add the remaining 1 tablespoon olive oil. Add the asparagus and red pepper flakes and sauté until the asparagus is crisp-tender, about 4 minutes. Return the shrimp and shallots to the pan, add the lemon zest, and combine well. Add the cream if using, and heat for a minute. Add ½ cup of the reserved pasta cooking water (¾ cup if you didn't use the cream), bring to a simmer, and season with salt and pepper.

4. Transfer the shrimp mixture to the pot with the pasta, add the butter (see Cooking Tip) and the lemon juice, and toss to combine everything well, making sure the butter melts throughout. Check the seasonings, and add a little more of the pasta cooking water if necessary to make sure the sauce coats the pasta nicely. Serve hot.

More Easy Pasta Dinners

Try the following combinations and adjust the cooking times accordingly. Mix and match any of the ingredients; this is just to get the gerbil up and running in the wheel. And while many of the suggested combinations do feature some sort of seafood or meat, this recipe blueprint also lends itself to infinite vegetarian combinations, like the last trio of ingredients.

Scallops + Peas + Lemon Juice & Zest

Cubed Chicken + Brussels Sprouts + Mustard

Cubed Pork + Broccoli Florets + Fresh Rosemary

Crumbled Sausage + Broccoli Rabe + Parmesan

Kale + Peppers + Fennel Seeds

Vegetable Lo Mein

FORK IN THE ROAD: Go for just the vegetables, or add chicken or pork or both for a meaty lo mein.

This lo mein made its debut to a group of 11- to 14-year-old boys, and I wasn't really paying attention to the meal as it unfolded. Afterward I asked them how they liked it on a scale of one to ten. Jack's friend Max said, "I give it a five. Because I had five plates of it." I'll take that score.

Use whatever vegetables you have around. Broccoli florets are great in this, diced kohlrabi (see Kohlrabi: The UFO of Root Vegetables, page 77), chopped broccoli rabe, mushrooms, spinach . . .

Kosher or coarse salt, to taste

1 package (1 pound) thin spaghetti

1½ cups vegetable broth, preferably low-sodium

¼ cup dry sherry

2 tablespoons soy sauce

1 tablespoon cornstarch

1 teaspoon sesame oil

1 teaspoon sugar

Freshly ground black pepper, to taste

2 tablespoons canola or vegetable oil

2 teaspoons minced garlic

½ cup thinly sliced celery

1 cup thinly sliced carrots

1 red bell pepper, stemmed, seeded, thinly sliced, and cut into 1-inch pieces

2 cups fresh sugar snap or snow peas

2 cups shredded napa cabbage

1 cup fresh bean sprouts (optional)

½ cup drained canned bamboo shoots (optional)

Yield

Serves 8

What the Kids Can Do

This is a nice opportunity to let kids pick the vegetables they like to include in the recipe. They can also measure and mix up the ingredients for the sauce.

Make Ahead

It's not a make-ahead dish, per se, but I have heated up leftovers that were stored in the fridge, covered, up to 4 days later to much happiness. You can heat the lo mein on the stove over medium heat, or in the microwave if that's easier.

Chicken version

A totally vegetarian
lo mein

1. Bring a large pot of water to a boil. Salt the water generously and add the pasta. Return the water to a boil and cook according to package directions, stopping 2 minutes or so before the pasta is fully cooked. Drain and set aside.

2. Meanwhile, combine the broth, sherry, soy sauce, cornstarch, sesame oil, sugar, and black pepper in a small bowl or container. Set the sauce aside.

3. ━◄ You can continue with Step 4 or see the Fork in the Road if you'd like to also add meat.

4. Heat the oil in a large skillet or wok over high heat. Add the garlic, celery, carrots, red pepper, and sugar snap peas and cook until everything becomes crisp-tender, 3 minutes. Mix in the pasta and cabbage.

5. Cook, stirring occasionally, until everything is combined and hot and the cabbage is a bit wilted, 2 minutes.

6. Add the sauce and toss until the noodles are cooked and absorb most of the sauce, and the rest of the sauce is slightly thickened, another 2 minutes or so. Stir in the bean sprouts and/or bamboo shoots if using.

This is one of those recipes you can turn to again and again if you have a vegetarian or two in the house.

FORK IN THE ROAD

Chicken or Pork Lo Mein

Before you start cooking the vegetables, cook 1 pound boneless chicken breasts or thighs (or pork loin), diced or cubed, in 1 tablespoon vegetable oil until most of the pink is gone. Add the chicken or pork to the pan when you add the sauce in Step 6 and allow it to finish cooking in the sauce. (You can use chicken broth in the sauce instead of vegetable broth.)

If you want to make the lo mein half vegetarian and half with meat, still use vegetable broth to make the sauce. After the cabbage has wilted in Step 5, separate out half the mixture into another skillet. Then add the partially cooked meat to one of the pans, divide the sauce between the two pans, and proceed, dividing any remaining ingredients between the two versions.

Fill 'em up.

A whole chapter for tacos and enchiladas? I guess that's a fair indication of how significant a role this genre of food plays in our family. If Jack had only one dish to eat over and over and over it would be tacos, and so it is to him that this particular chapter is dedicated.

Tacos & Enchiladas

Did I ever think my kids would ask for Fish Tacos on a regular basis? No, I did not, but was delighted to be proven wrong. In other filling news, shrimp (or chicken) is swathed in a robust tomato sauce and slow-cooked pork is shredded into either tacos or enchiladas—and we can't decide which we like better. Then there are slightly piquant chicken enchiladas in a cheesy white sauce, and surprisingly satisfying vegetarian Creamy Black Bean, Mushroom, and Zucchini Enchiladas. If your house is like mine, and the words "tacos" and "enchiladas" are the most repeated dinner requests, this should be a new arsenal of recipes for you to rely on.

Fish Tacos

FORK IN THE ROAD: Simple and clean fish tacos are a fabulous change of pace from meat tacos, and a choice of toppings makes them even more terrific.

My kids have had such a love affair with tacos—turkey, beef, pork, chicken—that it caused me some apprehension to rock the boat with fish tacos. Fish impinging on taco territory? That was looking for trouble.

The first time they encountered a fish taco was in Florida, near the ocean, and luckily they were extremely hungry. And lo and behold, fish entered the taco lexicon. We are now an equal opportunity taco family.

FOR THE TACOS

1½ pounds flaky white fish fillets such as cod, halibut, or red snapper, cut into about ¾-inch-thick slices

1 teaspoon ground cumin

1 teaspoon chili powder

Kosher or coarse salt and freshly ground black pepper, to taste

2 tablespoons plus 2 teaspoons canola or vegetable oil

1 clove garlic, finely minced

2 teaspoons fresh lime juice

4 cups very thinly shredded cabbage, preferably napa

2 tablespoons cider or rice wine vinegar

12 corn or flour tortillas (6 inches in diameter)

TO SERVE (PICK AND CHOOSE)

Diced or sliced avocado

Fresh cilantro leaves

Thinly slivered red onion

Lime wedges

Tomatillo (salsa verde) or regular salsa, and/or Pico de Gallo (page 222)

Lime Crema or Avocado Crema (page 348)

Serves 4 to 6

What the Kids Can Do

Help select toppings, sprinkle the fish with seasonings, toss the cabbage with the dressing, dice or slice the avocado with an age-appropriate knife, select additional toppings, and assemble their own tacos.

Make Ahead

The dressed cabbage can be made a day ahead of time and refrigerated, covered. The fish is best made right before serving, but leftover cooked fish can be refrigerated and quickly warmed in the microwave the next day.

Everyone creates their own fish taco magnum opus.

1. Sprinkle the pieces of fish all over with the cumin, chili powder, and salt and pepper.

2. Heat the 2 tablespoons oil in a large skillet over medium-high heat. Add the garlic, swish it around, then add the fish without crowding (in batches if necessary), and cook until cooked through, turning it as needed, about 5 minutes in all. The pieces may fall apart a little as you cook them; that's perfectly fine. Remove with a slotted spoon or spatula and place them on a serving plate and sprinkle with the lime juice.

3. Meanwhile toss the cabbage with the vinegar and remaining 2 teaspoons oil, and season generously with salt and pepper.

4. Just before serving, warm the tortillas (see Cooking Tip).

5. Place the toppings you like in individual bowls. Serve the warm tortillas with the fish, cabbage, and toppings and let everyone assemble their own tacos.

The Fork in the Road here is simply that everyone can top their tacos exactly how they see fit.

Cooking Tip

To warm corn or flour tortillas, wrap a stack of up to 12 in a very slightly dampened clean dish towel or paper towel and microwave 45 to 90 seconds, until heated through. You can heat a few wrapped stacks at once side by side; but add 10 seconds for each stack. You can also wrap them in a slightly damp paper towel and then in aluminum foil and heat them in a 350°F to 400°F oven for 5 to 8 minutes.

If you have time, warming tortillas individually for 5 to 10 seconds on each side in a dry skillet over medium-high heat brings out the flavor really nicely. This is particularly noticeable with corn tortillas.

Shrimp Tacos

FORK IN THE ROAD: Make tacos with shredded cooked chicken instead of the shrimp if you want a non-shellfish option, or offer both versions and it's a taco party.

Yield

Serves 6

What the Kids Can Do

Peel the shrimp and measure the spices. Deveining may end up being your job—sorry. If you are making the chicken version, they can shred the chicken.

The firm texture of shrimp is so fantastic in a soft tortilla, and my family absolutely loves the tangy, saucy tomato mixture that binds the filling together. If you're not thinking about tacos, this is also quite lusty served over a pile of hot rice or quinoa, or tossed with freshly cooked hot pasta.

2 tablespoons extra-virgin olive oil

2 pounds large (31 to 35 per pound) shrimp, peeled and deveined, or see the Fork in the Road for a chicken substitute

Kosher or coarse salt and freshly ground black pepper, to taste

1 large onion, finely chopped

1 large bell pepper (any color, see Bell Peppers, page 228), stemmed, seeded, and chopped

3 cloves garlic, very finely minced

1 can (8 ounces) tomato sauce

2 tablespoons tomato paste or ketchup

½ teaspoon dried oregano

½ teaspoon chili powder

½ teaspoon red pepper flakes (optional)

½ cup chopped green olives (optional)

1 to 2 tablespoons minced fresh flat-leaf parsley leaves

12 corn tortillas (6 inches in diameter), for serving

Sour cream or crème fraîche, for serving

Diced avocado, for serving

1. Heat 1 tablespoon of the olive oil in a large deep skillet over medium-high heat. Add the shrimp, season with salt and pepper, and sauté just until they start to turn pink, 2 minutes. Remove the shrimp with a slotted spoon to a plate and set aside.

This dish makes me selfishly pray for leftovers.

2. Return the skillet to medium-high heat and add the remaining 1 tablespoon olive oil. Add the onion and bell pepper and sauté until they start to soften, 2 minutes. Add the garlic and sauté until you can smell it, 1 minute more. Add the tomato sauce, tomato paste, oregano, chili powder, and red pepper flakes, if using. Cook, stirring occasionally, to blend the flavors, 5 minutes. Season with salt and pepper. Stir in the olives if using, the parsley, and the reserved shrimp and cook until the shrimp are cooked through, another 2 minutes.

3. Meanwhile, warm the tortillas (see Cooking Tip, page 216).

4. Serve the shrimp mixture with the tortillas and pass the sour cream and avocado on the side.

Chicken Tacos

In place of the shrimp, use 4 cups shredded cooked chicken. Skip the initial sautéing step (and the first tablespoon of olive oil), and just start with Step 2, adding the cooked chicken with the parsley and olives when you would have added the partially cooked shrimp. You may want to add shredded cheese to the topping options. BTW, the chicken filling is also fantastic in a hard tortilla shell.

Make Ahead

The whole dish can be made up to 2 days ahead, refrigerated, and heated gently over low heat. Heat the tortillas just before serving.

Carnitas

FORK IN THE ROAD: This makes a lot, which happily enough means if you plan right, you'll have enough to make carnitas tacos at the beginning of the week and a filling for enchiladas later on.

Don't you love when a dish that you've heard breathless praise about lives up to your expectations? Having fallen head over heels for pulled pork—unsurprisingly, since pork incites passionate feelings—the call of Mexico's carnitas had to be addressed. There are many heated opinions on the subject of what perfect carnitas should be. I took them all to heart, and then came up with this variation.

The key to carnitas is to start with a fatty piece of pork. First the meat is simmered in liquid, releasing the fat, and then after the liquid evaporates, the meat is caramelized in the same pot, in the fat that was rendered from the braising. If this sounds a little explicit, I'm sorry, but sometimes cooking and life are a little graphic, which we knew already.

*As with any recipe I offer
that is regional,
ethnic, classic, or pork-related,
I relinquish any claims
to authenticity.*

Yield

Serves 8 to 10 (or 4, with enough left over for enchiladas)

What the Kids Can Do

Juice the citrus, smash the garlic with a rolling pin, add the ingredients to the pot. Pull apart the meat once it is cooked and slightly cooled. Pick toppings. Assemble the enchiladas.

Make Ahead

You can make the carnitas a few days ahead of time, and keep it covered in the fridge. Reheat in a baking pan loosely covered with aluminum foil in a 300°F oven for 10 to 15 minutes.

Pickled jalapeños

Orange and lime wedges

Cubed avocado

Pickled onions

Cilantro

Coleslaw

Avocado Crema

Pico de Gallo

FOR THE CARNITAS

4 pounds boneless pork shoulder or pork butt, cut into 2- to 3-inch chunks

1 tablespoon ground cumin

4 teaspoons kosher or coarse salt

1 teaspoon freshly ground black pepper

Juice of 2 limes

Juice of 2 oranges

8 cloves garlic, peeled and smashed

TO SERVE (PICK AND CHOOSE)

Corn or flour tortillas, warmed (see Cooking Tip, page 216)

Salsa or Pico de Gallo (see Sidebar)

Slivered cabbage or coleslaw, store-bought or homemade (page 281)

Pickled jalapeños

Sliced or cubed avocado, or guacamole

Lime and orange wedges

Fresh cilantro leaves

Chopped onions or pickled onions

Avocado Crema (page 348), or Lime Crema (page 348), or sour cream

Shredded queso fresco (mild white cheese)

1. Toss the pork with the cumin, salt, and pepper. At this point you can put the meat in a sealed container and refrigerate it for up to 2 days (it's not necessary to season the meat ahead, but if you plan for it you will be rewarded with a deeper flavor).

2. Place the pork in a large stockpot or Dutch oven and add the citrus juices, garlic, and enough cold water to just cover the pork. Bring just to a boil, uncovered, over high heat, then reduce the heat so that the liquid is simmering. Simmer, uncovered, until the liquid is evaporated, 2 to 3 hours (a longish time frame, but it really varies, that's a fact). You don't have to monitor it much during this time; in fact the less messing around you do the better. You can skim off the slightly foamy stuff that will rise to the surface, but don't worry about it too much.

Pico de Gallo

If you like a lot of heat in your pico de gallo, leave some or all of the seeds in the jalapeño. Make the pico de gallo on the day it's being served, or a day before.

Yield

Makes about 2½ cups

Ingredients

2 medium-size ripe tomatoes, seeded and diced

1 jalapeño pepper, with or without seeds, finely chopped

¼ cup finely chopped onion

2 to 3 tablespoons minced fresh cilantro

1 tablespoon fresh lime juice

¼ teaspoon kosher or coarse salt, or to taste

¼ teaspoon freshly ground black pepper, or to taste

Combine the tomatoes, jalapeño, onion, cilantro, lime juice, salt, and pepper in a medium-size bowl. Serve right away or refrigerate, covered, until ready to serve.

3. Now the second part of the cooking process takes place, and here you need to pay attention. Cook the chunks of meat over medium-low heat in the fat that will have been released during the simmering. Flip the chunks every few minutes or so, so that all sides have a chance to be in contact with the hot bottom of the pan and brown up nicely. After about 30 minutes, the meat should be quite browned on the outside and start to fall apart—that's how you know it's done.

4. Remove the meat from the pan, let it cool a bit, and using your fingers or two forks, shred it into small pieces (see Note). Transfer the meat to a shallow bowl and serve with the warmed tortillas and the toppings you like.

Note: Definitely do not over-shred the meat, as you don't want little stringy bits: The pleasure of carnitas is the nice bites highlighting the contrast between the super-tender interior and the crispy caramelized exterior. Be still my heart.

FORK IN THE ROAD

Carnitas Enchiladas with Avocado Crema

UNLESS YOU ARE FEEDING a crowd, you'll likely have leftovers when you make carnitas as a filling for tacos. Use them to make this different dinner later in the week—leftovers are always a full-on gift, and something I always aim for in meal planning. The enchiladas also work beautifully with shredded leftover chicken.

Nonstick cooking spray

2 teaspoons vegetable, canola, or olive oil

1 cup chopped onions

5 cups shredded pork carnitas

2 cans (4 ounces each) chopped green chiles

1 can (14 ounces) pureed or crushed tomatoes

2 jalapeños, seeded and minced (optional)

¼ cup chopped fresh cilantro leaves (optional)

16 flour tortillas (6 inches in diameter), warmed (see Cooking Tip, page 216)

2 cups (8 ounces) shredded cheddar cheese

Avocado Crema (page 348)

1. Preheat the oven to 375°F. Lightly spray a 9 by 13–inch baking dish with nonstick cooking spray.

2. Heat the oil in a medium-size skillet over medium-high heat. Add the onions and sauté until tender, 4 minutes. Add the carnitas, 1 can of the chopped chiles, the tomatoes, and the jalapeños and cilantro if desired. Stir to blend and cook until warmed through, about 3 minutes.

3. Place about ⅓ cup of the carnitas mixture along the edge of one warmed tortilla and roll it up. Place it in the prepared pan seam side down. Repeat with the rest of the tortillas, lining them snugly one next to another. Place the last few perpendicular to the row of enchiladas once the row is full. Scatter the remaining can of chiles over the enchiladas and sprinkle the cheese on top. Bake uncovered until the cheese is melted and the top is nicely browned, 20 to 30 minutes.

4. Serve, passing the Avocado Crema on the side.

Two different meals from one dish— happiness.

Slightly Spicy Cheesy Chicken Enchiladas

FORK IN THE ROAD: Gently piquant, or more on the spicy side, or some of both.

Spicy red-sauced enchiladas are a favorite in my house, and there is a recipe for them in *The Mom 100 Cookbook* that has served us very, very well. But just for a change, I decided to make chicken enchiladas with a white and green sauce. The sauce starts with sautéed onions, peppers, and scallions, and the addition of flour provides thickening with a minimum of fat (saving the fat part for the sour cream and the cheese; I don't know why I am even pretending this is a low-fat recipe). If you want, pull out some of the sauce before you spike the rest of it with a nice amount of jalapeños and cayenne, to make some milder enchiladas, which will still have good flavor and an ever-so-slight kick.

This makes enough for a small crowd. And if you don't have a crowd, then you get leftovers. The bell peppers add nice pops of color, and build vegetables right into the dish.

Yield

Serves 6 to 8

What the Kids Can Do

Shred the cheese and chicken, help with the sauce (if they are old enough to be near a hot stove with supervision), mix the sauce with chicken, roll up the enchiladas and line them up in the pan, pour the sauce over, and sprinkle on cheese.

If you like a bubbly
brown top, run the
enchiladas under the broiler
for a couple of minutes
at the end.

Vegetable or canola oil or nonstick cooking spray, for oiling the baking pan

3 tablespoons unsalted butter

1 cup chopped onions

2 bell peppers (green, yellow, or red, or a combination), stemmed, seeded, thinly slivered, and sliced crosswise

5 scallions, trimmed, white and green parts sliced

3 tablespoons all-purpose flour

2 teaspoons ground cumin

2½ cups chicken broth, preferably low-sodium

¾ cup milk, preferably whole, or half-and-half

2 cans (4 ounces each) green chiles

Kosher or coarse salt and freshly ground black pepper, to taste

3 cups shredded Monterey jack cheese

¾ cup sour cream, low-fat or regular

1 jalapeño pepper, stemmed, seeded, and finely minced

½ teaspoon cayenne pepper, or to taste

4 cups shredded cooked chicken (preferably dark meat, or a mixture of dark and white)

14 corn tortillas (6 inches in diameter), warmed (see Cooking Tip, page 216)

Green or red salsa, or Pico de Gallo (page 222), or picante sauce, for serving (optional)

1. Preheat the oven to 350°F. Lightly oil a 9 by 13–inch baking pan, or spray it with nonstick cooking spray.

2. Melt the butter in a medium-size skillet over medium-high heat. Add the onions, bell peppers, and scallions and sauté until tender, about 5 minutes. Stir in the flour and continue stirring until it browns slightly, about 4 minutes. Stir in the cumin, then the broth. Add the milk, green chiles, and salt and pepper, and bring to a gentle simmer. Reduce the heat; simmer until the sauce is slightly thickened, about 4 minutes. Sprinkle in 2 cups of the cheese and simmer and stir until melted, about 1 minute. Remove the pan from the heat and stir in the sour cream.

Make Ahead

These enchiladas can be assembled and refrigerated in the pan(s), covered, for up to 1 day before baking. Take them out of the fridge and let them come to room temperature for about 20 minutes before baking (if you forget to do that, or don't have time, just add another 5 to 10 minutes to the baking time). Cooked enchiladas can be reheated in a 350°F oven for about 20 minutes (also bring them to room temperature, if possible, before reheating).

3. ⟍⟍ You can continue with Step 4 or see the Fork in the Road for less spicy enchiladas.

4. Blend the minced jalapeño and cayenne into the sauce. Place the chicken in a large bowl and mix in about 2½ cups of the sauce. Measure out ⅓ cup of the sauced chicken mixture, place it along the edge of one of the tortillas, and roll it up. Place it in the prepared baking pan seam side down. Repeat with the rest of the tortillas, using up all of the sauced chicken and lining up the enchiladas snugly. Place the last few perpendicular to the row of enchiladas once the row is full. Pour the rest of the sauce evenly over the enchiladas, tucking the pepper strips in the sauce between the enchiladas (there will be a lot of sauce—this is good).

5. Sprinkle the remaining 1 cup cheese evenly over the pan. Bake, uncovered, until the sauce is bubbly and the cheese is melted, about 40 minutes. If you want a browner top, broil the enchiladas for a minute or two after they finish baking.

6. Serve hot with salsa, Pico de Gallo, or picante sauce, if desired.

FORK IN THE ROAD
Gentler Creamy Chicken Enchiladas

For milder enchiladas, skip the jalapeño and cayenne.

To make both versions, bake the enchiladas in two 8- or 9-inch-square pans. After stirring in the sour cream at the end of Step 2, pour half of the sauce into a bowl. Add half a jalapeño, minced, and ¼ teaspoon cayenne to the sauce remaining in the pot. Combine 1¼ cups of this sauce with half the chicken and stir to mix well. Combine the remaining chicken with 1¼ cups of the remaining plain sauce and stir. Fill and roll 7 tortillas with the spicy mixture, then fill 7 more tortillas with the plainer mixture. Continue with the recipe, placing the enchiladas in the separate pans, topping them with their remaining sauce, and dividing the cheese between them. Be sure to keep track of which pan is which.

Bell Peppers

Bell peppers are members of the nightshade family of vegetables. In many cases, the peppers, regardless of color, are from the same species of plant, but it's their level of maturity that dictates the color and the flavor. Sometimes specific plants are cultivated for specific colors and flavors.

Bell peppers are related to hot peppers, but don't have capsaicin in them, the component that gives spicy peppers their heat.

1. **GREEN BELL PEPPERS** are, for the most part, peppers harvested before they are fully ripe, with a slightly bitter taste, which can be interesting in cooking. They get used a lot in sofritos (in many Hispanic cuisines), in Italian cooking, and are a firm part of the "holy trinity" of Southern Cajun and Creole cuisines. They are less expensive, sturdier, and readily available.

2. **RED BELL PEPPERS** are the most mature of all the peppers, quite rich in nutrients (such as beta-carotene and vitamins A and C), and are sweet and fruity in flavor.

3. **ORANGE AND YELLOW BELL PEPPERS** are most often just peppers that are more ripened than green (the yellow variety), and not quite as ripened as red (the orange variety). Their sweetness and fruitiness corresponds to their ripeness.

Creamy Black Bean, Mushroom, and Zucchini Enchiladas

FORK IN THE ROAD: If you want to make some of these non-veggie, they are a great way to use up all kinds of leftovers.

Yield

Serves 6

I made these for the first time for my vegetarian babysitter, my vegetarian mother, and my carnivorous kids and husband. The vegetarians loved them, and the carnivores didn't miss the meat for one minute. The tangy, creamy sauce that binds the filling together is pretty terrific, and there is a lot of textural interest.

Of course, if you are not looking for a vegetarian meal, these are a perfect vehicle for using up a couple of cooked chicken breasts or thighs (page 225) leftover steak (page 104), and a cup or two of carnitas (page 220).

Oil or nonstick cooking spray, for oiling the baking pan

1 tablespoon olive oil

1 teaspoon finely minced garlic

1 pound sliced mushrooms, any kind (about 5 cups)

Kosher or coarse salt and freshly ground black pepper, to taste

1 medium-size zucchini, sliced lengthwise and thinly sliced into half moons

1 can (15.5 ounces) black beans, rinsed and drained

3 ounces cream cheese (about ⅓ cup)

3 ounces goat cheese (about ⅓ cup)

1 teaspoon dried oregano

1 can (4 ounces) chopped green chiles

12 flour tortillas (6 inches in diameter), warmed (see Cooking Tip, page 216)

1 can (10 ounces) enchilada sauce

1. Preheat the oven to 375°F. Lightly oil a 9 by 13–inch baking pan or spray it with nonstick cooking spray.

2. Heat the olive oil in a large skillet over medium-high heat. Add the garlic and mushrooms, season with salt and pepper, and sauté until the mushrooms start to turn golden brown, about 8 minutes (see Cooking Tip, page 134). Add the zucchini and sauté until tender, 5 minutes more. Stir in the beans, cream cheese, goat cheese, and oregano and cook until the cheeses are melted and blended into the mixture, about 3 minutes. Stir in the chiles and remove the pan from the heat.

3. ➤═ You can continue with Step 4 or see the Fork in the Road to make the enchiladas for meat-eaters.

4. Measure out ⅓ cup of the mixture, place it along the edge of one of the tortillas, and roll it up. Place it in the prepared pan seam side down. Repeat with the rest of the tortillas, using up all the filling. Line up the enchiladas snugly and place the last few perpendicular to the row of enchiladas once the row is full. Pour the enchilada sauce evenly over the enchiladas. Bake until the tops start to brown, about 25 minutes. Serve hot.

What the Kids Can Do

Slice the mushrooms and zucchini with an age-appropriate knife and supervision. Scoop the mixture onto the tortillas and roll up the enchiladas. Pour the sauce over the rolled enchiladas.

Make Ahead

You can make the filling up to 3 days ahead of time; bring it to room temperature before filling and rolling the enchiladas. The enchiladas can be rolled and the baking dish covered and refrigerated for up to a day before baking. Bring the uncooked enchiladas to room temperature before cooking, and pour the sauce over just before baking. Or add a few minutes to the cooking time if you bake them straight from the fridge.

Non-Vegetarian Black Bean, Mushroom, & Zucchini Enchiladas

You can make these non-vegetarian in a wide variety of ways. Add 1½ cups chopped or shredded cooked chicken, pork, or steak, or diced cooked shrimp, to the vegetable mixture at the end of Step 2. You'll probably need 16 to 18 tortillas instead of 12.

You can also divide the filling into halves, and keep half vegetarian, and add ¾ cup meat or shrimp to the other half (plan to fill an extra 2 or 3 tortillas with the meat version). Bake them in two 8- or 9-inch-square pans to keep the two versions separate.

ONE-SKILLET BEEFY ENCHILADA NOODLE CASSEROLE, *page 239*

If you asked most people what they'd like for dinner on any given night, the answers would mostly fall into a category we all think of as comfort food. Many, many recipes in this book fit that description, but the ones in this chapter are so inherently comforting that they deserved a chapter all their own: A fork-tender pot roast with carrots and potatoes, crispy oven-fried chicken (maybe with a little spiciness if

I Need a Big Fat Hug

you like), a cold-weather chili with chicken and beans, and a beefy noodle-y enchilada skillet casserole that my family could eat weekly for the rest of their lives and never tire of it. Finally, one of my favorite dishes in the whole wide book is the Saucy Seafood Stew, which has been one of my go-to recipes for entertaining when I'm not trying to show off but just looking for a company-worthy dish that makes everyone feel extra loved.

Spanish-Style Beef Pot Roast

FORK IN THE ROAD: This doesn't have a Fork so much as a way to get a second soup meal out of a flavorful pot roast. More of a Spoon in the Road.

My family loves brisket dearly, but after years of the classic flavors (onions, tomatoes, carrots), I wanted to do something a little different. Also, and probably most important, I had bought a large tin of Spanish smoked paprika and had to find ways to make a dent in it.

My father always referred to brisket as pot roast, but the cut most often used in pot roast is beef chuck, which is nicely marbled and when cooked verrrrry slooooowly gets fork tender. I never really understood the difference between the two cuts, so I wanted to try a "real" pot roast.

You could really use whatever olives you like—the pimiento-stuffed green variety is the only kind of olives my whole family agrees on, though Gary likes them best when they are peeking up at him from the bottom of a vodka martini. They add nice flavor to the sauce, so even though some may pick them out, they are really worth tossing in there.

If you don't feel like browning the meat first, that's okay, but that little extra step will yield more flavor all around and an exterior that is still slightly crusty in contrast to the fall-apart interior.

Yield

Serves 8

Make Ahead

Like brisket, stews, chilis, many soups, and countless other dishes, this is even better made up to 3 days ahead of time. You can leave the roast in the cooking juices, then sometime in the following days, slice it and return it to the pot before heating it over medium-low heat (this also allows you the opportunity to remove the layer of fat that will have congealed on top of the cooking liquid). Chilling it before slicing also allows the soft slices to hold their shape a bit better.

If you turn the leftovers into soup, it will also keep in the fridge for several days, or can be frozen for up to 3 months.

2 tablespoons olive oil

1 chuck roast (4 pounds)

1 teaspoon kosher or coarse salt

1 teaspoon freshly ground black pepper

1 cup roughly chopped onions

1 cup sliced carrots

1 tablespoon finely minced garlic

1 tablespoon smoked Spanish paprika (see Smoked Paprika, at right)

1 teaspoon dried thyme

1 can (15 ounces) crushed tomatoes in juice, or tomato puree

½ cup beef or chicken broth, preferably low-sodium

½ cup dry red wine

2 tablespoons balsamic vinegar

Large pinch of saffron threads (see Saffron: The Rolls-Royce of Seasonings, page 253)

4 white or Yukon Gold potatoes (1 to 1½ pounds), scrubbed and cut into large chunks

1 cup small green olives stuffed with pimentos, rinsed (optional)

1. Preheat the oven to 275°F.

2. Heat 1 tablespoon of the olive oil in a large nonreactive pot, such as a Dutch oven or casserole with a lid, over medium-high heat. Sprinkle the meat all over with the salt and pepper. Add the meat to the pot and sear on the top and bottom, until both are nicely browned, about 4 minutes per side. Remove the meat to a plate.

3. Add the remaining 1 tablespoon olive oil to the pot and heat over medium heat. Add the onions, carrots, garlic, smoked paprika, and thyme and cook, stirring occasionally, until the vegetables start to become tender, 5 minutes. Stir in the tomatoes, broth, wine, vinegar, and saffron. Return the meat to the pan, placing it so that the liquid and vegetables come about halfway up the sides of the meat.

Smoked Paprika

Once most people discover this spice they have a "where have you been all my life?" reaction. Extremely popular in Spain, where it comes from, it's made from pimiento peppers that have been smoked and dried and then ground into powder. Sometimes it is labeled *pimentón* (just the Spanish word for paprika, so you'll have to check if it's smoked or not), *smoked pimentón,* or *Spanish pimentón.* It's very dark red in color, and has a strong smoky aroma and flavor, but it's not spicy hot— though a little does go a long way in most cases.

Smoked paprika is great in rubs, marinades, soups, stews, braises, barbecue sauces, dips, and even sprinkled over popcorn. It's a particularly great spice to use in vegetarian cooking if you're seeking that deep, smoky flavor that bacon and other rich, meaty ingredients can add to a dish.

4. Cover the pot, place in the oven, and braise the roast for 3 hours. Add the potatoes and olives, if using. Continue braising, covered, until a fork slides into the meat with hardly any resistance and the potatoes are tender, 45 minutes to 1 hour more. Taste the sauce and adjust the seasonings.

5. Remove the meat from the pan. (It may start to fall apart. That's okay; it means you did a good job cooking it.) Let it sit for 10 to 15 minutes, then slice it across the grain, knowing that the slices will not really hold together. Place the meat on a serving platter with sides, spoon the vegetables next to the meat, and pour some of the cooking liquid on top. You can pass some of the liquid from the pot on the side as well, but hold some back, as well as some meat, if you're interested in the ◼━◀≡ Fork in the Road soup.

What the Kids Can Do

Peel the carrots and scrub the potatoes, measure the spices, weigh in on the addition of olives.

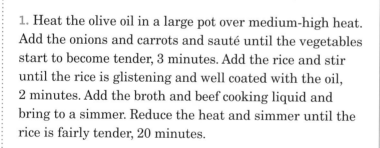

Spanish Beef and Rice Soup

Serves 4

ANY TIME YOU MAKE a roast, especially if there is braising liquid involved, save some of the meat and the juices and you have a second meal in the form of a soup just waiting to happen. After it's refrigerated you can remove the fat that hardens on top.

2 teaspoons olive oil

1 cup chopped onions

½ cup chopped carrots

¾ cup Arborio or other short-grain rice

3 cups beef or chicken broth, preferably low-sodium

1 cup liquid from cooking the pot roast

2 cups shredded leftover pot roast

Any extra carrots, potatoes, and onions from the pot roast

1. Heat the olive oil in a large pot over medium-high heat. Add the onions and carrots and sauté until the vegetables start to become tender, 3 minutes. Add the rice and stir until the rice is glistening and well coated with the oil, 2 minutes. Add the broth and beef cooking liquid and bring to a simmer. Reduce the heat and simmer until the rice is fairly tender, 20 minutes.

2. Add the shredded pot roast and any extra veggies you've salvaged from the pot. Simmer uncovered, stirring occasionally, for another 10 minutes. Serve hot.

One-Skillet Beefy Enchilada Noodle Casserole

FORK IN THE ROAD: Nicely seasoned for those who don't like a lot of heat, pumped-up seasoning options for those looking for some kick.

There is a recipe for One-Skillet Cheesy Beef and Macaroni in *The Mom 100 Cookbook* that not only is my husband's favorite from the book, and high on my kids' list, but also one of the recipes that people most often email me about, declaring it a staple in their weekly repertoires. It seems only right to try to follow it up with a beefy cheesy noodle-y encore. And so, I present for your

Yield

Serves 8

What the Kids Can Do

Measure the spices, cream, and cheese; dump things into the pan and stir (with supervision); sprinkle on the cheese.

consideration a Mexican twist on this much-loved dish, and a meal that is greeted in my house with thunderous applause. Okay, not thunderous applause, but requests for seconds, which is as close to thunderous applause as I can hope to get.

Nonstick cooking spray, for the skillet

1½ pounds lean ground beef

1 tablespoon olive, canola, vegetable, or peanut oil

2 onions, chopped

1 red, yellow, or orange bell pepper, stemmed, seeded, and diced

2 cloves garlic, minced

1 tablespoon chili powder

1 teaspoon ground cumin

1 teaspoon dried oregano

Kosher or coarse salt and freshly ground black pepper, to taste

2 to 3 cups chicken broth, preferably low-sodium

¼ cup tomato paste

1 can (28 ounces) enchilada sauce

1 package (1 pound) fusilli, rotini, or egg noodles

½ cup light or heavy (whipping) cream, or half-and-half

1½ cups shredded Monterey jack, cheddar cheese, or a Mexican blend

1. Spray a very large, deep (13-inch; 6 quart) skillet with nonstick cooking spray and place over medium-high heat. Add the ground beef and cook, stirring frequently and breaking up the meat, until it is crumbly and browned throughout, about 5 minutes. Transfer to a colander and drain.

2. Heat the oil in the skillet over medium heat. Add the onions, bell pepper, garlic, chili powder, cumin, oregano, and salt and pepper. Sauté until the onions are softened and the spices are nice and toasty and aromatic, 5 minutes.

3. Raise the heat to high, add 2 cups of the chicken broth, the tomato paste, and enchilada sauce, and bring to a

Make Ahead

You can make this casserole up to the point that the noodles are about halfway cooked, and refrigerate it, covered, for up to 2 days. Bring to room temperature and warm the casserole gently over low heat until the noodles are cooked through (you may need to add a bit more broth). When it is hot, stir in the cream (and the spicy ingredients if using) and finish it off with the cheese.

simmer. Reduce the heat to medium-high, add the drained beef and noodles, and stir well. Cover and bring to a simmer. Reduce the heat to medium-low and continue to simmer, covered, until the noodles are cooked, following the package directions. Stir once halfway through the cooking time. The liquid should be pretty much absorbed, but the mixture should still be moist looking. If the noodles absorb all of the liquid before they are cooked, add up to an additional cup of chicken broth to the pan, stir, and cover until the pasta is tender.

4. ●━━◄ You can continue with Step 5 or see the Fork in the Road if you want a spicy casserole.

5. Stir in the cream, and sprinkle over the cheese. Cover and cook until the cheese melts, just 1 or 2 minutes. Serve hot.

VARIATION:
You can also make this with ground turkey for a slightly lighter version.

FORK IN THE ROAD

Spicy Enchilada Casserole

When the pasta becomes tender at the end of Step 3, stir in about 1 tablespoon finely minced jalapeño pepper and 8 trimmed and chopped scallions (white and green parts) along with the cream, then sprinkle on the cheese. Cover and let the cheese melt.

For half spicy and half tame, before adding the cream and cheese, remove half of the mixture to a shallow serving bowl, stir in ¼ cup cream, and sprinkle on ¾ cup of the cheese, then cover and let the cheese melt. Then, to the mixture remaining in the skillet, stir in 1 to 2 teaspoons minced jalapeño and 4 chopped scallions with ¼ cup cream. Sprinkle with ¾ cup cheese, cover, and let it melt.

The main version has a nice level of flavor, but the Fork in the Road really gives your taste buds something to think about.

Simple Oven-Fried Chicken

spicy
Oven-Fried Chicken

Spicy (or Not) Oven-Fried Chicken

FORK IN THE ROAD: Hold back on the cayenne and dry mustard in the flour coating to make a less-spicy fried chicken.

During long car rides and other stretches of time when we're looking for ways to entertain ourselves, subjects come up like, "If you had a million dollars, what would you do first?" Or, "If you could pick one meal to eat for the rest of your life, what would it be?" In those food-centric conversations (I'm not saying they happen all the time, but as you might imagine . . .), the words *fried chicken* have been known to make an appearance. Right up there in the pantheon of best foods on the planet.

I wouldn't say I'm a big deep fryer in general, because it's messy and hard to justify on a regular basis. This is why I start the chicken in the pan, but finish it in the oven. This is also handy because when I am making fried chicken, I am usually making it for a crowd, so the notion of standing over a pot of bubbling oil for hours on end does not work for me.

The cornstarch gives the crust extra crunch, always a good thing in fried chicken. The key tips are to not crowd the pan, and to keep the oil at a lively bubble, but not smoking hot, so that the skin really crisps up. Start this recipe a day before you are going to cook it; the chicken needs to brine overnight.

Yield

Serves 8

What the Kids Can Do

Season the buttermilk, season the flour mixture, and dredge the chicken. Keep them away from the actual frying.

Make Ahead

Many people love fried chicken at room temperature, or even cold. If you do, then you can certainly make it a few days ahead and store it in the fridge. If you'd prefer it warm, reheat it in a 325°F oven for 10 to 15 minutes. Bring it to room temperature before reheating so that it reheats more quickly and evenly.

My nephew Alex mentioned my fried chicken in his bar mitzvah service. I was very excited.

8 cups (2 quarts) buttermilk

½ cup plus 2 teaspoons kosher or coarse salt

2 tablespoons freshly ground black pepper

6 pounds skin-on, bone-in chicken pieces (divide drumsticks and thighs; cut large breast halves in half)

5 cups canola or vegetable oil or more as needed, for frying

3 cups all-purpose flour

¼ cup cornstarch

2 tablespoons paprika

2 tablespoons dry mustard powder

1 tablespoon cayenne pepper

Cooking Tip

I had one of my proudest culinary breakthrough moments in the middle of the night. I dreamed that I was making fried chicken, but that I was combining the notion of a brine with the buttermilk bath that is the typical tenderizer of fried chicken. (I have very strange dreams; this is the most normal dream I can remember. Isn't that sad?)

And then, awake, in real life, I tried it, spiking the buttermilk with a hefty amount of salt, so that the buttermilk would take on brining properties (see To Brine or Not to Brine, page 246). This is as close as I've ever gotten to feeling like a genius. I know I can't be the only one to have come up with this, but I don't care, I'm still mightily pleased with myself for this.

1. Combine the buttermilk, the ½ cup salt (see Cooking Tip), and 1 tablespoon of the pepper in a very large bowl, stirring well to dissolve the salt. Add the chicken pieces to the bowl, making sure the chicken is thoroughly covered. Cover with plastic wrap and refrigerate for 24 to 36 hours, turning the pieces once or twice to make sure they're evenly submerged.

2. Preheat the oven to 350°F. Place wire cooling racks on each of 2 rimmed baking sheets.

3. ━━◀ You can continue with Step 4 or see the Fork in the Road for a less-spicy coating.

4. Combine the flour, cornstarch, paprika, mustard powder, cayenne, and remaining 2 teaspoons salt and 1 tablespoon pepper in a large bowl. Remove the chicken from the buttermilk, letting the excess liquid drip off (as you do, smooth out the skin, so it covers the chicken as best as possible). Dip each piece in the flour mixture to coat it very thoroughly. Shake off the excess, then place the chicken on the wire racks. (You will finish baking the chicken on the same wire rack–lined baking sheets.)

5. Pour oil to a depth of 2 inches into a Dutch oven, stockpot, or a skillet that's at least 4 inches deep (you may want to use 2 pots to speed up the process; you will need to double

the amount of oil). Heat over medium-high heat until the oil is bubbly around the edges, 365°F on a candy or frying thermometer. If you don't have a thermometer, just drop a cube of bread into the pan; when it turns brown pretty quickly (10 to 15 seconds), the oil is ready.

6. Ease the chicken pieces into the bubbling oil, making sure not to crowd the pan. Fry the chicken in batches with the oil at a moderately lively bubble, until light golden brown all over, about 4 minutes each side. Place each fried piece back on a wire rack, skin side up; the pieces can be close but not touching. Add oil to the pan as needed and bring it back to the proper temperature before adding more chicken.

7. Bake the chicken on the racks on the baking sheets until it is cooked through, 25 to 40 minutes. Thighs and breasts will register 170°F on an instant-read thermometer inserted near—but not touching—the bone. The time will depend on the size of the pieces, and dark meat will take longer than white. Thus, wings 25 minutes, thighs or big breasts 40 minutes. (You might want to bake the smaller white meat pieces on a different baking sheet from the larger or dark meat pieces so you can take them out earlier.) Serve hot, warm, or at room temperature.

FORK IN THE ROAD
Simple Oven-Fried Chicken

If you don't want to make the chicken spicy, just skip the mustard powder and cayenne pepper in the flour coating.

To make half and half, divide the flour, cornstarch, paprika, and pepper mixture between 2 bowls at the beginning of Step 4, and then add 1 tablespoon mustard powder and 1½ teaspoons cayenne to one of the bowls and stir. Dredge half of the chicken in the plainer flour mixture, half in the spicy flour mixture. Bake them on separate baking sheets so the pieces don't get mixed up.

To Brine or Not to Brine?

What is brining and what's the point? The most basic reason for brining is to add moisture and flavor to meat, especially lean meats that tend to get dry when cooked, such as certain cuts of pork or turkey. The most basic brine is simply water and salt. The third ingredient most often added is some form of sugar. And then you can add whatever your heart desires in terms of seasonings, from simple peppercorns, garlic, and bay leaves, to lemongrass, herbs, and citrus zest. (See page 108 for a Basic Brine.) I kind of love the results, but don't always have the time. Story of our lives, right?

Chicken and White Bean Chili

FORK IN THE ROAD: Make this into a vegetarian chili, or when you're serving a mixed crowd, make half of each.

When we know we'll be entertaining a crowd during cooler weather—post sledding or school play, or for the Super Bowl or Oscars—many of us turn to chili. It's easy to make in large quantities, not too strenuous on the wallet, and even better when made ahead. Plus the house smells great, plus people can serve themselves, plus everyone can add the toppings they like to make it their perfect bowl, plus leftovers are freaking awesome and freeze well. And pretty much everyone likes it. Well, except for the one time one friend who, upon finding out chili was that night's main course, went out, bought a burger, brought it back to my house, and ate it in the corner of the kitchen while we all ate chili. You know who you are. I still really love you . . . but seriously.

The tiny amount of flour thickens up the chili a bit, as does the mashing of the beans. Neither one is a game changer if you don't have the time. If the jalapeño makes you say "oh no, too spicy," skip it. This recipe doubles quite easily.

Yield

Serves 8

What the Kids Can Do

Measure the ingredients and rinse the beans. For the vegetarian version, they can crumble the tempeh, and perhaps dice the zucchini or squash with an age-appropriate knife.

FOR THE CHILI

   2 tablespoons olive, canola, or vegetable oil

   2 onions, chopped

   3 ribs celery, chopped

   2 yellow bell peppers, stemmed, seeded, and diced

   1 tablespoon minced garlic

   1 jalapeño, seeded and minced (optional)

   1 tablespoon chili powder

   1 teaspoon ground cumin

   1 teaspoon ground coriander

   1 teaspoon paprika, smoked or regular

   ¼ teaspoon cayenne pepper (optional)

   1 tablespoon all-purpose flour

   Kosher or coarse salt and freshly ground black pepper, to taste

   3 cups chicken or vegetable broth, preferably low-sodium

   1 cup whole milk

   3 cans (15.5 ounces each) white beans, such as cannellini, rinsed and drained

   1 zucchini or summer squash, cut into small cubes

   2 pounds skinless, boneless chicken breasts or thighs, cut into small cubes (about 4 cups), or ➤ see the Fork in the Road for vegetarian substitutes

   2 tablespoons fresh lime juice

   Hot rice to serve

FOR THE ACCOMPANIMENTS (PICK AND CHOOSE)

   Lime wedges

   Cilantro leaves

   Shredded cheese (such as white cheddar or Monterey jack)

   Diced avocados

   Chopped onions

   Sour cream or Avocado Crema (page 348)

1. Heat the oil in a large stockpot or Dutch oven over medium heat. Add the onions, celery, and bell peppers and sauté until the vegetables are softened, 5 minutes. Add the garlic, jalapeño (if using), chili powder, cumin, coriander, paprika, cayenne (if using), flour, and salt and pepper. Sauté until you can smell the spices and the garlic, 1 minute more.

A light, pretty chili— a little more delicate in flavor and palette than many tomato-based recipes

2. Stir in the stock and milk, raise the heat to medium-high, and cook just until the mixture comes to a simmer.

3. Meanwhile, pour 1 can of beans into a small bowl and mash them up a bit. Add them to the pot; this gives some body to the liquid. Reduce the heat to medium-low and add the remaining beans and zucchini.

4. ◗═══ You can continue with Step 5 or see the Fork in the Road for a vegetarian version.

5. Add the chicken and continue to gently simmer to cook the chicken through and allow the flavors to blend, 20 minutes. Stir in the lime juice just before serving.

6. Serve hot, over rice, with the accompaniments you like.

Make Ahead

This is even better made 1 or 2 days ahead of time (stir in the lime juice right before serving if possible, but if you are reheating portions with the lime juice already added, that's just fine) and it will keep in the fridge, covered, for at least 4 days. Reheat over low heat on the stove.

FORK IN THE ROAD

Vegetarian White Bean Chili

USE VEGETABLE BROTH. In Step 5, instead of the chicken, add the following with the remaining cannellini beans.

1 package (8 ounces) tempeh, crumbled (see What Is Tempeh?, page 197)
1 additional zucchini or summer squash, cut into small cubes
1 can (15.5 ounces) chickpeas , rinsed and drained
2 cups corn kernels, either fresh, frozen, or canned (drained)

If you want to make some of each, split the chili into 2 pots after you add the beans and zucchini. Add 2 cups cubed chicken to one of the pots, and half an 8-ounce package of tempeh and half the amounts of the vegetables listed above to the other. Simmer for 20 minutes, divide up the lime juice between the 2 pots, and serve.

The vegetables in this vegetarian variation will keep to the pale chili theme, but you can use other vegetables like carrots or tomatoes, if you prefer.

Saucy Seafood Stew

FORK IN THE ROAD: If you're looking for a gluten-free or lower-carb dish, try serving the stew over spaghetti squash instead of pasta.

T his stew is brightly flavored—thanks to the fennel and orange—and hearty—thanks to everything else. I love it, my husband loves it, and here's the confession: My kids don't love it. They will eat it, but they don't love it . . . *Yet*.

Yet. That's the operative word in so many parent/kid dinner situations, and I am not going to pretend that it doesn't happen in my house, too. This is, however, a dish I am going to serve, and serve again, in the hopes that one day a junior member asks for seconds. And if you're looking for an easy but impressive main dish to serve company, here's your answer.

Kosher or coarse salt

2 tablespoons olive oil

1 onion, finely chopped

2 carrots, finely chopped

1 bulb fennel, trimmed, cored, and finely chopped

3 cloves garlic, minced

4 anchovy fillets, rinsed and minced

1 cup dry red wine

1 can (28 ounces) crushed tomatoes

1½ cups low-sodium chicken broth

Freshly ground black pepper, to taste

1 pound tubular pasta, such as ziti or rigatoni, ➤ or see the Fork in the Road for a spaghetti squash option

1½ pounds firm white fish, such as cod, snapper, sea bass, or halibut, cut into 1-inch chunks

1 pound large shrimp (31 to 35 count), peeled and deveined

¼ teaspoon saffron (see Saffron: The Rolls-Royce of Seasonings, page 253), optional

Finely grated zest and juice of 1 orange

⅓ cup chopped fresh flat-leaf parsley

Chipotle Mayonnaise (page 355), for serving (optional)

Yield

Serves 6 to 8

What the Kids Can Do

Peel the carrots, cut the fish (with an age-appropriate knife), peel the shrimp, zest and juice the orange. If you make spaghetti squash instead of pasta and let it cool a bit, they will love creating the strands of squash with a fork.

1. Bring a large pot of water to a boil over high heat and season generously with salt.

2. Heat the oil in a very large pot or a very large and deep skillet over medium-high heat. Add the onion, carrots, and fennel and sauté until tender, 5 minutes. Add the garlic and sauté until you can smell the garlic, 1 minute more. Add the anchovies and red wine and simmer until the wine is reduced slightly, about 2 minutes. Add the tomatoes and chicken broth and bring to a simmer.

3. At this point if you want a smoother stew base, remove the pot from the heat and puree slightly: Use either an immersion blender and puree the soup in the pot, or transfer the stew in batches to a food processor or blender and pulse a few times, then return to the pot. (You don't want it super smooth—some texture is nice.) For a coarser texture skip this step (see Note). Season with salt and pepper (taste as you go; the anchovies add saltiness).

4. Meanwhile, add the pasta to the boiling water and cook it according to the package directions.

5. Simmer the tomato mixture over medium-high heat to blend the flavors, about 5 minutes, then add the fish, shrimp, saffron, and orange zest. Cook, stirring very gently, until the fish and shrimp are just cooked through, about 5 minutes. Gently stir in the orange juice and parsley (if the parsley will turn off anyone at the table, sprinkle over individual portions for those who like a fresh, herby finish).

6. Drain the pasta and place it in a large shallow serving bowl, or plate up individual bowls. Spoon the seafood stew over the pasta and pass the Chipotle Mayonnaise for people to dollop atop their servings as they wish.

Make Ahead

The soup base can be made through Step 3 and refrigerated for up to 4 days. Return to a simmer and continue with the recipe.

Note: I have an immersion blender, which I love, and I use it for this. Frankly, if I didn't have one, for this particular recipe I would not go through the trouble of pureeing.

Saucy Seafood Stew with Spaghetti Squash and Chipotle Mayonnaise

SOMETIMES YOU'RE LOOKING FOR a dinner that's lighter on the carbs, while still quite substantial. Or maybe you have a gluten-free member of the family. Instead of pasta, substitute cooked spaghetti squash—it has a great, naturally buttery flavor, great nutrition, and is just plain fun to make as well.

1 large (3 to 3½ pounds) spaghetti squash

1. Preheat the oven to 450°F.

2. Cut a large spaghetti squash in half and scrape out the seeds with a spoon. Place the halves cut side down on a rimmed baking sheet and bake for 45 to 55 minutes, until the halves look somewhat wrinkly and collapsed.

3. Remove the squash from the oven and allow it to cool for a minute or two. Using a fork, scrape, scrape, scrape the cut sides of the squash to release the insides from the skin. You'll see the squash form spaghetti-like strands as you do this; it's pretty cool. Transfer all of the squash to a serving bowl (or individual bowls), then top with the seafood stew and serve as above.

Saffron: The Rolls-Royce of Seasonings

The first time you go to purchase saffron you may well gasp and think, "There must be some kind of mistake." It often comes in a teeny tiny jar, or in a tiny pouch inserted in a regular-sized jar, and the price tag doesn't seem to reflect the volume of the spice. You're not wrong; it is in fact the most expensive spice in the world.

Here's why: Saffron is the labor-intensive collection of the itty-bitty stigmas of a particular crocus flower. For every acre of crocuses, the harvested stigmas yield only about 6 pounds of saffron. The best saffron comes from Spain and India, and it appears frequently in Indian, Persian, European, Arab, and Turkish cuisines. But a little saffron goes a long way: Most recipes call for a very small amount, but that little bit adds wonderful golden color and flavor. That's why the gram you'll buy will cover several recipes. There are a number of grades, and you'll find the one that fits most comfortably into your budget.

WARM ROASTED TOMATO, COUSCOUS, AND CHICKPEA SALAD, *page 271*

Increasingly I hear from fellow home cooks that there is a newly turned (or not so newly turned) vegetarian in the house, and that figuring out what to make for dinner has become even trickier. So, how can you cook one meal that will work for both the vegetarians and the carnivores? There are lots of recipes in the book that offer a vegetarian version as well as one for meat eaters. The recipes in this chapter are vegetarian at their core, but most of them can take a Fork in the Road and include meat for those who are craving it.

Vegetarian

I am besotted with Korean flavors, featured in the sesame tofu and mushroom dish. A Lazy Vegetable One-Skillet Lasagna is made completely on the stovetop, mushrooms serve as the base of cheesy, hearty "pizzas," and a main course salad featuring toothsome Israeli couscous, lots of vegetables, and chickpeas is one of those dishes that allows everyone to select the components they love, and skip those they don't. And in another do-it-yourself kind of dinner thought, a Baked Potato Bar also offers you a chance to use up all those little bits of leftovers in a brand-new meal.

CHAPTER 15

Cheesy, Crispy Pizza Portobello Mushrooms

FORK IN THE ROAD: An all-in-one vegetarian meal in its own great container—whether that container is a big fat portobello or an assortment of cute-as-a-button mini mushrooms.

Mushrooms are a mainstay of many a vegetarian's diet as they are substantial, have great texture, and provide that elusive and desirable umami flavor we all crave (even if we don't know exactly what umami is: See Umami? on page 258).

But not everyone loves mushrooms, and for some kids mushrooms are one of those acquired tastes ("acquired tastes" is parent code for "oh my god, if you don't take a few bites of this I am going to scream"). Keep going—they are such a great flexible food that they are worth putting a little elbow grease behind. Turning them into pizza isn't a bad place to start, because mushrooms are a great food to love, and a pretty important one if you are looking for hearty, healthy, meatless meals.

Yield

Serves 6

What the Kids Can Do

Scrape out the mushroom gills with a spoon, measure the ingredients, brush on the marinade, mix the filling, stuff the mushrooms, drizzle the sauce. This is a very good kid-involved recipe.

Make Ahead

You can bake the mushrooms for 15 minutes, and then cool, cover, and refrigerate them. They'll keep for 2 days. Reheat them in a 450°F oven for 5 to 8 minutes until hot throughout.

Vegetable oil or nonstick cooking spray, for oiling the baking sheet

6 large portobello mushrooms (about 5 inches), stemmed; or see the Fork in the Road for mini substitutes

4 tablespoons extra-virgin olive oil

2 tablespoons balsamic vinegar

2 teaspoons finely minced garlic

Kosher or coarse salt and freshly ground black pepper, to taste

¾ cup panko bread crumbs

¾ cup shredded mozzarella cheese

½ cup freshly grated Parmesan cheese

½ teaspoon dried oregano, or 1 teaspoon minced fresh oregano

½ teaspoon dried thyme, or 1 teaspoon minced fresh thyme

½ cup jarred pasta sauce or Super Simple Tomato Sauce (page 347)

1. Preheat the oven to 450°F. Lightly oil a rimmed baking sheet, or spray with nonstick cooking spray. Scrape the gills (soft ridgey parts) out of the mushrooms.

2. Whisk together 2 tablespoons of the olive oil, the vinegar, 1 teaspoon of the minced garlic, and salt and pepper in a small bowl. Brush this marinade over both sides of the mushrooms and arrange them, hollow side up, on the baking sheet.

3. Mix together the remaining 1 teaspoon garlic, the panko, mozzarella, Parmesan, oregano, and thyme in another small bowl. Drizzle the remaining 2 tablespoons olive oil over the cheese and panko mixture and toss well. Scoop some of the mixture into each mushroom cap, pressing it down slightly into the hollows and making sure it doesn't fall over the edges.

4. Bake the mushrooms until the cheese mixture is melted and browned and the mushrooms are tender, 15 to 20 minutes. Let sit for a minute or two before serving. Drizzle each with some of the tomato sauce or pass the sauce for people to serve themselves.

FORK IN THE ROAD

Cute-as-a-Button Mushroom Pizzas

A mushroom the size of a hubcap might be intimidating to some kids, or even grown-ups. It's easy to turn this recipe into a bunch of smaller, and more adorable, mini pizza mushrooms. Just use 2 pounds of good-size button or cremini mushrooms (sometimes labeled "stuffing mushrooms"). Use a small teaspoon to scrape out the gills and divide the mixture among the littler mushrooms. You should still be able to cook them all on one baking sheet, and they will be done in 10 to 12 minutes.

Umami?

There is some deep science behind the discovery and explanation of umami, which is widely considered to be the fifth flavor (sitting alongside sweet, sour, salty, and bitter). It's interesting reading, if you want to investigate. But suffice it to say, for the purposes of our book, that umami is basically defined as the flavor of savoriness. Think of miso paste, anchovies, Parmesan and other cheeses, seafood, and meat. Foods with depth and a concentrated flavor and richness. Mushrooms are great examples of the umami flavor, and since vegetarians choose to skip a number of foods with great umami taste, mushrooms are a good go-to ingredient for capturing that elusive and delicious flavor. Umami actually means "yummy" in Japanese, or "a pleasant savory taste," and if you don't want to dig further into the definition of umami, that's a pretty good one.

Baked Potato Bar

FORK IN THE ROAD: Baked potatoes—one for each person—and some great toppings, are the basis for a customized dinner.

Leftovers turn into full-on meals when they're merged with the right kind of starch as a base. They fill quesadillas, enhance stir-fried rice, top Asian Rice Bowls (page 189), and stuff steamy baked potatoes.

This simple baked potato has a crisp-chewy skin and a soft interior that is ready to be fluffed with a fork. Then it's ready to be topped with anything from a pat of butter and a sprinkle of salt to everything else you can think of.

Russet potatoes
Your choice of toppings (see Pile 'Em High, pages 260 to 261)

1. Preheat the oven to 375°F.

2. Scrub the potatoes, dry them, and remove any dark brown or greenish spots, or "eyes." Use a fork, skewer, or thin sharp knife to poke several holes all around each potato (Important! Unpoked potatoes can explode!). Bake the potatoes directly on the oven rack for 1¼ to 1½ hours, until a thin sharp knife slides easily into a potato. (You can also cook 3 to 5 potatoes in a microwave for anywhere from 15 to 25 minutes, depending on the level of power, but the skin will not have an exciting texture.)

3. Let the potatoes cool for a couple of minutes. Take a sharp knife and slit lengthwise down the middle of one potato. Give it a squeeze, spread it open, and use a fork to loosen up the insides a bit. Repeat to open all the potatoes. Top as desired (see Side Dish Variation).

Yield

Serves the number of people you make baked potatoes for.

What the Kids Can Do

Poke the potatoes with a fork, choose toppings, create their personal baked potato.

Make Ahead

The potatoes can be baked up to 3 days ahead of time, then reheated in a 375°F oven for 10 to 15 minutes until hot throughout. The potatoes can also be reheated in a microwave for about 2 minutes.

Side Dish Variation

If you want a simple baked potato side dish, bake the potatoes as directed, then top with a pat of butter and a pinch of salt and pepper, if desired. Sour cream is another classic potato topper, or try one of the cremas on page 348.

Pile 'Em High

Clearly not all of these toppings are vegetarian, but equally as clearly, a stuffed baked potato is a brilliant vegetarian meal notion. These are just a few combo ideas for inspiration—you are going to create your own, with whatever you and your family likes, and what you have in the fridge.

1. THE CLASSIC STUFFED POTATO: This is what the quintessential baked potato with all the works looks like: shredded cheddar, sliced scallions, crumbled bacon, and a big dollop of sour cream. This is bar food and comfort food rolled into one.

2. CHEESY GARDEN POTATO: If you have leftover steamed or sautéed vegetables, you're already on your way. Use any cooked veggies, such as broccoli, asparagus, broccoli rabe, spinach, tomatoes, kale, you name it, any kind of cheese, slivered or crumbled (manchego is pictured here), and maybe a dollop of pesto, such as this Sun-Dried Tomato Pesto (page 351).

3. TEX-MEX POTATO: The flavors of the Southwest continue to captivate us, and this potato brings them all together in one seriously savory package. Queso fresco, red onions, Salsa Verde (page 119), and cilantro make this a potato as fun to look at as it is to eat.

Queso fresco, sometimes referred to simply as *queso*, is a fresh cheese that is slightly tart and crumbly in texture; it provides a tangy note in this combo. You can substitute mild feta if queso is unavailable.

filling you like: Try the shrimp or chicken filling from the tacos on page 217.

Then top the whole thing off with Chipotle Mayonnaise (page 355), and fresh salsa, or your favorite selection of sour cream, grated cheese, scallions, salsa, avocado . . . or all of the above.

3. Tex-Mex Potato

2. Cheesy Garden Potato

1. The Classic Stuffed Potato

4. CARNITAS TACO POTATO: When is a taco not a taco? When a baked potato stands in for the tortilla shell. This Mexican-inspired potato is stuffed with carnitas (page 220), or any taco

5. MUSHROOM & RICOTTA SALATA POTATO: This is a pretty and unexpected filling, and will also cure that salt craving you've been having. Fill the potato with sautéed mushrooms (page 265), and any blend of olives, chopped or sliced, and top with shavings of ricotta salata (which is a pressed, salted, and aged version of ricotta, usually sold in firm wedges). A dusting of lemon zest adds some punch and brightness, and you can also give the warm potato a drizzle of vinaigrette for even more flavor.

MEATBALL–BAKED POTATO "SUB" (not pictured): Try your favorite frozen or homemade meatballs, or the chicken Parmesan meatballs (page 171). Cut large meatballs in half and tuck them into the opened potato. You can also make mini meatballs if you're looking for adorable. Top with a generous spoonful of tomato sauce (page 347), and a shower of grated Parmesan cheese. Big thumbs-up from the junior set on this one.

4. Carnitas Taco Potato

6. STEAK & CARAMELIZED ONION POTATO: A steak dinner often comes complete with a steaming baked potato and a pile of caramelized onions (see page 42) to top the meat. This version piles all of the components of the dinner right into the potato. You can use any cut of beef that you like: Try skirt, hanger, flank, sirloin, porterhouse, T-bone. (And this is a great way to use up that piece of leftover steak, page 104.) Serve with steak sauce,

Chimichurri sauce (page 104) or maybe sour cream, if desired.

5. Mushroom & Ricotta Salata Potato

CHUTNEY & FETA POTATO (not pictured): Exotic, vegetarian, and so simple to put together. Jarred chutneys can be spicy or sweet or tangy or a combination of all of the above. They feature all kinds of flavors and ingredients from cilantro to onions to coconut to mango to raisins to citrus juice, and they are an excellent way to jazz up all kinds of dishes. This works well with a regular russet but it's a great treat when made with a baked sweet potato.

PIZZA POTATO (not pictured): We will take pizza in any way, shape, or form. Using a baked potato for the base (instead of a dough crust) not only provides a gluten-free choice for those who want it, but bumps up the nutritional value as well. Spoon some jarred or homemade pizza or tomato sauce (page 347) over the potato, then add a nice layer of slivered

6. Steak & Caramelized Onion Potato

or grated fresh mozzarella and a sprinkle of dried oregano. You can play around with any toppings that you like on a pizza, from pepperoni to peppers, onions to olives. A shake of red pepper flakes is a nice finish. After the potatoes are topped, place them on a baking sheet and give them a quick run under the broiler to melt the cheese and give everything a bubbly finish.

HUMMUS & RED PEPPER POTATO (not pictured): Another vegetarian option, easily put together with store-bought hummus, which is available pretty much everywhere these days, or your own (page 41). This can be made with a regular russet potato, but it's really dazzling in looks and flavor when made with a sweet potato as the base. On top of the hummus, try some strips of roasted red pepper, or some red pepper puree (which can be made with roasted red pepper whirled up in a food processor with a touch of olive oil, or found in supermarkets or specialty stores). For texture you might want to sprinkle on some whole chickpeas.

Korean Sesame Tofu and Mushrooms

FORK IN THE ROAD: For a non-vegetarian version, try this with chicken.

Are you ready for something simple but immensely satisfying? A vegetarian weeknight dinner that is comforting, but the opposite of same-old, same-old? Why do I sound like a circus barker right now?

The use of sesame oil plus a bit of heat (here, the chili sauce or red pepper flakes) is common in many Korean dishes; when you taste this you'll know why it's such a good combination.

Tofu is also a big staple of Korean cooking. I often press it to remove excess water so it holds its shape and browns better, but in this case the firm but creamy texture of the unpressed tofu is really appealing. Even though you will be searing the tofu over high heat, the cubes will probably fall apart slightly; it's okay.

Serve the tofu and mushrooms over a pile of rice (white or brown or jasmine) or quinoa—your choice.

Yield

Serves 4

Make Ahead

This is best made right before serving, though leftovers can be heated in the microwave.

This is a great chance to explore the different types of mushrooms available: try shiitake, portobello, chanterelle, oyster, enoki, morels, black trumpet, matsutake—and plain old button or cremini work beautifully, too.

3 tablespoons reduced-sodium soy sauce (or 2 tablespoons regular soy sauce plus 1 tablespoon water)

1 tablespoon sesame oil

1 teaspoon Asian chili sauce or ½ teaspoon red pepper flakes, or to taste

½ teaspoon sugar

2 tablespoons sesame seeds (optional)

2 tablespoons vegetable or canola oil

3 to 4 cups (1 pound) sliced mushrooms (any kind, any mixture)

1 block (1 pound) firm or extra-firm tofu, blotted dry and cut into ½-inch cubes, ▬◄ or see the Fork in the Road for a chicken substitute

1 teaspoon minced garlic

8 scallions, trimmed, white and green parts finely chopped, plus additional for garnish (optional)

Hot cooked rice or quinoa, for serving

What the Kids Can Do

Slice the mushrooms and cut up the tofu with an age-appropriate knife, measure and mix the ingredients for the sauce, and sprinkle over the sesame seeds and scallions.

1. Combine the soy sauce, sesame oil, chili sauce, and sugar in a small bowl or container. Set aside.

2. Heat a large skillet, preferably nonstick, over medium heat. If using sesame seeds, add them and toast, stirring and tossing frequently, until they are golden brown and fragrant, about 2 minutes; watch carefully so they don't burn. Transfer the toasted seeds to a small plate.

3. Add 1 tablespoon of the vegetable oil to the skillet and heat over high heat. When the oil is hot, add the mushrooms and sauté (see Sautéing Mushrooms on the facing page) until the liquid is evaporated and the mushrooms are lightly browned, 8 to 10 minutes. Transfer the mushrooms to a plate with a slotted spoon.

4. Heat the remaining 1 tablespoon oil in the same skillet over high heat.

5. ▬◄ You can continue with Step 6 or see the Fork in the Road for a version using chicken.

6. When the oil is very hot, add the tofu, which should sizzle and sear (watch for splattering). Cook the tofu, not moving it so it has a chance to brown on the bottom, for at least 3 minutes. Flip the cubes using a thin metal spatula (knowing some cubes will break) and continue to cook until the tofu is hot and lightly browned on top and bottom, about 6 minutes in all.

7. Reduce the heat to medium, add the garlic and scallions and continue to gently flip the ingredients until the garlic and scallions are slightly softened and fragrant, about 2 minutes. Add the mushrooms, then the soy sauce mixture, and stir gently to combine. Serve hot over the rice or quinoa. Sprinkle with the sesame seeds and additional chopped scallions if desired.

FORK IN THE ROAD

Sesame Chicken & Mushrooms

Instead of tofu, you can use 1 pound skinless, boneless chicken breasts or thighs, cut into ½-inch dice. In Step 6, sauté white meat chicken for about 4 minutes, dark meat for about 6 minutes, until the chicken is partially cooked, then add the garlic and scallions and continue with the recipe.

If you want to make some with tofu and some with chicken, just divide the oil in Step 4 between two separate skillets, sautéing ½ pound tofu in one and ½ pound chicken in the other. Divide the scallions, garlic, cooked mushrooms, and sauce between the two skillets and serve.

P.S. I like it with chicken *and* tofu.

Sautéing Mushrooms

There's a very simple reason that sometimes sautéed mushrooms have a great texture and a rich, concentrated flavor, and sometimes they are just kind of limp and watery. Mushrooms have a lot of water in them, and when cooked over high heat they will start to release that water. You want to keep sautéing until the mushrooms are no longer giving out liquid, and then sauté them for a few minutes longer, so the water evaporates and they have a chance to brown.

BACKING UP ONE STEP FARTHER: Never submerge your mushrooms in water or run water over them. That will make them soak up even more liquid, and make them harder to brown. Instead, take a barely damp paper towel and wipe off any visible dirt from the mushrooms just before you prepare them.

Lazy Vegetable One-Skillet Lasagna

FORK IN THE ROAD: Go halvsies or double the recipe and make a chicken skillet lasagna at the same time.

We all love lasagna. But making it, I am perfectly willing to admit, sometimes, it's just a pain in the . . . tush . . . butt . . . [fill in the blank] . . . definitely south of the waist. But you know, those flavors, the noodles, we just can't turn away. So when you want . . . no, *must* heed the call and don't have time to layer, you can stir and shove.

I made this for the first time—a double batch, one vegetarian, one not—for my husband's birthday, which involved a large crowd of people, kids, and adults. Anyone who entertains will tell you not to experiment with a new dish when you are having guests, let alone 23 of them. But because I apparently spend a lot of time hanging around the corner of Do-What-I-Say Street and Not-What-I-Do Lane, this sage advice doesn't pertain to me.

I made the base ahead of time, and then as people were arriving I started to stick the broken noodles into the skillet. At first it did not seem like it was going to all come together, but then, it just did. Neatness doesn't count at all because the ingredients kind of sort themselves out at the end, and the sprinkling of cheeses on top camouflages all imperfections. So, worry not: This is a delicious crowd pleaser that is kind to the cook as well. My friend Jenny Mandel is spreading the word of this recipe like lasagna gospel.

Yield

Serves 8 to 10

Make Ahead

The sauce can be made up through Step 1, and refrigerated, covered, for up to 5 days, or frozen for up to 4 months. Defrost fully before continuing with the recipe. The lasagna can be made up through adding the remaining mozzarella and before the final 10 minutes of cooking, then cooled and refrigerated for up to 3 days. Bring it to room temperature, then simmer over medium heat for 10 minutes to complete the cooking. The fully baked lasagna can also be made ahead, refrigerated for up to 3 days, and then gently reheated over low heat on the stove.

"Once again, my life has been saved by the miracle of lasagna." —Garfield

2 tablespoons olive oil

1½ cups chopped onions

1 tablespoon minced garlic

1 teaspoon dried oregano

1 teaspoon dried basil

Kosher or coarse salt and freshly ground black pepper, to taste

2 cans (28 ounces each) crushed tomatoes

1 zucchini, sliced in half lengthwise and thinly sliced into half-moons

1 package (5 ounces) baby spinach leaves

1 package (8 or 9 ounces) no-boil lasagna noodles

3 cups (about 1 pound) shredded mozzarella, preferably fresh

1 container (16 ounces) ricotta cheese

About ¼ cup freshly grated Parmesan (optional)

½ cup chopped fresh basil leaves (optional)

What the Kids Can Do

Slice the zucchini with an age-appropriate knife, and shred the mozzarella. Distribute the final layer of mozzarella over the top, and Parmesan, if using, with supervision because of the hot pan (you may want to remove it from the stove, let them help, then return it to the stove for the final cooking). Sprinkle over the fresh basil, if using.

1. Heat the olive oil in a 12-inch (or larger) deep-sided skillet with a lid over medium-high heat. Add the onions and garlic and sauté until tender, about 5 minutes. Stir in the oregano, basil, and salt and pepper. Add the tomatoes, bring to a simmer, and let simmer for 10 minutes.

2. ▬◀ You can continue with Step 3 or see the Fork in the Road if you'd like to include chicken.

3. Stir in the zucchini and spinach. Cook until the vegetables are limp and well blended, 5 to 8 minutes.

4. Now the shortcut part begins: Break the noodles into halves or thirds—shards will fly, but you'll use them, too. Shove the pieces of noodle, including the shards, into

the sauce mixture, submerging everything as best and as evenly as possible. It will feel like it's not happening all that well, but it will absolutely all work out. Reduce the heat to medium, cover, and allow it all to simmer until the noodles start to soften, 10 minutes. Lift the lid and give the mixture a few pokes and stirs partway through to redistribute the noodles.

5. When the noodles have softened somewhat, stir in half of the mozzarella and all of the ricotta, using a spoon to fold and tuck in the cheeses between all the noodles, getting it toward the bottom of the mixture, swirling it around but not blending it completely at all. This is an imprecise science; that's what's so nice about the recipe.

6. Sprinkle over the rest of the mozzarella, and the Parmesan if desired, cover the pan again, and simmer until the noodles are tender and the whole thing looks like lasagna, another 10 minutes or so.

7. Let it sit, uncovered, to firm up for about 10 minutes before serving. Sprinkle over the fresh basil, if desired.

If you can buy fresh mozzarella and fresh ricotta, boy, you're in for a treat.

FORK IN THE ROAD

Chicken Skillet Lasagna

Chicken or chicken sausage can easily be added if you'd like a non-vegetarian lasagna meal. If you are adding it to the whole recipe, sauté 1 pound of diced skinless, boneless chicken thighs or breasts, or 1 pound of crumbled chicken sausage. Stir the cooked chicken into the sauce with the zucchini and spinach in Step 3.

If you want to divide the mixture in half and make 2 lasagnas, make the sauce in a smaller deep-sided 8-inch skillet, up through adding the vegetables in Step 3. Transfer half of the sauce to another similarly sized pan and add ½ pound cooked chicken or chicken sausage to one of the pans, and then proceed with the recipe as directed in Step 4, dividing the rest of the ingredients between the 2 pans.

Warm Roasted Tomato, Couscous, and Chickpea Salad

FORK IN THE ROAD: This summery main-course salad can easily be simplified for those looking for a less intricate meal. And the whole recipe is just a springboard for wherever your mood and pantry take you.

Don't know what's for dinner? A warm or room-temperature main-dish salad is a beautiful thing. In fact, two of the best busy-person dish concepts in the world, for vegetarians and non-vegetarians alike, are (1) soups and (2) main-course salads.

Look in your fridge and untether yourself from whatever might be holding you back. Fling open those vegetable drawers, reach for that spice you haven't used in a while, and create something uncomplicated and delicious. If you've seen the movie *The Sure Thing* (every now and then I like to date myself, making references to things that highlight my age), this is when Professor Taub would have poured forth her inspiring notions to get her students to cut loose and write from the gut, culminating in her classic line, "Make love in a hammock!"

Okay, back to the point at hand. Salad as a main course is a very important notion for anyone trying to move meat off of, or away from the center of, the proverbial plate. This is a starter recipe, and you have full permission to shuffle around the proportions, eliminate or swap out ingredients, and consider everything else about it just a suggestion so that you keep creating your own fabulous main-dish vegetable-y, grain-y, bean-y salads. Which, by the way, usually end up being fairly gorgeous and make fantastic buffet fare.

Yield

Serves 6 to 8

What the Kids Can Do

Cut the tomatoes and zucchini with an age-appropriate knife. Toss the tomatoes with the oil and season them. Whisk together the dressing. Arrange the spinach, toss the couscous salad, heap it on the spinach, arrange the various vegetables on the platter. Or, find substitutions for any ingredient in the recipe that you don't have or they don't care for.

Make Ahead

This can be made ahead and left, covered at room temperature, for about 2 hours, or refrigerated for up to a day and brought to room temperature before serving. Sprinkle on the feta, if desired, just before serving.

Does this recipe seem like a stretch for your kids? Try the simpler Fork in the Road version. And please see the Introduction on page vii. And, finally, ask them to help you put together a salad that's main-course worthy. But full disclosure: When Jack, my older son, saw this recipe as I was writing it, he winced. And then he gave me a bit of advice: "Mom, we're pretty decent eaters. We'll try most things. But if this is really meant to be a family cookbook, if you really want to reach kids, you need to not stray too far off course." *Fine!* The Fork in the Road is for him, and he's very happy with it.

2 pints cherry or grape tomatoes, halved

4 tablespoons extra-virgin olive oil

Kosher or coarse salt and freshly ground black pepper, to taste

2 zucchini, sliced in half lengthwise and then into half-moons (2 cups half-moons), or 2 cups small broccoli florets

2 cups corn kernels, fresh or frozen

3 tablespoons fresh lemon juice

1 tablespoon honey

1 tablespoon minced fresh oregano

3 cups cooked Israeli couscous (see Cooking Tip 1), or any other grain, warm or at room temperature

1 can (15 ounces) chickpeas, drained and rinsed

4 cups baby spinach

1 small red onion, slivered (optional)

1 cup crumbled feta cheese (optional)

1. Preheat the oven to 350°F.

2. Toss together the tomatoes with 2 tablespoons of the oil, ½ teaspoon salt, and black pepper to taste on a baking sheet. Arrange the tomatoes so that they are in a single layer, cut side down. Roast the tomatoes until they are soft and a bit collapsed, 30 minutes (for tomatoes that are more shriveled and concentrated in flavor, roast for up to 1 hour and 15 minutes). About 20 minutes before you want to take out the tomatoes, move them to one side of the baking sheet,

Cooking Tip 1

To make Israeli couscous, heat 1 tablespoon olive oil in a medium-size pot over medium-high heat. When the oil is hot, add 1½ cups Israeli couscous and cook, stirring occasionally, until it starts to color, about 3 minutes. Add 3½ cups water or vegetable broth and bring to a simmer. Lower the heat, cover the pot, and continue to simmer until the water is mostly absorbed, about 12 minutes. Turn off the heat and let sit, covered, for another 2 minutes.

add the zucchini and corn to the other side, spreading them out but keeping the vegetables grouped separately. Return the baking sheet to the oven and continue cooking till all the vegetables are cooked through.

3. Meanwhile, make the dressing: Whisk together the remaining 2 tablespoons olive oil, the lemon juice, honey, oregano, and salt and pepper.

4. Place the cooked couscous in a mixing bowl and add the chickpeas. Pour on the dressing, toss to combine, and taste for seasoning.

5. Spread out the spinach on a large serving platter. Mound the couscous mixture in the center of the spinach and top with the slivered onion if using. Surround the couscous with the roasted vegetables (see Note). Sprinkle on the feta or serve it on the side if using. Serve the salad warm or at room temperature, and let everyone choose the elements he or she likes.

Note: Instead of arranging the salad in components, you can toss every single ingredient together into one big bowl, from the spinach to the vegetables to the feta and it will be absolutely delicious. Not as elegant a presentation, and obviously fewer choices left to the individuals, but quite a nice thing to pack up for a work or school lunch, or a potluck buffet. This is what happens to any leftovers.

Cooking Tip 2

To roast broccoli florets, preheat the oven to 425°F. Toss 2 cups small broccoli florets with 2 teaspoons olive oil right on a rimmed baking sheet, and sprinkle with ½ teaspoon kosher or coarse salt. Roast until tender and slightly browned, about 25 minutes.

FORK IN THE ROAD

Simple Couscous Salad

Skip any ingredients your kids won't eat. My kids are very happy with a version that includes roasted zucchini and broccoli (see Cooking Tip 2), chickpeas, feta, onions, and the dressing. Hold the tomatoes and the corn. Though depending on his mood, Jack may pick around the chickpeas. It really never ends.

WARM BRUSSELS SPROUTS WITH BACON AND MUSTARD VINAIGRETTE, *page 288*

I promise not to mention *The Mom 100 Cookbook* more than a handful of times in this cookbook, but I would be remiss not to point out that in that book there are other recipes for vegetables that my kids and many, many other kids who have traveled through my home, have loved and eaten by the plateful. Roasted broccoli, cauliflower, and asparagus in particular stand out as the vegetables I could put on the table night after night without complaint. And any time any parent ends a sentence with the words *without complaint,* the rest of us should pay attention.

Vegetables

But back to the drawing board I went, and I respectfully submit these five recipes for your family table. Cauliflower puree isn't intended to fool anyone into thinking it's mashed potatoes, but if you should fail to ID it . . . well, you're only human. The warm brussels sprouts have converted many a brussels-basher; spinach sautéed with some Korean seasonings is bright and appealing; coleslaw appears in two possible guises, each a crunchy punctuation to a variety of meals; and raw carrots get a run for their money against a version where they are sautéed with a hint of honey and soy.

CHAPTER 16

Honey-Glazed Carrots

FORK IN THE ROAD: Lightly glazed and sweetened, or enhanced with some soy sauce and citrus zest.

When you need a little sweetness, when you need a little color on a plate, when you don't feel like turning on the oven (or the oven is full), when you don't have a lot in the fridge, but—hey!—there's that bag of carrots, here's a no-need-to-think side dish that will make everyone happy.

Leftovers can be pureed and heated to make them into a nice side dish later in the week. Or add some more chicken broth to the pureed carrots and you have a simple, smooth soup.

- 1 tablespoon canola or vegetable oil
- 2 pounds carrots, cut into 1-inch pieces
- 1 cup chicken or vegetable broth, preferably low-sodium; or water
- ⅓ cup honey (see sidebar)
- 2 tablespoons red wine vinegar
- Kosher or coarse salt and freshly ground black pepper, to taste
- 2 tablespoons unsalted butter

1. Heat the oil in a large skillet with a lid over medium-high heat. Add the carrots and cook, stirring occasionally until they just start to brown in spots, 3 minutes.

2. ◄ You can continue with Step 3 or see the Fork in the Road to amp up the glaze with soy sauce and orange zest.

3. Add the broth, honey, and vinegar, and season with salt and pepper. Bring the broth to a boil, cover, and lower the heat to medium-low. Simmer until the carrots are crisp-tender, 10 minutes. Uncover, increase the heat to medium-high, and continue to cook until the carrots are tender and the liquid is syrupy, about 7 minutes more. At the end, the

Yield

Serves 6 as a side dish

What the Kids Can Do

Peel the carrots, measure the ingredients, and zest the orange if using.

How to Get Honey Easily Off the Cup

Before you pour in the honey, give the measuring cup a quick spritz of nonstick cooking spray, and all of the honey will slide right out (and the measuring cup will be easier to clean, too). This works with all thick, sticky liquids, such as syrup or molasses. Use this tip when measuring out these ingredients with a spoon, as well.

carrots should be tender, well glazed, with barely any extra liquid. Stir in the butter until melted, check seasonings, and serve hot or warm.

Make Ahead

The carrots can be made up to the point where the butter is added; just take them off the heat right before they are fully tender and refrigerate them, covered, for up to 2 days. When ready to serve, add a couple of tablespoons of water, heat over medium-low heat until warmed through, and stir in the butter at the end.

FORK IN THE ROAD

Honey-Orange-Soy Glazed Carrots

For a more declarative carrot dish, add 1 tablespoon soy sauce with the broth and honey at the beginning of Step 3. (You will probably not need any additional salt; taste and see at the end.) After you uncover the pot and simmer down the liquid in Step 3, add 1 teaspoon finely grated orange zest along with the butter.

If you want to make half portions of each, divide the sautéed carrots between two pans at the beginning of Step 3. Add half of the remaining ingredients to one pan along with 1½ teaspoons soy sauce, and half to the other. Finish the cooking process, adding ½ teaspoon orange zest along with half of the butter to the first pan, the rest of the butter to the other pan.

Simple Honey-Glazed Carrots

Honey-Orange-Soy Glazed version

Cauliflower Puree

FORK IN THE ROAD: Smack in a beet or two and you'll end up with a crazy vivid pink vegetable side dish that will wake up a dinner plate pretty fast.

M any kids like cauliflower, and that's a good thing, because cauliflower is a powerhouse of a vegetable, nutritionally speaking. We are huge, huge cauliflower fans. We adore it roasted, but this dish, which is like a very close first cousin of mashed potatoes, makes us very happy.

And the Fork in the Road is a "whoa! what's that?" showstopper. If you have a small person in your house who happens to be fond of pink, this may be a nice way to slide a new pair of vegetables into the rotation.

> 1 large head cauliflower (about 2 pounds), trimmed and cut into florets
>
> 1½ cups vegetable or chicken broth, preferably low-sodium
>
> 3 tablespoons sour cream
>
> 1 tablespoon unsalted butter, at room temperature
>
> Kosher or coarse salt and freshly ground black pepper, to taste

1. ➤ Place the cauliflower and broth in a large pot, and maybe beets (see the Fork in the Road). Place over high heat, bring to a simmer, and reduce the heat to medium. Cover and simmer until the cauliflower is very tender and much of the liquid is evaporated, 15 to 20 minutes.

2. Transfer the cauliflower and whatever is left of the broth (there should be a few tablespoons) to a food processor or blender and puree until smooth. Add the sour cream, butter, and salt and pepper and puree just until blended. Serve hot or warm.

Yield

Serves 6 as a side dish

What the Kids Can Do

They can measure the ingredients, and maybe peel the beets. With supervision they can puree the mixture in the food processor or blender.

Cauliflower & Beet Puree

Like mashed potatoes, cauliflower is a blank canvas, one that takes well to all kinds of seasonings. Try this bright pink twist, which is even better for you because beets sport nice amounts of nutrients. Like many people, big and small, some folks in my house were beet-a-phobic, but this turned the beet around (sorry).

Trim, peel, and cut 2 beets into ½-inch chunks and add to the pot with the cauliflower, along with an additional ½ cup water. Simmer for 20 minutes, or until tender. (You can also use precooked or canned beets instead.) When you blend the vegetables, you can add 1 tablespoon jarred horseradish if desired, along with the sour cream.

And if you want to do the half-and-half thing, divide the cauliflower and broth into two small pots, and add 1 diced peeled beet to one of the pots. Proceed with the recipe, and when everything is tender, simply puree the two mixtures separately. Add 1½ teaspoons horseradish to the beet version, if desired.

Asian Slaw

Creamy Coleslaw

Creamy Coleslaw

FORK IN THE ROAD: The simple slaw can be turned into a bright, addicting, and vibrant Asian vegetable side.

This is the go-to slaw to serve alongside lightly seasoned grilled chicken or pork chops, a burger, or just about any protein when you want a side dish with crunch and presence. You can heap it on a sandwich, make a bed of it for kebabs, roll it up in a wrap, add it to tacos. And if you want a very simple, creamy, cooling slaw, just cut back on the chili powder and cumin.

Thinning the dressing with a bit of milk enables you to reduce the amounts of mayo and yogurt (or sour cream) in the mixture, and makes a less gloppy dressing that coats the vegetables more evenly.

And check out the Asian-inspired Fork in the Road for something very different. It's nice to offer up both versions at a barbecue or on a buffet; label them so people know there are two choices.

FOR THE SLAW

    1 large head green cabbage, quartered, cored, and thinly shredded
        (see Blades of Glory, page 282)
    4 large carrots, peeled and shredded
    1 large onion, finely chopped

FOR THE CREAMY DRESSING

    1 cup mayonnaise
    ⅔ cup plain Greek yogurt or sour cream
    3 tablespoons milk, preferably whole
    2 tablespoons white wine vinegar
    2 tablespoons Dijon mustard
    Kosher or coarse salt and freshly ground black pepper, to taste
    2 tablespoons chili powder
    2 tablespoons ground cumin
    ⅓ cup chopped fresh flat-leaf parsley

Yield

Serves 10 to 12 as a side dish

What the Kids Can Do

Peel the carrots, shred them and the cabbage if they can handle a hand grater (you can also use a food processor, and supervise them carefully), measure the dressing ingredients, add them to the container, shake, pour, and toss.

Make Ahead

You may make either dressing up to 2 days ahead and toss with the slaw mixture an hour or two before serving, to let the flavors and textures meld a bit. Or, if you like your slaw a bit less crunchy, the whole thing can be made a day ahead.

1. Make the slaw: Combine the cabbage, carrots, and onion in a large bowl.

2. ⬤━◀ You can continue with Step 3 (or see the Fork in the Road for an Asian dressing).

3. Make the creamy dressing: Combine the mayonnaise, yogurt, milk, vinegar, mustard, and salt and pepper in a container with a lid. Add the chili powder, cumin, and parsley to the container, cover, and shake well to combine.

4. Pour the dressing over the cabbage mixture and toss well. Taste and adjust seasonings as needed.

The Asian Version

Blades of Glory

I don't think there's a small kitchen appliance I love more than my food processor. If I had to name the times I love it the most, it would be when mincing onions, shredding large amounts of cheese, or potatoes for potato pancakes, and making slaw. The shredding blade is just a lifesaver, so if you have a food processor, don't forget that it came with more than one insert, and put all of those extra disks to good use. Just core the head of cabbage, cut it into small wedges, and shove them down the feed tube.

Asian Dressing

COLESLAW MIXED WITH THIS dressing is bright and refreshing, and oh-so-healthy. It makes a fantastic, easy side dish to any Asian-inspired meal. Finish the slaw with a sprinkling of ½ cup chopped fresh mint leaves if you like. Or add small cooked shrimp or cubes of grilled chicken to the slaw for a lovely, light warm-weather lunch or dinner. The dressing makes enough for the full slaw recipe.

¼ cup rice vinegar

2 tablespoons fresh lime juice

2 tablespoons fish sauce

2 tablespoons soy sauce, preferably reduced-sodium

2 tablespoons minced fresh ginger

1 tablespoon Asian (toasted) sesame oil

2 teaspoons sugar

1 teaspoon sriracha or other hot sauce, or to taste

Combine the vinegar, lime juice, fish sauce, soy sauce, sesame oil, ginger, sugar, and sriracha in a container with a lid. Cover and shake well. Pour over the cabbage as in Step 4 (page 282) and toss.

If you'd like to make half creamy coleslaw and half Asian-inspired, halve the ingredient amounts for the creamy dressing and the Asian dressing, then divide the slaw mixture into two bowls. Dress one with the creamy dressing and the other with the Asian dressing.

Serve the Asian Slaw with the Mustard and Maple-Glazed Pork Loin (page 107), Japanese Salmon Burgers (page 163), or the Spicy Asian Spareribs (page 115).

Korean Spinach

FORK IN THE ROAD: You can remove some of the spinach and keep it just delicately flavored with gently cooked garlic.

I f you've ever been to a Korean restaurant you might agree that the very best part of the meal is the *banchan,* which is the appealing name for the assortment of little plates that usually show up at the beginning of a meal. The word actually means "side dish," though they never really make it to the main meal in my experience. The last time I went with Charlie, we polished them off so quickly the lovely waiter wordlessly brought us a second round, clearly recognizing *banchan* strumpets when he saw them.

Typical *banchan* offerings are kimchi (Korean pickled cabbage), mung bean sprouts with sesame oil, a kind of seasoned fish jerky (so much more delicious than it sounds), and often an amazing cold sesame spinach dish. Since cold cooked spinach is not what speaks to the people in my house as loudly as it speaks to me, I wanted to take the habit-forming flavors of this little appetizer and affix them to simply sautéed spinach.

If you've never cooked fresh spinach before, you will think this is a very large amount of greens. And then you will cook it and think, "Where did it all go?" Spinach contains a lot of water, so when it cooks, it really shrinks down.

Yield

Serves 6 as a side dish

What the Kids Can Do

Measure and mix together the ingredients for the soy-sesame sauce.

Make Ahead

This is best made right before serving, though it's also nice at room temperature.

I could make
a full meal of this spinach,
with a little rice.

2 tablespoons canola or olive oil

3 large cloves garlic, thinly sliced

1 tablespoon Asian (toasted) sesame oil

2 teaspoons soy sauce

1 teaspoon rice vinegar

1 teaspoon fresh lemon juice

½ teaspoon sugar

2 pounds fresh baby spinach, washed and not totally dried

Kosher or coarse salt and freshly ground black pepper, to taste

1 tablespoon toasted sesame seeds (see Note), for serving (optional)

Note: To toast sesame seeds, heat a medium-size skillet, preferably nonstick, over medium heat. Add the sesame seeds and toast, stirring and tossing frequently, until they are golden brown and fragrant, about 2 minutes; watch carefully so they don't burn. Transfer the toasted seeds to a small plate.

1. Heat the oil in a large skillet over medium-low heat. Add the garlic and sauté gently until the garlic is soft and very lightly golden, but not browned (turn the heat down if it starts to brown too quickly), about 8 minutes.

2. ━━◀ You can continue with Step 3 or see the Fork in the Road for a simpler spinach dish.

3. Meanwhile, mix together the sesame oil, soy sauce, rice vinegar, lemon juice, and sugar in a small bowl or container.

4. Increase the heat to medium-high and add the barely damp spinach to the skillet, in batches if necessary, and stir until it wilts (tongs are helpful for this), seasoning lightly with salt and pepper, 3 to 4 minutes.

5. Add the sesame oil mixture and toss until the spinach is well coated and nicely glazed. Check for seasonings and serve hot, sprinkled with toasted sesame seeds if desired.

VARIATION:

Try this with thinly sliced kale, Swiss chard, or collard greens. Sauté them until quite well wilted, 8 to 10 minutes.

Simple Sautéed Spinach

Not interested in an Asian-flavored side dish? Don't make the soy-sesame mixture in Step 3 and skip the toasted sesame seeds at the end. Simply serve the spinach hot after Step 4 (you may want to give it a bit more salt and pepper). If you wanted to dust the finished garlic spinach with grated Parmesan, or sprinkle over some shaved ricotta salata, you could also do that, giving it an Italian bent.

To make both Korean Spinach and Simple Sautéed Spinach, just remove some spinach just as it's cooked at the end of Step 1 and season it with salt and pepper. Add the soy-sesame mixture, adjusting the amount to taste, to the spinach remaining in the skillet, and add sesame seeds to that version, if desired.

Serve with the Chicken in Orange Sauce (page 135), Stir-Fried Shrimp and Scallions (page 145), Thai Chicken Stir-Fry (page 176), and Korean Sesame Tofu and Mushrooms (page 263). Leftovers are excellent in Asian Rice Bowl, Many Ways (page 189).

Warm Brussels Sprouts with Bacon and Mustard Vinaigrette

FORK IN THE ROAD: Skip the mustard vinaigrette altogether for a very simple pan-roasted and braised brussels sprouts dish. (Or skip the bacon for a vegetarian side.)

As parents, we often fall into the trap of assuming our kids won't like something, and therefore we either don't serve it (not a good solution) or state aloud, "I don't think you're going to like this, but . . ." (also not a good solution). Brussels sprouts are high on the list of foods that many of us think will not be met with good cheer at the dining table. Often this is because when we were kids we were served an unappetizing version, probably overcooked and possibly underseasoned, and that's the way brussels sprouts have been cemented into our memories. Poor little brussels sprouts, so unfairly maligned. It's like if you went to a job interview with a terrible cold, and were not your best self, and that was the impression that you left on your prospective boss, and no matter what you said or did, that was how he was going to think of you forevermore. So very sad.

Those of us who love brussels sprouts will find these irresistible, and for those who are still on or nowhere near the fence, this recipe could make them converts. The bacon certainly doesn't hurt. I've used turkey bacon in this dish, and found it quite satisfactory. Once my son Jack and I ate the entire batch for lunch. And then the next time I made them, he forgot he liked them. Hashtag sigh.

Yield

Serves 8 as a side dish

What the Kids Can Do

Trim and halve the brussels sprouts with an age-appropriate knife, crumble the bacon, whisk together the vinaigrette, and dress the brussels sprouts.

Make Ahead

You can cook the brussels sprouts up to 2 days ahead of time (remove them from the heat just before they are tender). Reheat them on the stove just before serving and dress them while they are still warm or hot. Reheated leftovers (over low heat on the stovetop or in the microwave) are pretty delicious, too.

4 strips bacon

4 tablespoons olive oil

½ cup minced onion

2 pounds brussels sprouts, trimmed and halved

⅔ cup chicken or vegetable broth, preferably low-sodium

4 teaspoons white wine vinegar

1 tablespoon mustard

Kosher salt and freshly ground black pepper, to taste

Vegetarian Note:
If you're looking for a vegetarian side dish, you can use vegetable broth and leave out the bacon.

1. Cook the bacon in a large skillet over medium-high heat until crispy, about 4 minutes per side. (Or see How to Bake Your Bacon, on the facing page.) Drain on paper towels.

2. Discard the fat in the skillet. Add 1 tablespoon of the olive oil to the skillet and heat over medium-high heat. Add the onion and brussels sprouts and cook, stirring only occasionally, until the onion is tender and turning golden and the brussels sprouts begin to brown in spots, about 8 minutes.

3. Add the broth and cover the pan. Let the liquid come to a simmer, then reduce the heat to medium. Steam the brussels sprouts until you can easily slide a sharp knife into them and the broth is almost evaporated, 7 to 10 minutes more.

4. ━━◄ You can continue with Step 5 or see the Fork in the Road for mustard-free sprouts.

5. To make the vinaigrette, whisk together the remaining 3 tablespoons olive oil, the vinegar, and mustard in a small bowl and season with salt and pepper.

6. Pour the vinaigrette over the cooked brussels sprouts in the pan and toss to coat with the vinaigrette. Crumble the bacon, add it to the vegetables, and toss one more time before transferring to a serving dish. Serve hot or warm.

FORK IN THE ROAD

Braised Brussels Sprouts

Skip the vinaigrette in Step 5 and serve the very simply braised brussels sprouts as they are, with a sprinkle of salt and pepper, maybe a little of the crumbled bacon on top.

Or serve some plain, and then continue dressing the rest of the brussels sprouts with the vinaigrette, using as much dressing as you like.

How to Bake Your Bacon

Preheat the oven to 350°F. Set a wire rack in a rimmed baking sheet. Lay your strips of uncooked bacon in straight rows, just touching, not overlapping, on the rack. Bake until the bacon is as crispy as you like it, 15 to 20 minutes. Drain on paper towels.

Dear Carbs,
You are the Greatest.
Love, Everyone

LEMON-HORSERADISH POTATO SALAD, *page 307*

So, you've got a main course, you've picked a vegetable or made a salad, now how to round out the meal? And since we're always honest with each other, let's admit that it's the starch on the plate that many kids (and grown-ups) reach for first. I love that joke, "I went on a low-carb diet once . . . it was the hardest 15 minutes of my life."

Good Old Carbs

My family thinks cornbread belongs on the docket with almost anything, and you also have the option of elevating it by adding cheddar cheese, scallions, and maybe some jalapeño. A dense, creamy noodle kugel with its crisply browned top makes itself welcome at a brunch, for a dinner, as a snack, possibly even eaten cold while standing in front of the open fridge in an oversize T-shirt in the middle of the night.

Over to the potatoes. A great room-temperature standby is potato salad, here either classic and creamy, or snappy with a lemon-horseradish dressing. Sweet potato fries, plain or a scallion-ginger version, might edge into center stage. And when you need a potato dish that is both indulgent and sophisticated (but still very kid-pleasing), that's the moment to assemble a timeless potato gratin.

Scallion and Ginger Sweet Potato Fries

FORK IN THE ROAD: Plain or seasoned with scallions and ginger . . . and all made right in the oven.

One of the best reasons to have children is that the amount of French fries in your life goes up incrementally. You thought I was going to say something more touching, didn't you? I do have deeper thoughts on the matter, but I will say that I have actively enjoyed the fact that many more restaurant meals have ended up with fries on the table, without my having to actually order them, than before I became a parent. I suppose that's one of those things you should think and not say, but I am not always good at that "filtering" thing.

I have made "authentic" fries with my kids, double frying them in oil like they do in restaurants, and boy were they good. But that's just not going to happen on a regular basis, mostly because of the messiness than because of health awareness. But these fries we can embrace on all fronts—oven-baked (healthier and no mess) and delicious.

Nice to know that sweet potatoes have noteworthy amounts of vitamins B_6, C, and E and loads of beta-carotene, fiber, and a slew of other minerals.

4 scallions, trimmed, white and green parts cut into chunks

1 clove garlic, peeled

1 chunk (1 inch) peeled fresh ginger, sliced

Generous pinch of red pepper flakes or cayenne pepper

2 tablespoons vegetable or canola oil

Kosher or coarse salt and freshly ground black pepper, to taste

4 sweet potatoes (about 2½ pounds), peeled and cut into sticks about ¼ inch wide in each direction (see Note)

Yield

Serves 6

What the Kids Can Do

Add the ingredients to the food processor, and blend with supervision. Toss the fries with the seasonings.

Make Ahead

You can cut the potatoes into sticks a day ahead of time, but bake just before serving. Not that leftovers reheated in a 400°F oven aren't great, because they are. Store the uncooked potato sticks in a sealed container.

Tossed with a knock-out combination of scallions, ginger, and red pepper flakes

Simple and delicious sweet potato fries

1. Place a rack in the center of the oven and another on the next level down. Preheat the oven to 400°F.

2. You can continue with Step 3 or see the Fork in the Road for a seasoning-free version.

3. Combine the scallions, garlic, ginger, red pepper flakes, oil, and salt and pepper in a food processor or blender and process to form a paste. You can also mince all the ingredients with a knife and combine them in a small bowl, or use a mortar and pestle (see Sidebar).

4. Place the sweet potatoes on two separate rimmed baking sheets, add half the paste to each, and toss. Make sure all the fries have space between them (this is why you need two baking sheets). If your oven is large enough, place the baking sheets side by side on the center rack. If it isn't, place one baking sheet on the center rack and one on the rack below it. Bake until the potatoes are nicely browned and very tender, 10 to 12 minutes. They won't get super crispy; sweet potato fries have a hard time doing that. Serve hot.

FORK IN THE ROAD

Plain Sweet Potato Fries

Plain sweet potato fries are nothing to shrug at. Forgo the paste in Step 3 and just toss the fries with 2 tablespoons vegetable or canola oil and salt and pepper to taste. Or use half of the paste ingredients to season one sheet of fries and add 1 tablespoon oil and salt to the potatoes on the other sheet.

Mortar and Pestle

Do you have one of these primitive yet effective little tools? The mortar is a heavy bowl, usually made of stone or ceramic, sometimes wood. The pestle is a heavy club-shaped object, the bulbous end of which is used to crush and grind ingredients against the inside of the bowl.

The most common use I can think of for a mortar and pestle is to make authentic pesto (see page 350) with a great texture, but any spice or herb paste comes together quickly and beautifully with one of these. Kids have a good time grinding up everything, too.

Note: When cutting up the sweet potatoes, do not worry about perfect sticks. You are not entering a French fry–making contest. The easiest way to get nice long fries, however, is to peel the potatoes, cut them lengthwise into ¼-inch-thick slabs, then stack up a few of those at a time and cut them into long ¼-inch-wide sticks.

Potato Gratin

FORK IN THE ROAD: When a classic potato gratin isn't quite enough, try the mother of all potato gratins, layered with blue cheese and sautéed leeks. Seriously.

This is a rich and decadent dish. If you do not wish to serve a rich and decadent dish, please turn the page. My personal feeling is that a potato gratin should not be pared down in an attempt to be healthful; it should be eaten with relish on occasion, and served with lighter fare, such as grilled fish, chicken, and plain vegetables.

The rubbing-the-garlic-clove-around-the-pan thing is almost silly, but I first learned it from Patricia Wells, one of the most respected experts on French food in the world. If you're short on time or garlic cloves, skip it, but it makes me feel Parisian for some reason.

In closing, let me say that I will probably write about food for the rest of my life, but I will probably never be able to write the word *Gruyère* without having to spell-check it.

1 clove garlic, peeled and crushed

2½ to 3 pounds baking or russet potatoes, peeled and sliced crosswise as thinly as you can manage (see The Skinny on Mandolines, page 298)

2 cups half-and-half, or a mixture of whole milk and heavy (whipping) cream (see Note)

1½ cups shredded Gruyère cheese

Kosher or coarse salt and freshly ground black pepper, to taste

1. Preheat the oven to 350°F. Rub a 9 by 13-inch pan, or any shape 2- to 3-quart baking dish, with the garlic clove.

2. Layer half the potato slices evenly in the pan.

3. ◾━◄ You can continue with Step 4 or see the Fork in the Road if you'd like to make a blue cheese/leek version.

Yield

Serves 10

What the Kids Can Do

Grate the cheese, if they can handle the grater. Rub the pan with garlic. Layer the potatoes, half-and-half, and cheeses. Stay away from the mandoline.

Make Ahead

This can be made and baked a day ahead, then reheated, uncovered, in a 350°F oven for 20 minutes. Microwaved squares of gratin are also a great treat the next day.

Note: As with many dairy-based dishes, the percentage of fat you use depends on how indulgent you're feeling. A lot of heavy cream will give the richest flavor and texture, mostly milk will be lighter. You can play with the balance as your palate and your conscience dictate.

4. Pour over half of the half-and-half (tee hee), and sprinkle over half of the cheese. Season with salt and pepper. Repeat the layers ending with cheese.

5. Bake the gratin, uncovered, until the top is golden brown (cover the pan with aluminum foil if the top starts to brown too early) and a knife inserted into the middle glides easily through the potato layers, about 1 hour and 15 minutes.

6. Let the gratin sit on a wire rack for about 10 minutes until it sets up a bit and the cream has a chance to be absorbed by the potatoes.

VEGETARIAN

FORK IN THE ROAD

Blue Cheese & Leek Potato Gratin

This gratin version has enough presence to be a vegetarian main course all its own, with a big tossed salad (bracing lettuces like arugula or watercress or frisée or endive would be great, and a dressing tart with vinegar or lemon juice . . . yes, I know not everyone is into bitter lettuces; I'm just saying). Or, if it's a big-deal occasion and you listen very closely, you can probably hear this gratin saying, "Serve me with a big juicy steak." Plus a salad with vinaigrette.

Thinly slice and clean the white and light green parts of 3 leeks. Melt 1 tablespoon butter in a skillet over medium heat. Add the leeks and sauté until tender, 6 to 8 minutes. After you make a layer of potato slices in Step 2, then top the potatoes with the leeks. Sprinkle over ½ cup crumbled blue cheese instead of Gruyère, then half of the half-and-half. Make another layer of potatoes, leeks, blue cheese, and half-and-half. Bake as instructed above. (I use less blue cheese than the Gruyère—1 cup rather than 1½ cups—because the blue cheese flavor is stronger.)

You can make half the pan with Gruyère and half with blue cheese and leeks; use only ¾ cup Gruyère on one side, and half the amount of leeks and blue cheese on the other. Know that the people who get the slices in the middle of the pan may be in for a bit of a gratin potluck, which is kind of fun. You could also use two 8-inch-square pans.

The Skinny on Mandolines

You should be able to read the paper through that potato slice!

Okay, that's asking a lot, but you do want to take the time to make the slices of potato as thin as possible. This can certainly be achieved with a cutting board and a sturdy knife, but if you're going to make a habit of thinly slicing things, you may want to invest in a mandoline, an apparatus that allows you to slide produce and other foods across a blade and get even, super delicate slices (or thicker slices; the blade is adjustable).

Conversations about mandolines usually go something like this: There are excellent pricey ones (a varied bunch of them, with some fancy attachments), but chefs and avid home cooks alike praise the Benriner as a very efficient and effective cheap mandoline, also with an adjustable knob. Start with that, and if you get addicted to thinly slicing things, and feel like you want more, treat yourself to a fancy one.

And it just needs to be said: Be careful, pay attention, and never look away when you are slicing.

This noodle kugel comes loaded with memories.

Noodle Kugel

FORK IN THE ROAD: This makes a delicately sweet and fragrant kugel that serves as a great side for a hearty meal, but you can bump up the sweetness and flavorings for a more dessertlike casserole.

I have such nostalgia for noodle kugel. First, because my father's mother used to make it. This is particularly notable because she wasn't much of a cook. In fact, I can't think of anything else she made other than that ubiquitous Jell-O mold filled with jarring chunks of canned fruit that was so perplexingly popular for so long. I remember being served a big quivering slab of the Jell-O, and using a spoon to scrape around the unpleasantly hard indistinguishable fruit cubes to salvage whatever amount of the otherwise perfectly good Jell-O I could.

But her kugel was really quite good. My grandfather would hold up his pinky and ask us, "Can you guess what's in here that makes it special?" "Orange," we'd sigh. We had been down this road before. "Orange!" he'd say triumphantly, finger poking into the air. He never seemed to notice our lack of proper admiration for this smart addition to a plain old kugel. Now I get it.

However, there is a coda to this story of nostalgia and food. When I made it for my mother, after finally feeling like I nailed it, she said to me: "You know your grandmother never made that kugel. Her housekeeper did." Apparently I have nostalgia for my Nana's housekeeper's kugel. I think I'm okay with that. (For more kugel memories, see Proust Had It Right, page 303.)

Yield

Serves 10

Make Ahead

The kugel can be baked up to 2 days before serving; reheat in a 300°F oven for 15 minutes or so. You can also make the kugel and refrigerate it unbaked for up to a day, and then bake it right before serving.

8 tablespoons (1 stick) unsalted butter, cut into pieces, plus extra for buttering the pan

1 cup raisins

Grated zest and strained juice of 1 orange

1 package (12 ounces) wide egg noodles

6 large eggs

2 cups cottage cheese, preferably full-fat (see Note)

2 cups sour cream (see Note)

2 cups whole milk

½ cup sugar

1 teaspoon ground cinnamon

1 teaspoon pure vanilla extract

½ teaspoon kosher or coarse salt

1. Preheat the oven to 350°F. Butter a 9 by 13-inch baking pan.

2. Combine the raisins and the orange juice and set aside to soak. Cook the noodles according to the package directions.

3. Whisk together the orange zest, eggs, cottage cheese, sour cream, milk, sugar, cinnamon, vanilla, and salt in a medium-size bowl. Add the plumped raisins and up to 1 tablespoon of any remaining juice.

4. ━━◄ You can continue with Step 5 or see the Fork in the Road for a more dessertlike version.

5. Drain the noodles and return them to the pot. Add the butter in pieces and toss until melted. Add the cottage cheese mixture and stir gently until well combined. Transfer the noodles to the prepared pan.

6. Bake the kugel until a bit bubbly around the edges, well set, and pretty well browned, 1 hour and 15 minutes. Broil it for 1 or 2 minutes if you like a really crunchy top.

7. Transfer the kugel to a wire rack and let cool for at least 15 minutes before serving.

What the Kids Can Do

Measure the ingredients, zest and juice the orange, crack the eggs, stir together the cottage cheese mixture, stir into the noodles.

Note: **Can you use reduced-fat sour cream here in place of regular? Can you use low-fat cottage cheese? Sure you can. I rarely do—I try to be an eat-the-good-stuff-in-reasonable-amounts person, most of the time—but it's all up to you.**

FORK IN THE ROAD If you want to make this sweeter and more dessertlike, whisk in an additional 2 tablespoons sugar, 1 teaspoon ground cinnamon, 1 teaspoon orange zest, and 1 teaspoon vanilla. Or divide the creamy mixture into two bowls, add half of the aforementioned additional amounts, and divide the buttered noodles between the two bowls. Bake in two buttered 8-inch-square pans for 50 to 60 minutes, finishing under the broiler if desired.

Proust Had It Right

I'm not prone to wallowing in the past, but I do know that so many of my best memories have food attached to them. The roasted vegetable tart I made for my mom's sixtieth birthday in France, which I shopped for using my horrible French. The fondue I made recently in a hotel room for friends, using the fondue pot Jean and David had just given me for the holidays (with the qualifier that "this was really a present for us"). The time we lost power and fled to the house of Jennifer and Charlie carting the entire contents of our fridge and freezer—I asked them to buy a bag of rice and when I got there I made two huge paellas, which we ate with other blackout refugees. And then some less happy, but still super-potent memories. The cascade of dishes I (and others) cooked for my father when he was sick and losing his appetite, trying to find something to tempt him. The food others cooked for me and my family after Dad died.

I also have a very soft spot for noodle kugel because after the planes hit the buildings in New York City on 9/11, after I raced home from hearing the news at work to be with 1½-year-old Jack, with Gary stuck out of town, I (like every other New Yorker, and citizen of the world) absolutely didn't know what to do with myself. I found myself in the kitchen with baby Jack, him sitting on the counter carefully guarded from the edge by my body, while I numbly made a noodle kugel, because those were the ingredients I had at hand. I stirred and dumped, and Jack grabbed raisins with his fat little hand and threw them into the noodle mixture. It was the first thing we ever cooked together, and it seemed like the only thing that felt comforting and even close to the right thing to be doing during such an out-of-body moment in time.

The version in this book took several—many—tries but it tastes like my memory of Nana's kugel, and those rare moments when you can capture a meaningful memory with food are pretty great. Just ask Proust.

Jacked up
with cheddar,
jalapeños, and
scallions.

A lovely plain
cornbread.

Cornbread

FORK IN THE ROAD: A simple, lightly sweetened cornbread is a joy. A jalapeño and cheddar–spiked cornbread is a joy with a little kick.

Homemade cornbread mixes up and bakes so quickly; it's really an immediate-gratification quick bread. And how much do we parents love immediate gratification? You do not need any special equipment for this; you can bake it in any ovenproof skillet, or an 8-inch baking pan, square or round. But, if you need one single reason to buy a cast-iron pan, or to take the one you have out of retirement, this would be it. What a beautiful crust you'll get; you'll see.

This cornbread is slightly sweet, making it a perfect accompaniment to pretty much anything you can think of. If you want to make almost any meal feel fully pulled together, make a pan of cornbread to go with it. Chili (page 247) and cornbread. Fried chicken (page 244) and cornbread. Soup (pages 88 to 99) and cornbread. You know you'd be thrilled if someone plunked down a piece of cornbread next to whatever you were eating.

4 tablespoons (½ stick) unsalted butter

1¼ cups cornmeal

¾ cup all-purpose flour

2 teaspoons baking powder

1 teaspoon kosher or coarse salt

2 tablespoons sugar

1 large egg

1¼ cups milk, buttermilk (see Note), or plain yogurt

1. Preheat the oven to 375°F.

2. Put the butter in a medium-size ovenproof skillet (preferably cast-iron) or an 8-inch-square or round baking pan and place it in the oven to heat until the pan is hot and the butter is melted, about 4 minutes.

Yield

Serves 8

What the Kids Can Do

Measure all of the ingredients and blend the batter. Pour it into the hot pan, with supervision.

Make Ahead

The cornbread can be made ahead and kept, well wrapped, at room temperature for up to 2 days.

3. Meanwhile, combine the cornmeal, flour, baking powder, salt, and sugar in a large bowl. In a smaller bowl, mix the egg and milk together. Pour the melted butter from the pan into the egg and milk mixture and whisk to combine (but don't wipe out the excess melted butter in the pan).

4. ⟍⟍⟍ You can continue with Step 5 or see the Fork in the Road to kick it up with cheddar and jalapeño.

5. Stir the milk mixture into the dry ingredients, stirring just until they are barely combined. Scrape the batter into the pan that you used to melt the butter, and spread it evenly.

6. Bake the cornbread until the top is lightly browned and a toothpick inserted into the center comes out clean, about 25 minutes. Place the skillet on a wire rack to cool for at least 10 minutes. Serve the cornbread hot or warm.

Note: Don't have buttermilk, but like the slightly tart flavor? You can easily make a perfect substitute. Just take 1¼ cups milk at room temperature (if you need to microwave it for a little bit to get it to room temp, that's fine), and blend in 1 tablespoon white vinegar or fresh lemon juice. Let it sit for 10 minutes or so.

Never mind that you spent 4 hours making Carnitas (page 220), the cornbread is what they'll remember.

FORK IN THE ROAD

Cheddar-Jalapeño Cornbread

This is decadent and a bit spicy and truly the kind of thing that people will talk about after eating at your house. Skip the jalapeño if you want cheesy but not so spicy.

When combining the wet and dry ingredients in Step 5, mix in ⅔ cup grated extra-sharp cheddar cheese, ¼ cup chopped scallions (both the white and green parts), and 1 teaspoon seeded and finely minced jalapeño pepper. Then, right before the cornbread goes into the oven, sprinkle another ¼ cup grated cheddar on top, if you like.

If you want to make some cornbread plain and some cheddar-jalapeño, it's best to double the basic recipe ingredients. Melt 4 tablespoons unsalted butter in each of two ovenproof skillets; but then you add both skillets of melted butter to the egg/milk mixture. After pouring half of the batter into one of the skillets or pans, quickly blend the additional cheddar-jalapeño ingredients into the remaining batter and pour into the second pan.

Lemon-Horseradish Potato Salad

FORK IN THE ROAD: Skip the horseradish dressing and go for the classic, creamy summertime side dish.

Whenever I say, "Wow, this is good!" or something of that nature about something I've cooked, Jack is quick to point out that it's not really my place to say. His comments range from, "Wow, that's humble," to "You should really wait for someone else to make this statement."

It's a valid point, and no one should walk around on a regular basis complimenting their own work, but by the same token, if I don't like what I cook, then why should I expect anyone else to? I would also like my dentist to feel good about his professional skills, you know what I mean?

I really like both versions of potato salad offered here, and after Jack is done making sure my sense of self-worth has been corralled (thank goodness for teenagers, otherwise we parents would walk around with sadly overinflated egos: dancing freely at weddings, singing along with the radio with unbridled gusto, talking about pop culture in public places), he will also tell me that he really likes them both, too.

I'd like to put in a good word about the Lemon-Horseradish Dressing. It has so much flavor you will be licking your fingers or the spoon or whatever else touches the dressing. But remember this dressing even when you're not thinking of potato salad: drizzled over green salads, as a dunk for radishes or crudité, and wow, was it good when I served a dollop alongside seared scallops.

Yield

Serves 6 to 8

What the Kids Can Do

Scrub the potatoes (there's something quite satisfying about watching your children engage in manual labor of this sort), juice the lemon, measure and combine the dressing ingredients, toss the warm potatoes with the dressing.

2½ pounds red or white new potatoes, scrubbed and cut into quarters

Kosher or coarse salt, to taste

½ cup sour cream, regular or low-fat, or plain Greek or regular yogurt, or a combination

2 tablespoons bottled horseradish

2 tablespoons Dijon mustard

1 tablespoon fresh lemon juice

⅓ cup finely minced onion

Freshly ground black pepper, to taste

1. Place the potatoes in a large saucepan with a lid and add cold water to cover and a generous seasoning of salt. Cover, place over high heat, and bring to a simmer. Reduce the heat to medium to maintain the simmer and cook, uncovered, until the potatoes are tender and a sharp knife slides easily in, about 15 minutes.

2. While the potatoes are cooking, make the dressing: Mix together the sour cream, horseradish, mustard, lemon juice, and onion in a medium-size bowl. Season generously with salt and pepper. ●━━◀ Or see the Fork in the Road for a classic creamy dressing.

3. Drain the potato quarters well and let them sit until they are cool enough to handle. Cut them into ½-inch dice. While they are still slightly warm, toss them in a large serving bowl with the dressing. Serve at room temperature.

Make Ahead

Most creamy potato salads are best served the day they are made, and if you can avoid refrigerating them at all, the texture will be amazing. This is not to say that leftover potato salad can't be refrigerated, covered, for a few days—it certainly can. Bring to room temperature before serving.

Classic Potato Salad

LOOKING FOR A MORE basic potato salad? Here it is. You could halve both dressings and mix half of the potatoes with each version if you want to try both.

CLASSIC DRESSING

⅓ cup mayonnaise, regular or low fat

¼ cup sour cream, or regular or low-fat yogurt

¼ cup buttermilk

1 tablespoon mustard, any kind

1 tablespoon sweet relish

½ teaspoon sugar

¾ cup minced celery

½ cup finely minced red onion

2½ pounds red or white new potatoes, prepared as per facing page

Mix together the mayo, sour cream, buttermilk, mustard, relish, sugar, minced celery, and onion in a medium-size bowl. Toss with the slightly cooled potatoes in a large serving bowl. Serve at room temperature.

Look how happy this potato salad makes me.

CHOCOLATE CHUNK AND CRYSTALLIZED GINGER
OATMEAL COOKIES, *page 323*

and

HONEY-ROASTED PEANUT COOKIES, *page 315*

Cookie Monster may have said it best: "Today me will live in the moment unless it's unpleasant in which case me will have a cookie."

I wish Cookie Monster would come over for cookies. I would love to show off for him with a batch of Big Chewy Brownie Cookies, maybe even with some peanut butter or chocolate filling layered in. But I might also make One-Pot, No-Bake Oatmeal Peanut Butter Cookies if I didn't feel like turning the oven on, or maybe he'd like the bar cookie of the year in my house, One-Pot Raspberry Oatmeal Bars. And if raspberry wasn't his thing, they could be blueberry- or strawberry- or apricot-filled—the recipe is open to interpretation.

CHAPTER 18

Cookies

The new homey-but-elegant cookie that has been on the top of my list lately is the one that combines oatmeal, chocolate chunks, and crystallized ginger. Sure you can skip the ginger in some, if your cookie monster is more of a purist. It's all good. That's what the Fork in the Road is all about. Crystallized ginger for you, plain and simple for traditionalists. But most important, cookies for everyone.

One-Pot, No-Bake Oatmeal Peanut Butter Cookies

FORK IN THE ROAD: *A handful of chopped dried fruit adds even more interest to these chunky cookies.*

There are moments in life when turning on the oven is just plain unthinkable, whether it's because of relentless heat, lack of baking energy, time constraints—or maybe the oven is already on, but it's occupied by a large turkey or something of that nature. These are the cookies for those moments. They are sweet and nicely crumbly and surprisingly rich.

- 8 tablespoons (1 stick) unsalted butter
- ½ cup milk
- 1¾ cups sugar
- ¼ cup unsweetened cocoa powder
- ½ teaspoon kosher or coarse salt
- 1 teaspoon pure vanilla extract
- ⅔ cup peanut butter, preferably crunchy
- 3 cups old-fashioned or quick oats

1. Line 1 or 2 rimmed baking sheets with parchment or wax paper.

2. Melt the butter in a medium-size pot over medium heat. Add the milk, sugar, cocoa powder, and salt and bring the mixture to a simmer. Stir in the vanilla, then stir in the peanut butter. Continue cooking and stirring until everything is just melted and smooth (bits of crunchy peanut notwithstanding), 2 to 3 minutes. Stir in the oats.

Yield

Makes about 24 cookies

What the Kids Can Do

Measure, stir (with supervision, paying attention to a hot pot), and form the cookies.

It's kind of funny that these no-bake cookies are sitting on a cookie sheet. . . .

3. ⚓ You can continue with Step 4 or see the Fork in the Road for the dried fruit option.

4. Drop the dough by heaping tablespoons onto the baking sheets and use your fingers to form the cookies into nice flat, round shapes (not necessary, but this does make them look pretty); they can be very close to each other since they will hold their shape. Let them sit until completely cooled and set, about 20 minutes.

FORK IN THE ROAD

One-Pot, No-Bake Oatmeal Peanut Butter & Fruit Cookies

Add 1 cup chopped dried fruit to the batter after you add the peanut butter in Step 2. Or divide the mixture in half, and add ½ cup chopped dried fruit to half of the mixture. Try chopped dried apricots, dates, and prunes, or whole raisins, dried blueberries, or dried cranberries.

These are the cookies to make when your kid tells you he needs to bring cookies to a bake sale during a heat wave.

Honey-Roasted Peanut Cookies

FORK IN THE ROAD: You can also try a salty-sweet peanut butter cookie, using salted peanuts instead of honey-roasted.

M any schools are nut free, and with valid reason, so sometimes I realize that a baked good I grew up with hasn't been introduced to my kids (who, knock wood, are allergy free). An example is peanut cookies, and that's surprising because all the members of my family are peanut freaks. (You don't want to get between us and a 5-pound bag of peanuts in the shell. Sometimes the floor in front of the TV is littered with so many shells, it looks like some sort of saloon. I actually had to go to the hospital once because I cracked open a peanut so enthusiastically, I got part of the shell in my eye. I don't know why I feel compelled to share all of this.)

1¼ cups all-purpose flour

1 teaspoon baking soda

½ teaspoon salt

8 tablespoons (1 stick) unsalted butter, at room temperature

½ cup creamy peanut butter

½ cup packed dark or light brown sugar

½ cup granulated sugar

1 large egg

1 teaspoon pure vanilla extract

1 cup crushed honey-roasted peanuts (see Cooking Tip, page 317), or see the Fork in the Road for a salty alternative

1. Preheat the oven to 325°F.

2. Combine the flour, baking soda, and salt in a small bowl.

Yield

Makes about 18 cookies

What the Kids Can Do

Measure the ingredients; crack the egg; dump, stir, and blend the batter; form and crosshatch the cookies.

Make Ahead

These cookies can be kept in a sealed container at room temperature for up to 7 days. Balls of the uncooked dough or the baked cookies can be frozen for up to 4 months. You can also refrigerate the dough (wrapped in plastic wrap) for up to 4 days before baking.

3. Beat the butter, peanut butter, brown sugar, and granulated sugar until creamy in a medium-size bowl using an electric mixer. Beat in the egg, then the vanilla. Add the flour mixture and beat just until blended. Mix in the crushed peanuts.

4. Form the dough into about 18 (1½-inch) balls and divide them between two baking sheets. Use a fork to press down on the cookies, creating a crosshatch pattern as you flatten them to about ½-inch thick.

5. Bake the cookies until very lightly browned, 12 to 14 minutes—they will still be soft to the touch but will firm up as they cool. Let them cool for 1 minute on the baking sheets and then transfer them to a wire rack to cool completely.

Time to bake another batch.

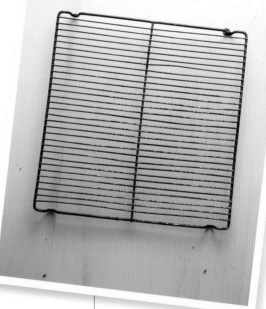

Cooking Tip

For 1 cup of crushed peanuts, place 1½ cups of whole and half peanuts in a sturdy zipper-top bag and gently whack with a rolling pin or a wine bottle or something of that nature. Don't crush them into a powder; you want some texture.

FORK IN THE ROAD

Salted Peanut Cookies

Salty-sweet is all the rage—many of us can't get enough of the fabulous and titillating contrast between sweet and saline. So, instead of using honey-roasted peanuts, use salted cocktail peanuts.

Or, divide the dough in half and add ½ cup salted peanuts to one half and ½ cup honey-roasted to the other. Proceed the same way with baking. You could also use a combo of the two kinds of peanuts in the entire batch. *That's* a peanut cookie.

Big Chewy Brownie Cookies

FORK IN THE ROAD: A creamy peanut butter filling turns these into very special, rich sandwich cookies.

Did this name stop you in your tracks? Well, yeah. I know. It's not like I'm immune to such enticing words all strung together. The first time I made these my husband was on a low-carb diet. I haven't seen that much naked desire in anyone's eyes since our honeymoon. Maybe not even then.

8 tablespoons (1 stick) unsalted butter

2 ounces unsweetened chocolate

1 package (12 ounces) semisweet chocolate chips

1½ cups all-purpose flour

½ teaspoon baking powder

¾ teaspoon kosher or coarse salt

4 large eggs

1½ cups sugar

2 teaspoons pure vanilla extract

1. Preheat the oven to 350°F. Line a baking sheet with parchment paper, if you have it; otherwise leave the baking sheet ungreased.

2. Place the butter, unsweetened chocolate, and chocolate chips in a small saucepan and melt over low heat, stirring frequently, just until everything is smooth. Set aside to cool slightly.

3. Meanwhile, combine the flour, baking powder, and salt in a small bowl. Beat the eggs and sugar in a large bowl with an electric mixer until creamy and light yellow, about 1 minute. Beat in the vanilla. With the mixer on low speed, blend the

flour mixture into the egg mixture in 3 batches, blending after each addition, just until barely combined. Add the chocolate mixture to the bowl and beat just until combined; the dough will be very thick.

4. Scoop out heaping tablespoons of the dough and create 12 mounds on a rimmed baking sheet. Bake until the tops are crackly and the edges are set, 9 to 11 minutes. Remove the cookies from the oven and firmly tap the pan against the counter. Let the cookies sit for 1 minute on the baking sheet (they will sink slightly), then transfer them to a wire rack to cool completely. Repeat to bake three sheets of cookies in all.

Make Ahead

You can make the dough up to 3 days ahead and store it, wrapped in plastic wrap, in the fridge. Or freeze the cookie mounds on a baking sheet covered with aluminum foil until solid, about 1 hour, then transfer them to a freezer-safe, zipper-top bag with the air pressed out, and store in the freezer for up to 2 months. Let the frozen cookie mounds thaw and press them down slightly before baking. Baked cookies will last for 5 days in a sealed container at room temperature, or for 1 month well wrapped and frozen. The filling will last for up to 1 week in the refrigerator.

FORK IN THE ROAD

Chocolate Brownie Sandwich Cookies with Peanut Butter Filling

Makes 16 sandwich cookies

THERE IS NOT MUCH more to say about these. You can, of course, spread some cookies with the filling, and not others.

⅔ cup peanut butter, smooth or chunky

¼ cup confectioners' sugar

1 tablespoon unsalted butter, at room temperature

32 Big Chewy Brownie Cookies

1. Blend together the peanut butter, confectioners' sugar, and butter in a small bowl with an electric mixer until smooth and fluffy.

2. Carefully spread about 1 tablespoon filling on the flat side of one cookie, then press the flat side of a second cookie onto the filling to make a sandwich. Repeat.

Big Chewy Brownie Cookies.

Peanut butter filling

Chocolate Chunk and Crystallized Ginger Oatmeal Cookies

FORK IN THE ROAD: If the sweet and spicy taste of the ginger is not to everyone's taste, leave it out.

These cookies have a truly compelling mix of flavors and textures. If you haven't introduced crystallized ginger to your baking pantry, you are in for a delicious awakening. It's a little spicy, a little sweet, a little chewy, and a lot delicious. It was exciting to find that it made such an excellent partner to chocolate. When you find that anything is an excellent partner to chocolate, it's always a little thrilling.

1½ cups all-purpose flour

1 teaspoon baking soda

½ teaspoon ground cinnamon

½ teaspoon ground ginger

½ teaspoon kosher or coarse salt

1 cup (2 sticks) unsalted butter, at room temperature

¾ cup packed light or dark brown sugar

½ cup granulated sugar

2 large eggs

1 teaspoon pure vanilla extract

2½ cups old-fashioned oats

1 cup chopped crystallized ginger

1 cup semisweet chocolate chunks

1. Preheat the oven to 350°F.

2. Combine the flour, baking soda, cinnamon, ground ginger, and salt in a medium-size bowl.

Yield

Makes about 30 cookies

What the Kids Can Do

Everything that kids can do with all cookies! Measure, dump, stir, blend, crack, scoop, and transfer to wire racks once baked.

3. Blend the butter and both sugars together in a large bowl with a hand mixer (or a standing mixer) until light and fluffy, about 2 minutes. Beat in the eggs one at a time, then beat in the vanilla. Add the flour mixture gradually, mixing on low speed until incorporated.

4. With a spoon (see Cooking Tip) blend in the oats, then the crystallized ginger and chocolate chunks. (━━◣ Or just one of them—see the Fork in the Road.) Mix until evenly blended.

5. Drop rounded tablespoons of the dough 3 inches apart onto ungreased baking sheets. Bake until the cookies are golden brown but still soft in the middle, 11 to 13 minutes. Let them sit on the baking sheets for 2 minutes before transferring them to a wire rack to cool completely (or almost completely . . . warm oatmeal cookies . . . yum).

FORK IN THE ROAD — Plain, or Just Chocolate Oatmeal, or Just Ginger Oatmeal Cookies

Skip the chocolate and crystallized ginger. Or skip one or the other.

If you want to make some of each, divide the batter in half, and just add ½ cup chocolate to one half and ½ cup ginger to the other. Or swap out the chocolate for raisins. Nothing wrong with an oatmeal cookie any which way.

Make Ahead

The cookies can be made up to 4 days ahead, and kept in a tightly sealed container. You can also freeze mounds of the dough on cookie sheets, and when firm (after about an hour or so) transfer them to a container and keep in the freezer for up to 2 months. Thaw and press them down a bit before baking.

Cooking Tip

If you're using a hand mixer in Step 3, at the point you add the oats, ginger, and chips in Step 4, switch over to a spoon. The beaters will chop up the final ingredients in an unwanted way, leaving you with unsatisfying bits of oats and chocolate in your cookies and compromising the texture. And we can't have that. Stand mixers with paddles are okay; they won't chop up the ingredients.

One-Pot Raspberry Oatmeal Bars

FORK IN THE ROAD: Or try a thin layer of chocolate in the middle.

Bar cookies, you rock. You rock for your one-batch-and-we're-done quality, for your simplicity, for your homeyness. These are Jack's addiction. I love them because you can use whatever preserves, jam, or jelly speaks to you—they will be consistently wonderful and different. This has become my favorite recipe when I find myself in possession of a new jar of fantastic preserves, found at a farmstand or given to me by a friend. Latest version was strawberry rhubarb. Thanks, Sarah.

And the entire recipe comes together in just one pot, no extra bowls. How lovely.

Unsalted butter or nonstick cooking spray, for greasing the baking pan

1 cup (2 sticks) unsalted butter

1 cup packed light or dark brown sugar

1½ cups all-purpose flour

1 teaspoon baking soda

½ teaspoon kosher or coarse salt

1½ cups old-fashioned rolled oats

1 jar (10 to 12 ounces) raspberry or blueberry or whatever jam, preferably seedless; ━━◟ or see the Fork in the Road for a chocolate variation

1. Preheat the oven to 350°F. Butter an 8-inch-square baking pan, preferably metal (see Note), or spray it with nonstick cooking spray.

2. Melt the butter in a medium-size saucepan over medium heat. Remove the pan from the heat, add the brown sugar,

Yield

Makes 16 squares

What the Kids Can Do

Measure ingredients, and if you let the mixture cool enough, press the oat mixture into the pan; spread the jam (let them pick the kind), then do the top layer of oatmeal crumbs.

and stir until dissolved. Stir in the flour, baking soda, and salt, then blend in the oats; the mixture should be very crumbly.

3. Measure 2½ cups of the mixture (a little more than half) and press it into the bottom of the baking pan so that it is evenly distributed. Spoon the jam over the top of the crumb base, using the back of the spoon to spread it evenly. Evenly distribute the remaining crumb topping over the top, pressing it lightly into the jam (it will just cover the filling).

4. Bake until lightly browned on top and firm, about 40 minutes. Cool completely in the pan set on a wire rack. Cut into 16 squares.

FORK IN THE ROAD

One-Pot Chocolate Oatmeal Bars

Use 1 cup mini semisweet chocolate chips in place of the jam. Just sprinkle them on the bottom oatmeal layer in Step 3 for a light sheet of chocolate. Or double the recipe and do one pan of jam and one pan of chocolate.

Make Ahead

These will last in a tightly sealed container for up to 4 days.

Note: A metal pan will create a firmer crust on the cookie, but glass will also work— you'll probably need to add an extra 5 to 8 minutes to the baking time.

Raspberry is just
one filling idea—
any kind of jam
or jelly would be
brilliant.
Let the kids
weigh in on
the flavor.

POUND CAKE, *page 330,* **and BLUEBERRY POUND CAKE,** *page 331*

People are impressed by fancy-looking desserts, but people *love* to eat homey desserts. Not desserts created to win beauty pageants or cooking showdowns. Rather, desserts that scent the kitchen while they're baking, desserts that have simple flavors that aren't novel for the sake of being novel, just happy-making and delicious.

CHAPTER 19

Homestyle Desserts

Gingerbread, that most humble and fragrant of treats, carrot cupcakes with chocolate cream cheese frosting (psst, leave off the frosting and you have carrot muffins), and pound cake, king of the simple desserts, with or without blueberries.

My kids fell in love with rice pudding in recent years, so there's a recipe for it, and you can quickly turn it into a sweet potato–cinnamon rice pudding, raisins optional. And then, there's a new brownie, chocolaty, slightly cakey, and with an optional rocky road twist. Julia Child put it best: "A party without cake is just a meeting."

Pound Cake

FORK IN THE ROAD: **Buttery simplicity or studded with blueberries.**

Pound cake in its simplest form is satisfying and buttery and homey, and the perfect ending to any meal. And it's so easy to make that those of us who grew up with a box of Entenmann's pound cake (or maybe Sara Lee) in our kitchens will be pleasantly surprised.

Cake flour produces a more tender pound cake, but if you don't have it on hand you won't find anything lacking in a cake made with regular all-purpose flour.

A slice on its own is terrific, and for a midafternoon snack, a piece lightly toasted is perfect—the toasting brings out the flavors, especially if the pound cake is a few days old. And if you want to serve it with generous dollops of sweetened whipped cream, as well as some sliced fresh peaches or berries, then you have a dessert you would feel good serving a visiting dignitary, should you have dignitaries passing through your home. (My editor Suzanne also recommends a scoop of ice cream.) This sturdy cake travels well, so it's a great potluck offering.

1 cup (2 sticks) unsalted butter, at room temperature (but not too soft; see Note on the facing page), plus more for buttering the pan

1¾ cups cake flour (not self-rising) or all-purpose flour

1 teaspoon kosher or coarse salt

1¼ cups sugar

4 large eggs, at room temperature

2 teaspoons pure vanilla extract

Yield

Serves 10

What the Kids Can Do

Butter the pan, measure ingredients, crack eggs, work the mixer, add the blueberries, pour the batter into the pan.

Make Ahead

You can store this cake, wrapped tightly in plastic wrap, at room temperature for up to 3 days, or freeze it for up to 2 months.

1. Preheat the oven to 325°F. Butter a 9 by 5-inch loaf pan.

2. Stir together the flour and salt in a medium-size bowl.

3. Cream together the butter and sugar in a large bowl with an electric mixer until light and fluffy. Add the eggs one at a time, beating well after each addition. Beat in the vanilla and scrape down the sides of the bowl. With a wooden spoon (or if you're feeling lazy, the mixer on very low), beat in the flour mixture in three batches, beating each batch just until it is incorporated and scraping down the sides after each batch. Stop beating as soon as the last batch has been incorporated and don't be tempted to overbeat.

4. ━━◖ You can continue with Step 5 or see the Fork in the Road to make Blueberry Pound Cake.

5. Scrape the batter into the prepared pan. Bake until a wooden skewer inserted into the center comes out clean, 1 hour and 10 minutes to 1 hour and 20 minutes. Cool the cake in the pan on a wire rack for 15 minutes, remove the cake from the pan, and cool completely on the wire rack.

Note: Try to make sure the butter is soft enough to beat, but not super melty soft. This is the difference between butter that blends with the sugar in a fluffy way, trapping air into the batter and allowing the cake to rise to its fullest potential, and overly-soft butter that results in less airy batter, and a flatter, denser cake. Sometimes it's referred to as cool room temperature.

FORK IN THE ROAD

Blueberry Pound Cake

Add 1½ cups rinsed and dried blueberries to the batter at the end of Step 3, before transferring it to the pan. Bake for the same amount of time.

You can make this in three 5 by 3–inch mini loaf pans as well, which allows you to make one or two plain mini pound cakes, and one or two blueberry-studded pound cakes. If you want to make one plain, fill one tin with batter, then add 1 cup blueberries to the rest of the batter before dividing it between the remaining two pans. For one mini blueberry loaf, fill two pans, then add ½ cup berries to the remaining batter. Bake the mini loaves for 40 to 50 minutes.

Rocky Road Brownies for my mom

One-Pot Cocoa Powder Brownies for Abby

One-Pot Cocoa Powder Brownies for Abby

FORK IN THE ROAD: A simple brownie is a pure joy. A rocky road brownie is my mother's definition of bliss.

For *The Mom 100 Cookbook* I tested many different versions of brownie recipes, searching for what I thought was the perfect one-pot brownie. I think I got there and many agreed . . . but others begged to differ. Well, not others. Just my friend Abby Schneiderman. While most people loved the Fudgy One-Pot Brownies, Abby could not stop talking about a recipe I had made that used only cocoa powder, no other chocolate, and which certainly made things quite easy. Abby made and enjoyed almost every recipe in the first book, but was not to be swayed in her nutty loyalty to the cocoa brownie recipe that I thought was second best. She brought them to parties, made them for celebrations, and all the while told everyone how wrong I was to have chosen the other brownie recipe over this one.

Well, I went back and found the recipe, and made them. I'm not saying she was right. I'm saying she has a point. My friend David Schiller, who finds the right words for everything, pronounced this an excellent morning brownie, after eating one at 10 a.m.

1½ cups (3 sticks) unsalted butter, plus more for buttering the baking pan

2½ cups sugar

1¼ cups unsweetened cocoa powder

6 large eggs, at room temperature

2 teaspoons pure vanilla extract

1 cup all-purpose flour

1 teaspoon baking powder

1 teaspoon kosher or coarse salt

Yield

Makes 24 brownies

What the Kids Can Do

As with almost all baking recipes, there is plenty of measuring and stirring to help with. If you are making the rocky road version, there is also scattering to do.

Make Ahead

These keep in a tightly sealed container for about 5 days, and can also be frozen.

1. Preheat the oven to 350°F. Generously grease a 9 by 13-inch baking pan.

2. Melt the butter in a medium-size saucepan over medium heat. Remove the pan from the heat and stir in the sugar and cocoa powder. Add the eggs one at a time, beating well after each addition. Stir in the vanilla. Stir in the flour, baking powder, and salt, mixing until the batter is completely smooth.

3. You can continue with Step 4 or see the Fork in the Road to go the rocky road route 30 minutes into the baking.

4. Pour the batter into the baking pan, smoothing the top. Bake until a toothpick or a skewer inserted into the middle of the pan comes out almost clean, 35 to 40 minutes.

5. Let the brownies cool completely in the pan on a rack before cutting them into 24 squares.

Whisper the words "rocky road" to my mother and she will do anything you ask.

FORK IN THE ROAD

Rocky Road Brownies

After 30 to 35 minutes of baking, when the brownies are almost done, remove the pan from the oven and scatter evenly over the top a mixture of 1 cup mini chocolate chips; 1 cup chopped walnuts, hazelnuts, or pecans; and 2 cups mini marshmallows. Return the pan to the oven and bake another 3 to 5 minutes. If you'd like everything toasted, run the pan under the broiler for just 1 minute. Cool completely in the pan on a wire rack.

Or you can divide the batter into two greased 8-inch-square pans (the brownies will be slightly thinner), and put them in the oven. After 30 minutes, remove one pan and cover with half the amounts of the rocky road ingredients above. Return to the oven and bake another 3 to 5 minutes.

Old-Fashioned Gingerbread

FORK IN THE ROAD: Sweet and simple, or packed with nuts and raisins.

My father and my father's father were ginger freaks, and clearly this is a hereditary trait. My grandfather, born in 1903, used to nibble crystallized ginger as a regular treat. He knew way back before other people in the West knew such things that ginger has medicinal benefits and a soothing effect on the stomach. Ancient Chinese wisdom from a Brooklyn-born Jewish milliner.

The flavor of this gingerbread smoothes out and gets rich and deeper after a few days, and just . . . better, really. This is the perfect recipe to remember when you want to make something ahead of time. And on top of that, it's a great traveler—it's one of those things you can whip up when you need to mail someone a little holiday cheer, or a treat to a sleepaway camper.

Unsalted butter or nonstick cooking spray for greasing the baking pan

2¼ cups all-purpose flour

2 teaspoons baking soda

½ teaspoon kosher or coarse salt

1 tablespoon ground ginger

1 teaspoon ground cinnamon

¼ teaspoon ground cloves

¾ cup (1½ sticks) unsalted butter, at room temperature

¾ cup sugar

¾ cup molasses

2 large eggs

1 cup boiling water

Yield

Makes 24 nice-size squares

What the Kids Can Do

They can measure, stir, blend, crack eggs, blend some more, pour, smooth, and cut into squares.

1. Preheat the oven to 350°F. Butter a 9 by 13-inch baking pan, or spray with nonstick spray.

2. Combine the flour, baking soda, salt, ginger, cinnamon, and cloves in a large bowl. In another large bowl, combine the butter, sugar, and molasses with an electric mixer until blended. Blend in the eggs, one at a time, beating well after each addition. Add the flour mixture to the sugar mixture and blend on low speed until combined. Pour in the boiling water and beat on low until combined and smooth.

3. ━━◀ You can continue with Step 4 or see the Fork in the Road for Dressed-Up Gingerbread.

4. Pour the batter into the pan and smooth the top. Bake until a toothpick or a wooden skewer inserted into the middle comes out clean, 32 to 35 minutes. Cool in the pan on a wire rack until completely cool, then cut into 24 pieces (or more).

FORK IN THE ROAD

Dressed-Up Gingerbread

For a richly studded gingerbread, add 1 cup chopped pecans and 1 cup raisins to the batter. Or, make one pan of plain and one pan with nuts and raisins. Use two 8-inch-square pans instead of the bigger pan, and pour half the plain batter into one prepared pan, then add ½ cup chopped pecans and ½ cup raisins to the bowl, stir to blend, and pour the second half of the batter into the second pan. Bake for 25 to 30 minutes, and cool as directed. The gingerbread will be slightly thinner.

Make Ahead

Not only is this a recipe you can make ahead, it (like stews and chilis, interestingly) gets better over the next day or two or three.

Carrot Cupcakes with Chocolate Cream Cheese Frosting

FORK IN THE ROAD: With the frosting, they are cupcakes. Without the frosting, these are muffins. (You always knew this secretly in your heart, didn't you?)

Change is good, new ideas are welcome, and no one wants to be bored at the dinner table. But when it comes to desserts I've found that most of us are very, very happy with great versions of old favorites. A fancy dessert at a restaurant is definitely fun, but at home, simple baked goods seem to be the most appreciated. This is Gary's new birthday favorite: wonderfully old-fashioned carrot cake in the form of cupcakes, with intensely chocolaty cream cheese frosting for a modern update.

2 cups all-purpose flour

2 teaspoons baking powder

1 teaspoon baking soda

2 teaspoons ground cinnamon

1 teaspoon kosher or coarse salt

2 cups finely shredded carrots

2 cups sugar

1¼ cups vegetable or canola oil

4 large eggs

1 can (8 ounces) crushed pineapple in juice (not syrup), drained (1 cup)

¾ cup raisins (optional)

½ cup chopped pecans or walnuts (optional)

Chocolate Cream Cheese Frosting (recipe follows)

Yield

Makes 24 cupcakes

What the Kids Can Do

Measure, scoop, dump, stir, and frost.

1. Preheat the oven to 350°F. Line 24 muffin cups with paper liners.

2. Stir together the flour, baking powder, baking soda, cinnamon, and salt in a large bowl. Stir in the carrots, sugar, oil, eggs, and pineapple. Stir in the raisins and/or nuts if using.

3. Scoop the batter into the muffin liners, filling each a generous three-quarters full. Bake until a toothpick or a wooden skewer inserted into the middle of a cupcake comes out clean, 20 to 25 minutes.

4. Cool in the muffin pans on a wire rack for 10 minutes, then remove the muffins from the pans and finish cooling on the wire racks.

5. ➤ You can continue with Step 6 or see the Fork in the Road for another suggestion.

6. When cool, frost with the cooled frosting.

After this photo was taken, how many minutes do you think this cupcake lasted?

Chocolate Cream Cheese Frosting

Makes about 3 cups

This is a rich frosting, my friends. Milk chocolate chips are another option for a softer, less bittersweet chocolate option.

1 package (12 ounces) semisweet chocolate chips

1 cup sour cream

1 package (8 ounces) cream cheese, at room temperature

2 teaspoons pure vanilla extract

Place a small saucepan inside a larger saucepan and add water to the larger pan so that it comes up about ½ inch around the sides of the smaller pan. Add the chocolate chips to the small pan and heat over medium-high heat, whisking occasionally, until the water is gently simmering and the chips are melted. Stir the sour cream and cream cheese into the chocolate and continue whisking until the mixture is smooth and blended. Whisk in the vanilla. Allow to cool to room temperature (the frosting will thicken as it cools).

FORK IN THE ROAD

Carrot Muffins

You can skip the frosting and keep the muffins on hand for breakfast or snacks (see Make Ahead). You can also cut the frosting recipe in half, frost some for a celebration, and keep the other dozen for snacks down the road.

Sweet Potato-Cinnamon Rice Pudding

FORK IN THE ROAD: Here, the plainer rice pudding is the Fork instead of the one that's all dolled up.

In some areas of the country, especially the South, sweet potatoes make regular appearances at the end of the meal (think sweet potato pie), but to many of us it's a surprise to see them in dessert form. But they are called sweet potatoes for a reason, and not only do they add flavor but also a nice nutritional boost to this comforting, attractively hued rice pudding.

The amount of cinnamon is small, but Charlie is a rice pudding purist, and he makes the point that the cinnamon distracts from the perfect simpleness of plain rice pudding. Therefore, it's optional, and when I'm going for a no-frills rice pudding, I skip that along with the sweet potato and the raisins.

5½ cups milk, preferably whole or 2%

¾ cup rice, preferably Arborio or other short grain white rice, though long grain is fine, too

⅔ cup sugar

½ teaspoon kosher or coarse salt

1 large sweet potato, peeled and cubed; or leftover sweet potato (see Note, facing page); or skip the sweet potato altogether (➤ see the Fork in the Road)

1 large egg yolk, at room temperature

1½ teaspoons pure vanilla extract

½ teaspoon ground cinnamon (optional)

1 cup raisins (optional)

1. Place 5 cups of the milk, the rice, sugar, and salt in a large heavy saucepan and heat over medium-high heat, stirring frequently, until tiny bubbles begin to appear around the

Yield

Serves 4 to 6

What the Kids Can Do

Peel the sweet potato, measure the ingredients, work the blender or food processor with supervision, separate the eggs (be prepared to pitch in and help here), blend the egg mixture, add the raisins.

Make Ahead

The pudding can be made up to 3 days ahead of time and kept, covered, in the refrigerator. Serve chilled or let it return to room temperature before serving. It does thicken up considerably as it cools, especially if it's chilled.

edges of the milk. Reduce the heat to medium-low and gently simmer, uncovered, stirring occasionally, until the rice is tender and the milk is mostly absorbed, about 30 minutes. Stir frequently toward the end.

2. Meanwhile, place the sweet potato in a small saucepan with water to cover and bring to a simmer over medium-high heat. Lower the heat to medium-low, cover the pot, and simmer until the sweet potato is tender, about 20 minutes. Drain and puree the sweet potato in a food processor or blender with the remaining ½ cup milk. Set aside.

3. Whisk the egg yolk with the vanilla and ground cinnamon if using, in a small bowl. Add ½ cup of the warm rice mixture to the egg mixture and quickly whisk to combine, then stir the egg-rice mixture back into the pot of warm rice, stirring constantly until well blended. Stir in the sweet potato puree (see the Fork in the Road).

4. Simmer the pudding over medium-low heat, stirring frequently, until the mixture is thick and the rice tender, about 5 minutes more. Stir in the raisins, if desired, during the last few minutes of cooking.

5. Transfer the pudding to one large serving bowl or individual bowls, and serve warm, at room temperature, or chilled.

Note: If you happen to have a leftover roasted sweet potato, you are welcome to peel and puree it with the milk instead of cooking one from scratch.

FORK IN THE ROAD — Cinnamon Rice Pudding

If you just want a plain rice pudding, then skip the part about cooking and pureeing the sweet potato (Step 2) and leave out the puree in Step 3.

If you want half plain pudding and half sweet potato, use half a sweet potato and ¾ cup milk for the puree. After adding the egg mixture to the rice pudding, pour half the pudding into another small pot. Add the sweet potato puree to one of the pots, and proceed with the recipe, simmering both pots for 5 minutes and adding raisins as desired.

KEY:

① Super Simple Tomato Sauce

② Cilantro Lime Sauce

③ Pico de Gallo minus cilantro (page 222)

④ Sun-Dried Tomato Pesto

⑤ Chipotle Mayonnaise

⑥ Lemon Mint Cream (page 119)

⑦ Chimichurri (page 104)

⑧ Mustard-Maple Sauce minus rosemary (page 108)

⑨ Soy Wasabi Ketchup (page 165)

⑩ Chopped tomatillos and jalapeños

Some of the go-to recipes that turn "What in the world am I going to make for dinner?" into "Oh, I know what we can have for dinner!" are in this chapter: Two Asian sauces (Cilantro Lime Sauce and Ginger Scallion Sauce), two cremas—a fancy term for sour cream mixed with a couple of other things (Avocado Crema and Lime Crema), a Super Simple Tomato Sauce, a Chipotle Mayonnaise, and two pestos—a basic Basil Pesto and a Sun-Dried Tomato Pesto.

Sauces & Basics

Any of these can turn a package of chicken breasts, or a leftover piece of steak (page 105), or Carnitas (page 220) into another meal, and a great meal at that.

With these items, or maybe the Mustard Maple Sauce on page 108, or the Rémoulade on page 143, and a handful of others (see the photo, opposite), you are now officially master of your kitchen domain. Give yourself permission to experiment, and solve tonight's "What's for dinner?" question in your very own way.

Super Simple Tomato Sauce

This is an adaptation, a slightly simplified and lighter version of a most basic and delicious tomato sauce created by the inimitable Marcella Hazan, the grande dame of authoritative Italian cookbooks, who died in 2013. She was wise and quite opinionated and a staunch proponent of the classics. If you haven't discovered her books, you are in for a treat. I taught myself how to make homemade pasta from her book, *The Essentials of Classic Italian Cooking*, when I was 12. It involved 8 pages of detailed instructions, which I followed to the letter.

2 tablespoons unsalted butter

1 yellow onion, finely minced

1 can (28 ounces) pureed tomatoes

Kosher or coarse salt, to taste

1. Melt the butter in a medium-size saucepan over medium heat. Add the onion and sauté until softened and just barely golden, 3 minutes.

2. Add the tomato puree. Bring the sauce to a simmer over medium heat, then lower the heat and keep it at a slow, steady simmer for about 20 minutes. Remove from the heat and add the salt.

Yield

Makes 4 cups

What the Kids Can Do

Mix the ingredients in the saucepan, taste to see how much salt is needed.

Make Ahead

This will keep for several days, well covered in the refrigerator, or you can freeze it in sturdy containers for up to 3 months.

A wonderful reminder that 3 ingredients— plus salt, of course— can make something magical.

Two Cremas

*C*rema is Spanish for "cream." Both recipes are simply blends of sour cream with a couple of other ingredients. And both are welcome on any kind of taco, or enchilada, or Mexican-oriented dish. Put these on the table and you'll feel like you've opened up a wonderful little Mexican restaurant right in your own house.

Avocado Crema

Avocados are one of the sexiest, most luxurious fruits around (I know, weird, right?). I don't know that this will be a selling point for your kids, but it's true.

1 avocado, preferably Hass, peeled, pitted, and cut into chunks

½ cup sour cream, crème fraîche, or plain Greek yogurt

1 tablespoon fresh lemon or lime juice

1 tablespoon extra-virgin olive oil

Kosher or coarse salt and freshly ground black pepper, to taste

Place the avocado, sour cream, juice, olive oil, and salt and pepper in a food processor or blender and blend until smooth.

Yield

Makes about 1 cup

What the Kids Can Do

Peel and cut up avocado, juice the citrus, stir or blend in a food processor with supervision.

Make Ahead

The crema can be made up to a day ahead of time.

Lime Crema

Creamy with a burst of citrus and a touch of heat, it's an easy little upgrade for your sour cream.

½ cup sour cream, crème fraîche, or plain Greek yogurt

1 tablespoon fresh lime juice

Kosher or coarse salt, to taste

Pinch cayenne pepper (optional)

Stir together the sour cream, lime juice, salt, and cayenne if using, in a small bowl.

Yield

Makes about ½ cup

What the Kids Can Do

Juice the lime, measure the ingredients, and stir.

Make Ahead

The crema can be made up to a day ahead of time.

Avocado Crema

Lime Crema

Two Pestos

Most people are familiar with green basil pesto, and this is a nice thick version. But other herbs and ingredients can also star in a pesto, and here's a ruddy red sun-dried tomato version just for kicks. You could make some festive crostini for the holidays, using a swipe of both pestos across little toasts.

Basil Pesto

A classic with garlic, basil, Parmesan, and pine nuts (if you want them).

2 cloves garlic (see Note)
2 cups packed fresh basil leaves (see Cooking Tip)
¼ cup pine nuts (optional)
⅓ cup extra-virgin olive oil
Kosher or coarse salt and freshly ground black pepper, to taste
½ cup freshly grated Parmesan cheese

1. Place the garlic and basil in a food processor or blender and pulse until everything is roughly chopped (another option is a mortar and pestle; see Mortar and Pestle on page 296). Add the pine nuts, if using, the oil, and salt and pepper and process, scraping down the sides of the bowl partway through, until everything is well blended.

2. At this point, for the best texture you should transfer the pesto to a small bowl or container before stirring in the Parmesan, but if you throw it into the food processor and pulse it a few times, no one will be the wiser.

Yield

Makes 1 cup

What the Kids Can Do

Pull the basil leaves off the stems, peel the garlic cloves, use the food processor with supervision.

Make Ahead

Keep the pesto, lightly covered with oil and sealed, in the fridge for up to a week.

Note: **If the sharpness of raw garlic is too much for the taste buds of your people, try this: Chop the garlic and sauté it in the olive oil in a small pan over very low heat just until it is soft and golden but not browned, 5 to 10 minutes. This will take some of the bite out. Cool, then proceed with the recipe.**

Cooking Tip

If you care about your pesto being and staying bright green, you can blanch the basil leaves. Bring a medium-size pot of water to a boil, plunge in the basil, drain after 5 seconds, then plunge into a waiting bowl of ice water. Pat the basil dry before proceeding.

Sun-Dried Tomato Pesto

The concentrated flavor of sun-dried tomatoes makes this a tangy pesto.

½ cup oil-packed sun-dried tomatoes

2 tablespoons freshly grated Parmesan cheese

1 tablespoon extra-virgin olive oil

4 fresh basil leaves

Kosher or coarse salt and freshly ground black pepper, to taste

Place the sun-dried tomatoes, Parmesan, olive oil, basil, and salt and pepper in a food processor and process until pureed.

Yield

Makes ½ cup

What the Kids Can Do

Pull off the basil leaves, measure, and work the food processor with supervision.

Make Ahead

This will last in the fridge for about 10 days, lightly covered with olive oil.

Pestos are great to have on hand to add to sandwiches, soups, stews, or just dollop on simply cooked foods, like salmon or a chicken breast. Dilute with some pasta cooking water, add an extra glug of olive oil, and toss with hot pasta.

Ginger Scallion
Sauce

Cilantro Lime
Sauce

Two Asian Sauces

Either of these two sauces helps you to turn a bowl of rice and some simple or Asian-influenced leftovers (such as Chicken in Orange Sauce, page 135, or Korean Sesame Tofu and Mushrooms, page 263) into another meal. These also would make nice dunks for cooked shrimp or simple chicken or beef skewers.

Cilantro Lime Sauce

Bright and refreshing. You could also make this with parsley if cilantro isn't your thing.

- ¼ cup fresh lime juice
- 3 tablespoons vegetable or canola oil
- 3 tablespoons minced fresh cilantro
- 1 clove garlic, finely minced
- 1 teaspoon honey
- ½ teaspoon kosher or coarse salt

Place the lime juice, oil, cilantro, garlic, honey, and salt in a small bowl or container. Blend well, or cover the container and shake to mix.

Ginger Scallion Sauce

Every once in a while you come across a sauce or a condiment you want to slather on or dip into or drizzle over everything. This is one of those times. This is a thick sauce and a bit intense, so go with small amounts to start.

Yield

Makes ⅓ cup

What the Kids Can Do

Juice the limes, measure, and mix.

Make Ahead

This will last for up to 3 days, covered, in the refrigerator.

10 scallions, trimmed, white and green parts cut into
  2-inch pieces

1 piece (3 inches) ginger, peeled and thickly sliced

⅓ cup vegetable or canola oil

2 tablespoons soy sauce, preferably reduced-sodium

1 teaspoon sesame oil (optional)

Kosher or coarse salt and freshly ground black pepper
  to taste

Place the scallions, ginger, vegetable oil, soy sauce, sesame oil
(if using), and salt in a blender or food processor and process
until pureed.

Yield
─────────────
Makes ⅔ cup

What the Kids Can Do
─────────────
**Peel the ginger with a
spoon (see page 124), cut
the scallions with an age-
appropriate knife, measure,
and blend with supervision.**

Make Ahead
─────────────
**This will last for up to 3 days,
covered, in the refrigerator.**

You could add a little dollop of this
Ginger Scallion Sauce to Chicken in Orange Sauce
(page 135) or Korean Sesame Tofu and
Mushrooms (page 263).

Chipotle Mayonnaise

This condiment is one of the most versatile to have on hand—it will turn almost any sandwich or wrap into something memorable—think roast beef, turkey, tuna fish, leftover chicken or pork loin, you name it. If you want to swap out some of the mayo in exchange for plain Greek yogurt or sour cream you can, especially if you're using it as a dollop on Saucy Seafood Stew (page 251), or a baked potato.

1 cup mayonnaise, regular or low-fat

3 cloves garlic, finely minced

1 teaspoon fresh lime or lemon juice

2 teaspoons chipotle puree (see Note)

Kosher or coarse salt and freshly ground black pepper, to taste

Whisk together the mayo, garlic, lime juice, and chipotle puree in a small bowl. Season with salt and pepper. This will keep covered in the fridge for up to 1 month.

Yield

About 1 cup

Make Ahead

Store in a covered container in the fridge for up to 1 month.

Note: To make chipotle puree, pour the contents of a 7-ounce can of chipotles in adobo into a food processor and puree until smooth. This puree will keep covered in the fridge for weeks, and adds smoky heat to all kinds of soups, stews, sauces, and other dishes.

Conversion Tables

Approximate Equivalents

1 STICK BUTTER = 8 tbs = 4 oz = ½ cup = 115 g

1 CUP ALL-PURPOSE PRESIFTED FLOUR = 4.7 oz

1 CUP GRANULATED SUGAR = 8 oz = 220 g

1 CUP (FIRMLY PACKED) BROWN SUGAR = 6 oz = 220 g to 230 g

1 CUP CONFECTIONERS' SUGAR = 4½ oz = 115 g

1 CUP HONEY OR SYRUP = 12 oz

1 CUP GRATED CHEESE = 4 oz

1 CUP DRIED BEANS = 6 oz

1 LARGE EGG = about 2 oz or about 3 tbs

1 EGG YOLK = about 1 tbs

1 EGG WHITE = about 2 tbs

Please note that all conversions are approximate but close enough to be useful when converting from one system to another.

Weight Conversions

U.S./U.K.	METRIC	U.S./U.K.	METRIC
½ oz	15 g	7 oz	200 g
1 oz	30 g	8 oz	250 g
1½ oz	45 g	9 oz	275 g
2 oz	60 g	10 oz	300 g
2½ oz	75 g	11 oz	325 g
3 oz	90 g	12 oz	350 g
3½ oz	100 g	13 oz	375 g
4 oz	125 g	14 oz	400 g
5 oz	150 g	15 oz	450 g
6 oz	175 g	1 lb	500 g

Liquid Conversions

U.S.	IMPERIAL	METRIC
2 tbs	1 fl oz	30 ml
3 tbs	1½ fl oz	45 ml
¼ cup	2 fl oz	60 ml
⅓ cup	2½ fl oz	75 ml
⅓ cup + 1 tbs	3 fl oz	90 ml
⅓ cup + 2 tbs	3½ fl oz	100 ml
½ cup	4 fl oz	125 ml
⅔ cup	5 fl oz	150 ml
¾ cup	6 fl oz	175 ml
¾ cup + 2 tbs	7 fl oz	200 ml
1 cup	8 fl oz	250 ml
1 cup + 2 tbs	9 fl oz	275 ml
1¼ cups	10 fl oz	300 ml
1⅓ cups	11 fl oz	325 ml
1½ cups	12 fl oz	350 ml
1⅔ cups	13 fl oz	375 ml
1¾ cups	14 fl oz	400 ml
1¾ cups + 2 tbs	15 fl oz	450 ml
2 cups (1 pint)	16 fl oz	500 ml
2½ cups	20 fl oz (1 pint)	600 ml
3¾ cups	1½ pints	900 ml
4 cups	1¾ pints	1 liter

Oven Temperatures

°F	GAS MARK	°C	°F	GAS MARK	°C
250	½	120	400	6	200
275	1	140	425	7	220
300	2	150	450	8	230
325	3	160	475	9	240
350	4	180	500	10	260
375	5	190			

Note: Reduce the temperature by 20°C (68°F) for fan-assisted ovens.

Menus

Even people who love to cook can get stymied by putting together a menu. This is understandable. Figuring out what goes together in a pleasing way, both visually and flavor-wise, not to mention timing-wise, is an acquired skill for most. Here are a few *Dinner Solved!* menus to get the ball rolling.

A Brunch for Company

Berry Banana Smoothie, page 4

Berry Streusel Coffee Cake with Sweet Vanilla Drizzle, page 15

Scrambled eggs (throw in some fresh herbs or chives if you like)

Sliced melon

The Mother's Day Dinner I Would Love

Baked Shrimp and Grits with Caramelized Fennel and Leeks, page 186

Light Green Crunchy Salad, page 75

Pound Cake, page 330

The Father's Day Dinner Gary Would Love

Buffalo Chicken Wings, page 61, and Honey Garlic Chicken Wings, page 63

Spicy Asian Spareribs, page 115

Creamy Coleslaw, page 281

Cornbread, page 305

Big Chewy Brownie Cookies, page 318

A Make-Ahead Cold-Weather Meal

Sweet and Spicy Peanuts, page 56

Chicken and White Bean Chili, page 247

Pickle-y Cucumber Salad, page 72

Cornbread, page 305

One-Pot Cocoa Powder Brownies for Abby, page 333

A Summer Lunch

Cobb Salad with Creamy Pesto Dressing, page 83

Plain Old Quinoa, page 80

One Pot, No-Bake Oatmeal Peanut Butter Cookies, page 312

A Holiday Open House Buffet

Herbed Spiced Nuts, page 58

Savory Zucchini Puff Pastry Tarts, page 67

Deviled Eggs (at least one version), page 48

Indian-Spiced Butternut Squash-Carrot Soup, page 89, kept warm on the stove

Kale and Quinoa Salad with Dried Cherries, page 78

An assortment of cheeses and sliced charcuterie

Crudité platter

Chocolate Chunk and Crystallized Ginger Oatmeal Cookies, page 323

One-Pot Raspberry Oatmeal Bars, page 325

A Show-Off Dinner

An Asian-Inspired Meal

A Kid's Birthday Party

A Taco Party

A Vegetarian Salad Buffet

An Italian Menu

During the Week

Here are ten weeknight dinner menus. While most of this book is designed to answer that persistent "what's for dinner" question on any average day of the week, if you need a quick hit list, this should help. You'll notice that a couple of these "menus" consist of a single dish. That's because in my house, your house, and most houses, on an average Tuesday night, one dish equals a menu. Also, you'll see that desserts aren't listed (and your kids will see it even faster) — that's because weeknight dessert (whether it exists, whether it revolves around fruit) is a highly personal matter, and you know what makes sense in your house. In my house, on a weeknight, "dessert" comes later in the evening in the form of a huge pot of stovetop popcorn.

Weeknight Dinner #1
Fish Tacos, page 214
Light Green Crunchy Salad, page 75

Weeknight Dinner #2
Stupid Easy Chicken and Broccoli Pasta,
page 202

Weeknight Dinner #3
Spanish Pork Chops, page 109
Honey-Glazed Carrots, page 276
Roasted or mashed potatoes

Weeknight Dinner #4
Maple-Barbecue Pork Meatballs, page 169
Simple Sautéed Spinach, page 287
Cooked rice or Plain Old Quinoa, page 80

Weeknight Dinner #5
Asian Rice Bowl Many Ways, page 189
Two Asian Sauces (pick one), page 353

Weeknight Dinner #6
Vegetable Lo Mein, page 209

Weeknight Dinner #7
Korean Sesame Tofu (or Chicken) and
Mushrooms, page 263
Simple green salad
Cooked rice

Weeknight Dinner #8
Caesar-Roasted Salmon, page 151
Cauliflower Puree, page 278

Weeknight Dinner #9
Chicken in Orange Sauce, page 135
Korean Spinach, page 284

Weeknight Dinner #10
Cheesy, Crispy Pizza Portobello Mushrooms,
page 257
Pickle-y Cucumber Salad, page 72

And There's More

Because I'm running out of pages, but have more to say (Can you feel my kids' eyes rolling? I can.), I'd like to direct you to themom100.com where you will find the following lists:

- Recipes That Take 30 Minutes or Less
- Under-an-Hour Main Courses
- Dishes Geared Toward Pickiest Eaters
- Make-Ahead Dishes
- Cooking to Impress
- One-Pot Dishes
- Super-Freezable Dishes
- Healthy Dishes
- Portable Dishes
- Recipes That Make Great Leftovers
- Mediterranean-Inspired Recipes
- Asian-Inspired Recipes
- List of Chicken Recipes
- List of Pasta Recipes
- List of Meat Recipes
- List of Vegetarian Recipes

Index

roasted, couscous, and chickpea salad, warm, *254, 270,* 271–73
sauce, super simple, *344, 346,* 347
sun-dried, pesto, *344,* 351, *351*
tempeh Bolognese, 197
Tortilla(s):
black bean, corn & chicken stew, 95
breakfast wraps, *10,* 11
chicken soup, Mexican, *93,* 93–95
scoops with minty pineapple-jalapeño salsa, 45–47, *46*
warming, 216
see also Enchilada(s); Taco(s)
"To taste," meaning of, 60
Turkey burgers, Cajun or plain & simple, 161
Turmeric, 125

U
don (noodles), 98
chicken soup, shortcut, *86,* 97–98
soup, vegetarian, 98
Umami, 258

V
anilla drizzle, 16, *18,* 19
Vegetable(s), 275–91
Brussels sprouts, braised, 291
Brussels sprouts, warm, with bacon and mustard vinaigrette, 288–91, *289*
carrots, honey-glazed, 276–77, *277*
carrots, honey-orange-soy glazed, 277, *277*
cauliflower & beet puree, 279, *279*

cauliflower puree, 278–79, *279*
cheesy garden potato, 260, *260*
coleslaw, creamy, *280,* 281–83
coleslaw with Asian dressing, 282, *283*
lo mein, 209–11, *210*
one-skillet lasagna, lazy, 266–69, *267*
potpie, 185
spinach, Korean, 284–87, *285*
spinach, simple sautéed, 287
see also Sides; *specific vegetables*
Vegetarian options (main dishes), 255–73
black bean, mushroom, and zucchini enchiladas, creamy, *229,* 229–31, *231*
black bean burgers, Southwestern, *156,* 166–68
cheesy, crispy pizza portobello mushrooms, *256,* 257–58
Cobb salad, *84,* 85
kale and quinoa salad with dried cherries, 78–80, *79*
potato, baked, bar, 259, *260–61*
rice bowl, Asian, many ways, *189,* 189–91, *190*
sesame tofu and mushrooms, Korean, *262,* 263–65
tempeh Bolognese, 197
tempeh joes, 31
tofu in orange sauce, 137
tofu stir-fry, Thai, *177,* 178
tomato, roasted, couscous, and chickpea salad, warm, *254, 270,* 271–73
udon soup with tofu, 98
vegetable lo mein, 209–11, *210*
vegetable one-skillet lasagna, lazy, 266–69, *267*
vegetable potpie, 185
white bean chili, 250
see also Fish & seafood; Shrimp
Vinaigrette, mustard, 288–91, *289*

W
asabi, 165
avocado crema, 165
soy ketchup, 165, *344*
Wheat germ, 52
granola bars, 51–52, *53*
White bean:
and chicken chili, *247,* 247–50, *248*
chili, vegetarian, 250
& kale soup, vegetarian, 100
sausage, and kale soup, 99–100, *101*
Whole grains, 82
Wraps, breakfast, *10,* 11

Y
ogurt:
berry banana smoothie, 4, *5*
granola parfaits, 52
see also Cremas

Z
a'atar, in Middle Eastern deviled eggs, *49,* 50
Zucchini:
black bean, and mushroom enchiladas, creamy, *229,* 229–31, *231*
lazy vegetable one-skillet lasagna, 266–69, 267
puff pastry tarts, savory, *54,* 54, 67–69, *68*
roasted tomato, couscous, and chickpea salad, warm, *254, 270,* 271–73
vegetarian white bean chili, 250